# Migrating to Oracle
*Expert Secrets for Migrating from SQL Server and MySQL*

*Oracle In-Focus Series*

*Ben Prusinski*

I would like to dedicate this book to my parents, friends, and everyone whom I have met as well as to fellow Oracle professionals who, night and day, work tirelessly to support database systems everywhere.

- Ben Prusinski

# Migrating to Oracle
*Expert Secrets for Migrating from SQL Server and MySQL*

By Ben Prusinski

Copyright © 2008 by Rampant TechPress.  All rights reserved.
Printed in the United States of America.
Published in Kittrell, North Carolina, USA.
**Oracle In-focus Series**: Book 33
**Series Editor**: Donald K. Burleson
**Production Manager**: Robin Rademacher
**Technical Editor**: Paulo Ferreira Portugal
**Production Editor**: Valerre Aquitaine
**Cover Design**: Janet Burleson
**Printing History**: September 2010 for First Edition

ISBN 10: 0-9797951-6-8
ISBN 13: 978-0-9797951-6-9
Library of Congress Control Number: 2009930093

# *Table of Contents*

## Chapter 8:  Understanding the Oracle Database Migration Utilities291

## Chapter 9:  Testing and Verification of Database Migration ..........314

# Using the Online Code Depot

Purchase of this book provides complete access to the online code depot that contains sample code scripts. Any code depot scripts in this book are located at the following URL in zip format and ready to load and use:

**rampant.cc/oracle_migration.htm**

If technical assistance is needed with downloading or accessing the scripts, please contact Rampant TechPress at rtp@rampant.cc.

# Conventions Used in this Book

It is critical for any technical publication to follow rigorous standards and employ consistent punctuation conventions to make the text easy to read. However, this is not an easy task. Within database terminology, there are many types of notation that can confuse a reader. For example, some Oracle utilities such as STATSPACK and TKPROF are always spelled in CAPITAL letters, while Oracle parameters and procedures have varying naming conventions in the database documentation. It is also important to remember that many database commands are case sensitive, are always left in their original executable form and never altered with italics or capitalization. Hence, all Rampant TechPress books follow these conventions:

**Parameters:** All database parameters will be lowercase italics. Exceptions to this rule are parameter arguments that are commonly capitalized (KEEP pool, TKPROF); these will be left in ALL CAPS.

**Variables:** All procedural language (e.g. PL/SQL) program variables and arguments will also remain in lowercase italics (*dbms_job, dbms_utility*).

**Tables & dictionary objects:** All data dictionary objects are referenced in lowercase italics (*dba_indexes, v$sql*). This includes all *v$* and *x$* views (*x$kcbcbh, v$parameter*) and dictionary views (*dba_tables, user_indexes*).

**SQL:** All SQL is formatted for easy use in the code depot, and all SQL is displayed in lowercase. The main SQL terms (select, from, where, group by, order by, having) will always appear on a separate line.

**Programs & Products:** All products and programs that are known to the author are capitalized according to the vendor specifications (CentOS, VMware, Oracle, etc.). All names known by Rampant TechPress to be trademark names appear in this text as initial caps. References to UNIX are always made in uppercase.

# Acknowledgements

This type of highly technical reference book requires the dedicated efforts of many people. Even though we are the authors, our work ends when we deliver the content. After each chapter is delivered, several Oracle DBAs carefully review and correct the technical content. After the technical review, experienced copy editors polish the grammar and syntax.

The finished work is then reviewed as page proofs and turned over to the production manager, who arranges the creation of the online code depot and manages the cover art, printing distribution, and warehousing.

In short, the authors play a small role in the development of this book, and we need to thank and acknowledge everyone who helped bring this book to fruition:

**Paulo Ferreira Portugal** for technical expertise and review.

**Robin Rademacher** for the production management including the coordination of the cover art, page proofing, printing, and distribution.

**Valerre Q Aquitaine** for help in the production of the page proofs.

**Janet Burleson** for exceptional cover design and graphics.

**John Lavender** for assistance with the web site, and for creating the code depot and the online shopping cart for this book.

**Don Burleson** for providing me with the opportunity to write this book.

With my sincerest thanks,

Ben Prusinski

# Introduction to Oracle Migrations

*"So you want to migrate to Oracle?"*

## Migrating to Oracle

Welcome to the world of database migrations! An exciting adventure is about to begin. As database administrators (DBAs), there are a plethora of daily challenges that keep them on their toes from database recoveries to performance issues to security tasks. However, of the millions of tasks that DBAs are required to complete, there is no single task as complex, or daunting, as that of a full-blown database migration from a non-Oracle environment to an Oracle environment.

The goal of this book is to provide a blueprint, roadmap and toolkit to complete even the most painful database migration. Because one could easily fill an entire library of texts on database migration, the topics here will focus on database migrations from MySQL and Microsoft SQL Servers to the Oracle 10g database platform using Oracle 10g Migration Workbench tools.

## Overview of Database Migration

Database migration is the process of moving from one database platform to a different database platform. In contrast, a database upgrade would be a movement from one particular database version to a new and later release of database software. There are many similarities between a database migration and a database upgrade. In this book, database migration will be represented in terms of moving from Microsoft SQL Server 2000 to Oracle 10g.

Most database vendors provide upgrade tools such as the Oracle Database Upgrade Assistant (DBUA) and custom scripts to perform upgrades. However, the in-house tools to perform the more difficult and challenging migration processes from one particular database vendor to a new platform are extremely limited and require senior database technical knowledge. Database migrations may be performed due to budget constraints such as the licensing costs that could be saved with a migration from SQL Server 2000 to Oracle or from IBM DB2 to MySQL platforms.

Another factor that currently drives the requirement for database migrations is that a particular database vendor may not support specific features. Such might be the case with a standby database or real time replication which makes the client need to migrate off of one database platform to another that provides real time replication and disaster recovery features.

One example is with the MySQL database environment which currently lacks the robust capabilities of disaster recovery standby databases and replication that are available with Oracle 10g Streams based replication and Oracle 10g Data Guard standby database. For a larger, higher performance transaction environment that processes millions of transactions per second, a database migration to Oracle 10g from MySQL would make a lot of sense.

# Manual Procedures for Database Migration

Database vendors such as Microsoft and Oracle provide database utilities that assist the database migration process. However, there are also times when a manual process is either required or optimal for completing the database migration. For example, if an application environment has legacy and homegrown code that must be ported from Teradata to Oracle, to use an automated tool would prove nearly impossible.

Another reason for manual database migration procedures would be the fine-grain level of control and customization that is possible with a bare bones custom process of migration scripts and manual conversion methods. Yet another reason may be due to cost and budget if third party tools are too expensive for a customer's budget.

In order to provide a comprehensive list of manual procedures for database migration to Oracle, the following methods will be discussed:

- Export and Import
- Server level copy and clone
- Database Replication
- Schema Copy and DDL Generation

## Export and Import Method for Database Migration (Data Pump)

In this method, the database technician applies native database utilities for export and import to complete a manual data pump migration to Oracle. For example, with Microsoft SQL Server 2000, a custom BCP script or DTS package could be used to export the database definitions and data for later import into an Oracle database. The database structure and schema for all of the database objects would need to be generated using MS SQL Server Transact SQL (T-SQL) scripts and stored procedures. Then a new database structure would need to be created within the future Oracle 10g database environment.

The downside to this approach is that experienced development and database time would be required to complete the manual translation of T-SQL scripts and data types to the Oracle environment. Transportable tablespaces can also be used with Oracle 10g migrations either from within export or recovery manager (RMAN) scripts. However, the limitation is that a direct migration from MySQL or Microsoft SQL Server to Oracle is not possible through transportable tablespaces.

## Server Level Copy and Cloning Method

In this technique of manual database copy and cloning, operating system level and disk-based utilities may be used to complete part of the migration to Oracle from another environment such as IBM DB2. For example, if the particular environment uses EMC or Hitachi SAN based storage, then an image copy of the entire operating system and data files can be taken as a snapshot and cloned to a new platform.

The downside of server level copy and cloning is that a great deal of manual coding and database changes must still be performed to migrate the database structures and schemas to Oracle. Because of this, this is not a recommended approach for migration. Server level copy at the SAN or NAS level is best used with like-to-like cloning of Oracle-to-Oracle databases rather than as a pure migration solution.

## Replication for Database Migrations to Oracle

This method is possibly one of the best approaches for completion of manual database migrations to Oracle from SQL Server and MySQL. With the built-in facilities in Oracle 10g, database replication methods using Oracle Streams and Oracle Transparent Gateways offer a viable manner to complete database migration.

Changes can be captured from the source database platform across a TCP/IP network connection and queued to Oracle Streams queues for processing. However, due to the level of complexity and resources to deploy replication and gateways, replication migrations pose special challenges for the busy database administrator.

## Schema Copy and DDL Generation

With schema copying and DDL generation, the DBA can utilize the native database system stored procedures and functions within MS SQL Server or MySQL to copy out the database structures, mappings, and schema DDL for the current environment. This can all then be mapped to the new Oracle database platform. Though this manual process provides a potential way to complete the manual migration to Oracle, it is time consuming and contains a large margin of possible error.

# Third Party Tools for Database Migration to Oracle 10g

As an alternative to the four mentioned methods of migration, there are three helpful tools to assist in Oracle migrations:

- GoldenGate Software
- Quest Shareplex
- SwisSQL

Now explore each option in detail and see how they assist in Oracle migrations.

## GoldenGate® Software

GoldenGate Software provides a comprehensive software solution for application and database migrations, upgrades, and disaster recovery. The software is available for most database and server vendor platforms including: HP NonStop (Tandem), DB2/UDB, MS SQL Server, MySQL, Sybase, and NCR Teradata environments. A multitude of custom implementation solutions are possible with the GoldenGate software.

For further details on GoldenGate, visit the site at: www.goldengate.com.

The main advantage of GoldenGate software is that zero downtime is possible while migration is completed to Oracle 10g. This is because even with complex migrations, the DBA can run the database that is being migrated from concurrently with Oracle 10g. This keeps the systems synchronized, minimizing risk associated with migrations.

> 🔔 For more details on Shareplex, visit the site: www.quest.com/shareplex_for_oracle/.

## Quest® Shareplex

Quest software is a replication product that may provide a solution for migrations to Oracle by using log-based technology to mine data from the transaction log files for use with Oracle environments.

## Swis® SQL

SwisSQL provides an excellent toolkit for conversion of non-Oracle SQL and stored procedures to Oracle 10g. While it is not a comprehensive migration product, it may provide assistance with the migration of complex database application code to Oracle 10g.

> 🔔 For details on SwisSQL, please visit the site at: www.swissql.com/database-migration-solution.html.

# The New Oracle 10g Database Workbench Migration (OMWB)

Now that third-party solutions have been introduced to perform migrations to Oracle, begin with an introduction to the Oracle 10g Database Migration Workbench (OMWB). In order to migrate to Oracle 10g and 11g from MySQL and SQL Server databases, Oracle provides a free utility, OMWB. This handy tool performs most of the challenging operations to migrate the source database structures and code to Oracle database structures. With the latest incarnation of the Oracle Migration tools available with SQL Developer, large databases from MySQL and Microsoft SQL Server platforms can be migrated with ease. The following figure example shows the welcome screen for OMWB.

**Figure 1.1:** *Oracle Migration Workbench Welcome Screen*

With all of the challenges of completing a complex and difficult database migration from MySQL or MS SQL Server, what alternative is available to third party tools and manual custom procedures? Enter the new OMWB tool, now available from Oracle, to complete the most difficult database migrations from MySQL and MS SQL Server to Oracle 10g. The OMWB tool provides a rich assortment of robust utilities that automate a majority of the database migration tasks. This is extremely helpful since these tasks would otherwise consume large amounts of time with manual processes.

Now an overview of the primary benefits and features for the Oracle Migration Workbench will be provided. The new OMWB utility provides the following features to assist with the database migration to Oracle 10g:

- Automated scripts to perform database migration from MySQL and SQL Server to Oracle 10g

- Wizards and editors to customize non-Oracle SQL and stored procedures to Oracle 10g SQL statements and Oracle 10g PL/SQL stored procedures

- Wizards and editors to convert non-Oracle database architectures and structures to Oracle 10g database structures and architecture

- Troubleshooting wizards to correct errors before, during and after a database migration from MySQL and SQL Server to Oracle 10g

- Ability to perform on-line database migration and capture between MySQL and SQL Server to Oracle 10g with no downtime

- Offline capture features and database migration functionality from MySQL and SQL Server to Oracle 10g

- The ability to create reports of all phases of database migration for review and analysis

- Available for migrations to either Oracle 9i or 10g

- Feature to generate DDL creation scripts for the migration to Oracle 10g

---

A comprehensive list of features for the Oracle 10g Migration Workbench is available on the Oracle website URL listed below: www.oracle.com/technology/tech/migration/workbench/index.html

# Preparation for Database Migration to Oracle 10g

"By failing to prepare, you are preparing to fail."- *Benjamin Franklin*

---

       **User ID = book, Password = reader**

---

This section consists of the following activities that are essential to basic training and planning for migration to 10g:

- Project planning for database migration to Oracle 10g
- Staffing requirements for database migration
- Tasks involved
- Backup and Recovery tasks before and after migration

## Database Migration to Oracle 10g Project Planning

Due to the complex nature of database migrations from MySQL and MS SQL Server platforms to Oracle 10g, project planning is an essential, and often ignored, aspect of migration. In order to complete a successful migration to

Oracle 10g, major players should first be assigned. Closely following, a kick-off project meeting must be held early in the game to ensure successful migration.

Tools such as Microsoft Project are useful for the documentation of complex and ever changing migration project plans. For example, the project and application/development management teams will first need to scope out the full life cycle of the project. This includes key milestones and delivery dates. Weekly team planning sessions are highly encouraged to manage all phases of the migration project. These sessions serve to promote knowledge transfer between all of the key applications, databases, and user community members.

If outside vendors or consultants are brought in to perform part of the project, it is even more critical to develop a statement of work (SOW) that will be implemented in concert with the overall migration project plan. Many projects either fail completely or accrue costly expenditures due to inadequate scoping or project management. Lack of adequate resource planning for staffing of large migration projects can also hinder migration. Because of this, being prepared early with effective program management and project plan design is needed to avoid the consequences of a failed migration project.

EXAMPLE CASE: On a recent database migration project where the author was the technical DBA manager for a software company, the senior management never realized how expensive licensing costs would be in contrast to hardware costs for migrating hundreds of databases from MS SQL Server to Oracle 10g! In fact, once this author provided the total licensing costs involved to the senior vice president, the entire migration program was cancelled.

## Staffing Requirements for Database Migration

There is a useful, tried and true rule of thumb to remember how to successfully staff for a large and complex database migration to Oracle 10g from non-Oracle platforms such as MySQL and MS SQL Server. The secret ingredient is to multiply the number of current non-Oracle databases and applications that will be migrated by a factor of two.

For example, if 100 databases need to be migrated to Oracle 10g and there are five database administrators on the team, an additional five database and application administrators would be required to complete the large scale migration on time and under budget. One solution for IT shops that are short staffed and want to maximize productivity on a short time table would be to bring in outside vendor(s) or consultants to complete part, or all, of the database migration. This is because senior level consultants with years of experience will be able to hit the ground running and complete a large migration to Oracle 10g in half the time that a junior level administrator or small staff could accomplish.

Tasks involved with the migration to Oracle 10g:

- Project Planning and Kick Off Meeting
- Staff Development and Resource Staffing
- Pilot Migration and Testing
- Backup and Recovery Test Before the Migration
- Installation and Configuration of Migration Tools
- Initial Data Capture from Production System
- Migration Data Application to Target System
- Final Backup and Recovery Tests After the Migration
- Data Verification and QA Testing

## Project Planning and Kick-Off Meeting

This is the first major step to a successful migration to Oracle 10g from MySQL or Microsoft SQL Server. All of the key players from the various technical teams should attend the kick-off meeting for the database migration. This includes technical leads from the database and application groups as well as project management and even executive or director level management.

A baseline project plan and scope should be created before the kick-off meeting and reviewed. After this, the project plan and milestones can be finalized and placed into a standards document available to the technical and business leaders as necessary.

## Staff Development and Resource Staffing

This aspect of a migration project is mentioned because of the fact that it is the single most neglected item outside of project/program management. When staffing and development are ignored, the risk of failure is increased by a huge magnitude. Technology professionals already are short staffed and overworked with all of the mergers and downsizing from the last several years. Why set them up to fail? By investing in the team, one ensures a much greater chance of success for the migration project.

Migrations are messy, complicated and difficult; they are not a walk in the park. This being, there are several ways to invest in technical teams. If one DBA has experience in Oracle, but zero experience in MS SQL Server or MySQL, send them to a DBA course on the legacy platform. This will assure that the migration is completed with fewer issues and less chance of failure. A few dollars spent in advance can mitigate the risk of a colossal and expensive failure.

## Pilot Migration and Testing

Many firms and technical teams rush head long into a migration with live production systems. In doing so, they fail to test or plan the migration resulting in an already daunting task that quickly becomes a nightmare. This being, the wise and sagely advice is to perform a pilot migration and test. Similar to a proof of concept, the pilot test can serve as a quick checkpoint and benchmark in terms of time, resources, and level of effort to complete a large migration. In addition, by taking this baby step of migration with a subset of production database systems, the recommended staff development and project management can be coordinated in a timely and effective manner.

For example, if the current set of production databases is on Microsoft SQL Server 2000 and MySQL 4.1, only two low cost servers are required to perform the pilot test migration. One server would be required on Windows 2003 server, for the SQL Server 2000 database to Oracle 10g, and the other could be a small Linux server running MySQL to perform the initial testing and migration in parallel, thus saving time and up front hardware and software costs.

## Backup and Recovery Test before the Migration

Of all the myriad of tasks that database and application professionals face, none are as important as backup and recovery. Disaster recovery testing should be the mantra of a DBA's existence.

In fact, one's job may depend on it. If something goes wrong in the migration process and recovery is not possible, precious data may be lost. This can cause serious financial and corporate data loss. Not only may one not have a job much longer, but the boss may even be terminated if a disaster strikes during the migration process and the DBA was responsible for keeping a time tested backup and recovery program in place.

EXAMPLE CASE: I once heard a similar story from an executive of a large financial services firm where I used to work about a former DBA who had done such a thing. He failed to not only take backups for the mission-critical production Oracle systems, but also neglected testing backups. One day a disaster struck, and the DBA was unable to bring the database and application back online. The CIO, or chief information officer, did a conference call with all of the team and fired both the careless DBA and his manager on the spot. As a senior level DBA, I can appreciate the value of tested backups before performing a major upgrade or migration.

EXAMPLE CASE: One evening several years ago on New Year's Eve while I was working as the lead production DBA for a large financial services company, I was paged by the help desk about a database that was down. The previous DBA had not tested backups, nor had he documented backup and recovery/DR procedures.

Luckily, I was the designated driver that evening and was able to intelligently login and resolve the problem. It was stressful and I had my boss, the CIO and the data center VP on the horn asking me if and when the database would be back up. Had I not tested the backups and DR process, all would have been lost, not to mention my job.

As the example cases above show, never neglect backup and recovery testing before starting database migration to Oracle 10g. In the event of a database migration failure, it is best to restore from a backup. Though senior DBAs already know the importance of this, it is worthwhile to repeat the mantra:

"backup, backup, backup". Be sure and test the backup before and after the migration!

## Installation and Configuration of Migration Tools

When planning for the database migration to Oracle 10g, several installations and configuration processes are required to ensure a successful migration. First, the Oracle 10g Database Migration Workbench suite of tools will need to be downloaded from the Oracle technical website. Second, the binaries for the Oracle migration workbench (OMWB) will need to be unzipped and configured on the source and target systems. Third, the required capture scripts will need to be configured and tested against the source non-Oracle database.

## Initial Data Capture from Production System

The Oracle 10g Migration Workbench (OMWB) provides two methods to perform the initial data capture from the source production environment. If the source, non-Oracle database must remain online, the online capture utility can be used with the source database to conduct the initial capture phase of data. However, if the source database can be taken offline after business hours, such as for a maintenance weekend, then an offline capture can be deployed using either the Oracle Migration Workbench suite of utilities or offline scripts can be used with MS SQL Server or MySQL.

These offline capture scripts provide direct hooks into the source, non-Oracle system to capture data and store it in a format that the Oracle migration workbench can use to perform the apply phase of the migration. For example, in the case of Microsoft SQL Server, Oracle provides a series of canned BCP scripts to log directly into the Microsoft SQL Server database. This will pipe out data and source database definitions to interface with the Oracle migration workbench during the target apply phase of the migration.

## Migration Data Application to Target System

As is similar to the case for the initial data capture, Oracle provides a series of methods to perform the migration data apply phase to the target Oracle 10g system. Both offline and online applications are possible with the Oracle 10g

Migration Workbench because it allows a fine level of customization for the migration process.

## Final Backup and Recovery Tests After the Migration

Once the final round of migrations is completed, an essential task to finish the process is the ever-important database backup of the newly migrated system to Oracle 10g. Both online hot and cold backups are possible as well as backups using the powerful Recovery Manager (RMAN) tool with Oracle 10g.

There are several choices for the final round of backups. For one, skip the user managed hot backup scripts and head straight full steam ahead with a well crafted RMAN hot and cold backup program. RMAN provides a feature rich list of backup and recovery tools that are essential for a solid backup and recovery environment. Implement an RMAN catalog if there are many databases that have been migrated to Oracle 10g.

 Warning: This bears the importance of repeating the venerated mantra of senior DBAs once again - always take a full database backup before and after the database migration.

This will make keeping track of the backups much easier and allow performing certain tricky recoveries, i.e. lost of control files, much safer and less prone to risk.

## Data Verification and QA Testing

Next to neglected backups and failed, or lack of, project planning and resource allocation, failures in the data verification and quality assurance testing are among the necessary, and often missed, actions for successful migration. While one does not have to be a white box or black box fanatic when it comes to testing and verification process for the database migration, the bare basics should be covered.

Communication and timely planning between the application, database (DBA), QA team, and project manager should occur. When done correctly, this can provide a standard measure of the phases and procedures to be conducted before, during, and after the database migration to Oracle 10g. The only thing worse than no backups is worthless data. This is why making sure QA and verification testing is done in a meticulous manner is so important! The end users, business analysts and executive management will be eternally grateful.

# Database Architecture Differences and Oracle 10g

One of the biggest challenges in the database migration from a non-Oracle platform to Oracle 10g lies in the architecture change between platforms. Both Microsoft SQL Server and MySQL have radical differences between their particular database architectures in contrast to that of Oracle. The good news is that the OMWB is such a potent tool that it resolves 99% of these architecture differences with pure automation. However, it is that remaining 1% that makes life both interesting and challenging with the migration from MySQL and MS SQL Server to Oracle.

For example, Oracle 10g uses the concept of tablespaces and data files for the logical physical structure of its database. Microsoft SQL Server uses datafiles and file groups instead, which have a different structure. As for transaction log mechanisms, Microsoft SQL Server only has one log-based mechanism, which is the transaction log file. Oracle, in contrast, has two types of transactional log based systems: online redo log files and archive log files.

In order to prepare for the migration to Oracle 10g, it is beneficial to first discuss the various database architectural differences between Microsoft SQL Server 2000, MySQL and Oracle 10g. This being, it is important to first discuss the core differences between platforms in order to address the key migration issues moving forward from MySQL and Microsoft SQL Server environments to that of Oracle 10g.

# Oracle 10g Database Architecture

Oracle 10g has a unique architecture that is both complex and logical in contrast to the database implementations from Microsoft and MySQL. The concept for database layout in Oracle contains both an instance and a database. In Oracle 10g, the Oracle instance specifically refers to the collection of special memory, buffers, and background processes. Together, these components allow database operations to proceed within an Oracle 10g system. While a detailed education of the Oracle 10g database architecture is beyond the scope of this book, a brief examination is in order.

The primary memory components of the Oracle 10g instance include the Oracle System Global Area, or SGA, which is implemented via shared memory segments in system memory, or RAM. The SGA provides communication with the other Oracle background processes and system buffers via interprocess communication (IPC) mechanisms. It contains both the database buffer cache and the redo log buffer cache. The Oracle SGA communicates with other background processes such as PMON and SMON. In addition to these buffer caches, the SGA contains the shared pool, Java pool, large pool (optional buffer cache), data dictionary cache, and the Oracle Streams pool for Streams based replication functions. The following figure diagram provides an overview of the Oracle database architecture.

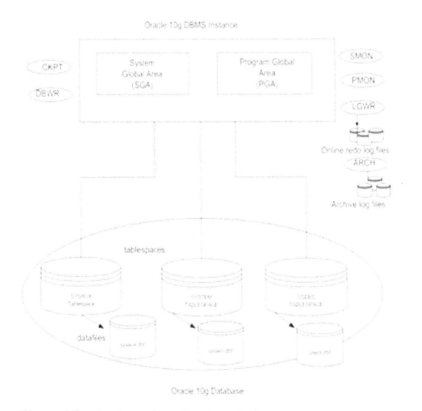

**Figure 1.2:** *Oracle 10g/11g Database Architecture*

Other key ingredients of the Oracle 10g database instance include the Program Global Area, or PGA. The PGA within an Oracle 10g instance contains various buffers to manage server processes with special attention to application database queries with SQL and PL/SQL. The PGA has a Private SQL Area to process information between the instance and database for SQL and PL/SQL queries such as cursor memory management. The PGA provides sorting and processing of SQL statements in memory as well as process management and session management functions.

In contrast to other database vendors such as MySQL and Microsoft SQL Server, Oracle 10g differs architecturally in another fundamental way. This difference is the numerous background processes that communicate with the Oracle 10g memory management areas of the SGA and PGA and database proper. These key background server level processes include SMON, PMON, LGWR, ARCH, CKPT, and DBWR.

The first series of processes, System Monitor (SMON), provides a host of cleanup and instance recovery functions for the entire Oracle 10g database instance. PMON (Process Monitor) is a close cousin of the SMON process. PMON is responsible for the management and recovery of user processes that fail from time to time. In addition to cleanup of failed user sessions, PMON also provides services to communicate with Oracle Network services, such as communication functions between the instance and network listener, for example.

The Checkpoint Process (CKPT) performs updates to all of the headers for the Oracle data files whenever a checkpoint operation is called by the DBWR process. The Archiver process (ARCH) is an optional background process that performs archival of online redo log files to archive logs either on disk or tape. In contrast, the log write (LGWR) process performs management of the critical online redo log files. In terms of communication, LGWR writes log files out to disk from the redo log buffer, which is located in the SGA of an Oracle instance.

One of the most important of the Oracle 10g background processes, the database writer process (DBWR), performs the essential task of writing data blocks from the database buffer cache located in the SGA out to the Oracle datafiles.

Besides the various background processes and memory buffers of an instance, other files play a key role in the operation of an Oracle instance. These files include the online redo log files, archive log files, Oracle 10g password file, Oracle 10g parameter file, and network configuration files and network services. The online redo log files contain all of the database transactions and play a key role in database recovery and storage. In order to take advantage of archival and advanced disaster recovery, copies of these critical online redo log files can be imaged and copied to the archive log files for future recovery purposes.

The Oracle 10g instance also contains special configuration files called parameter initialization (pfile) and static parameter files (spfile) for database instance operation configuration. These are flat text and binary files located as part of a standard Oracle 10g installation. In addition to these files, Oracle 10g has a set of critical files called control files. Control files can be used to store information for Oracle RMAN backups even if a catalog is used by RMAN.

The Oracle 10g network services play a key role in the operation of both the Oracle 10g instance and database. The network services include both the Oracle 10g listener as well as a series of network configuration files. The listener communicates via TCP/IP ports to both the instance and database, while the configuration files manage network communication traffic.

In addition to the Oracle 10g instance, the Oracle 10g database completes the picture for Oracle 10g architecture. In contrast to the instance, the Oracle 10g database consists of the Oracle datafiles, online redo log files, and Oracle control files. These physical database structures complement the logical database design laid out as tablespaces within an Oracle 10g database. As mentioned earlier, control files serve as markers in an Oracle 10g database to contain information on the database configuration.  This relationship is essential for maintenance and recovery operations.

Online redo logs contain the transactional data for an Oracle 10g database. If these were lost, the database would be in an inconsistent state and in grave danger. As such, the prudent DBA will multiplex the control files to protect against loss of one or more control files along with a backup of the datafiles and control files using either RMAN or another backup utility. The Oracle 10g database also contains an error log file, called the alert log, which is needed for reporting the status of the database and instance. The Oracle data files provide the key storage mechanism for application and database related data on disk.

 For further details on the inner workings of the Oracle 10g database architecture, a review of the Oracle 10g Concepts Guide is available for free download on the Oracle technical site: otn.oracle.com.

In addition to these physical database structures, Oracle also uses a logical method to assign these datafiles to a mapping using a system of tablespaces. Tablespaces are like file folders in a cabinet and the Oracle 10g database is split into multiple tablespaces. By default, each database within a standard Oracle 10g environment contains both a SYSTEM and SYSAUX tablespace. Further application data is stored in user created tablespaces designed by the database and application team. These tablespaces hold key data dictionary and database internals for the Oracle 10g database and should not be used for application related data.

# Microsoft SQL Server Architecture

**Figure 1.3:** *Microsoft SQL Server 2000 Database Architecture*

Microsoft SQL Server provides a robust, if simpler, configuration for enterprise database applications. This contrasts from the database architecture that is present with the Oracle 10g database platform. Also in contrast to the instance management required with Oracle 10g, most of the internal database operations are transparent to the user and database professional. Microsoft SQL Server uses a set of kernel-based libraries to manage the internal database operations. Whereas Oracle 10g provides a set of datafiles and tablespaces with a mapping to an Oracle instance, Microsoft SQL Server divides its mechanism for data storage into the concept of physical and logical storage into the physical medium of file groups, files, transaction logs and the logical aspect into databases. Each database within a SQL Server environment is assigned to its own set of filegroup and transaction logs stored on disk. Unlike an Oracle 10g environment that has a one-to-one correlation of one instance per database, the Microsoft SQL Server 2000 architecture is quite a bit different.

For example, a single MS SQL Server 2000 server installation, which would correspond to a single non-RAC cluster-based Oracle 10g instance, may contain hundreds of different SQL Server databases on one server. This being, each instance of a SQL Server may span multiple SQL Server databases. SQL Server uses a file group to store data on disk in the same manner as Oracle 10g stores data on disk into data files. These file groups are system level files that correlate in a one-to-one mapping per each SQL Server database. They also cannot be shared with other databases, much in the way a single data file within an Oracle 10g database is assigned to only one tablespace instead of multiple tablespaces.

SQL Server 2000 further categorizes the management of data, within its database architecture, into several system level databases: master, msdb, tempdb, pubs and Northwind. This is similar to Oracle 10g which uses the two default required tablespaces of SYSTEM and SYSAUX as well as TEMP tablespaces. The function of the SQL Server 2000 master database is to store system level data dictionary and system database information on the server database internals and catalogue. Most veteran SQL Server DBAs know that a time tested backup of the master database is critical to prevent data loss.

In addition, the msdb database functions provide all of the scheduled jobs and alerts used by the SQL Server 2000 database and SQL Server agent. These functions also offer information for processing replication activities between SQL Server databases. In much the same way that Oracle 10g maintains temporary sorting data processing via its TEMP tablespace, Microsoft SQL Server 2000 uses a special database called tempdb to provide a facility for sorting and temporary storage operations. The other two databases, pubs and Northwind, are installed by default with SQL Server 2000. These databases provide training and test database areas similar to the sample Oracle 10g schemas for Scott and hr, for example.

Since the scope of a detailed technical engagement of the SQL Server 2000 database architecture is beyond the level of this text, further explanations of the internal workings of SQL Server 2000 can be referenced on the Microsoft SQL Server 2000 Books Online as well as the free documentation available on the Microsoft SQL Server technical support site.

 The above information on Microsoft SQL Server 2000 can be found online at: http://technet.microsoft.com/en-us/sqlserver/default.aspx

## Introduction to the MySQL Database Architecture

The MySQL database architecture is quite different from that present in Oracle 10g and Microsoft SQL Server 2000. For easier introduction, the newer releases of MySQL 4.x and 5.x will be the ones referred to in order to avoid any confusion.

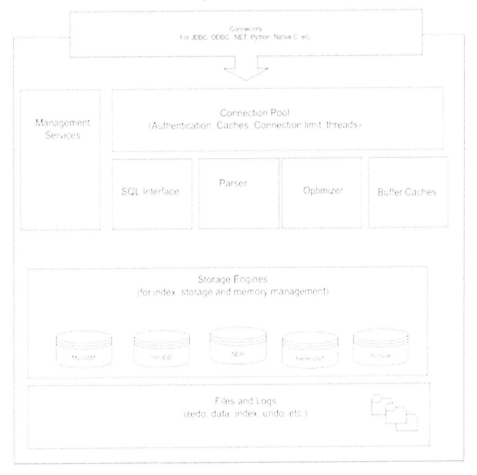

**Figure 1.4:** *MySQL Database Architecture*

In essence, many of the core architectural differences were borrowed from Oracle in terms of memory and data management. The MySQL environment is composed of various management services similar to those in an Oracle 10g instance such as connectors for access to development environment APIs like JDBC, ODBC and .NET as well as storage engines and physical data storage of application data into files and log files. First begin with a quick review of the MySQL storage engines which play a key role in database administration functions of a standard MySQL installation.

## The MySQL 4.x/5.x Storage Engine Architecture

Within a standard MySQL environment, data is stored within multiple storage engines. These storage engines include the following types:

- myISAM
- InnoDB
- Memory
- NDB

First of all, the myISAM storage engine functions as the default disk storage environment. The advantage of using myISAM is that it places a limited footprint. However, it does not provide built-in support for transaction management. In contrast, the InnoDB storage engine within MySQL provides a disk based and fully compatible ACID transaction management system.

The Memory storage engine provides the best speed, in terms of its operation, due to the nature of its method for storage into memory and RAM on the MySQL server.

The NDB, or cluster storage engine for MySQL, functions similar to other clustering database features such as those found with Oracle 10g RAC (Real Application Clusters) and Microsoft SQL Server 2000 Clustering Services. The NDB engine provides a suite of highly available services as well as ultra performance features across multiple nodes for large MySQL clustered environments. Within the MySQL database, files are stored on disk along with log files.

Before version 5.0 of the MySQL platform, usage of serious code development for enterprise database systems was limited due to the lack of stored procedure development features. As for application development with MySQL, it was not until the recent version of MySQL 5.0 that stored procedures entered the picture. MySQL has also recently implemented a new database engine for the SAP R/3 Basis and MySQL environment. This new engine called MAXDB runs many new features of the MySQL platform for SAP customers and has been optimized for SAP applications.

| | Configuration | Storage | SQL/Stored Procedures |
|---|---|---|---|
| Oracle | Instance | Datafiles/tablespaces | SQL, PL/SQL |
| SQL Server | Database | Filegroups | SQL, T-SQL |
| MySQL | Mgmt services | Files,logs | SQL, MySQL SPs |

**Table 1.1:** *Database Architectures for Oracle 10g, SQL Server, and MySQL*

# SQL Differences and Oracle SQL

Besides the challenges involved with migrating different architectures for MySQL and Microsoft SQL Server 2000 to an Oracle 10g platform, both MySQL and Microsoft SQL Server pose unique obstacles in terms of SQL code to Oracle 10g.

None of these vendors are fully compliant to the ANSI-92 SQL Standard. However, they are slowly but surely catching up to a close approximation. All three provide most constructs focused on the ANSI-92 standard for join conditions and DML queries. Nevertheless, the devil is in the details as shall soon be seen.

## MySQL SQL Versus Oracle SQL Constructs

With respect to SQL application syntaxes keeping with the ANSI-SQL 92 standard for database design, both MySQL and Oracle have their quirks. Previous versions of the MySQL platform lacked essential database application functionality such as stored procedures and view implementations. With MySQL 5.0, many new features were added to the MySQL database engine to be more competitive against major database vendors including Oracle and Microsoft SQL Server. Application developers can now write complex stored procedures and views for their open source applications.

The differences between Oracle and MySQL database SQL constructs will be briefly covered to better appreciate the "gotchas" for migration to Oracle 10g from MySQL. In MySQL there are limits on view implementation. For example, it is not possible to create indexes on a view in the MySQL database environment. In Oracle 10g, on the other hand, indexes can be implemented in a view. Oracle 10g also provides features such as materialized views. Materialized views allow complex query aggregations to be stored for future processing; MySQL lacks the mechanism for a materialized view.

Another difference in SQL between the two environments lies in the method of processing database subqueries. The MySQL environment poses special restrictions on how a subquery may be implemented and processed. For instance, a subquery contained within a FROM clause in MySQL cannot be used as a correlated subquery.

Another limitation and difference concerns how database cursors are processed and implemented. With MySQL, as opposed to Oracle, cursors are read-only and cannot be used to update rows in a table. Oracle 10g, on the other hand, allows more cursor functionality to process database tables.

| | MySQL | Oracle 10g |
|---|---|---|
| Support for Views | Limited | YES |
| Materialized Views | NO | YES |
| Stored Procedures | YES (5.x and later) | YES |
| Triggers | Limited | YES |
| Functions | Limited | YES |
| Having Clause | Limited | YES |
| Cursors | Read Only | Both read and write |

**Table 1.2:** *SQL Differences for MySQL and Oracle 10g*

Now that the main differences in SQL syntax have been covered between MySQL and Oracle, next up is a brief examination of the differences between Oracle SQL and Microsoft SQL Server.

# Microsoft SQL Server 2000 SQL versus Oracle SQL

Earlier, the differences between MySQL and Oracle in terms of SQL design were explained. Now to be examined is how Microsoft SQL Server has implemented their version of ANSI-92 related SQL code within their database management system. With this, one can also discover how it differs from that of the Oracle 10g SQL environment. Microsoft SQL Server has a robust SQL database engine that allows for full application and database development of complex triggers, functions, UDFs (Universal Disk Formats), and stored procedures.

The implementation flavor of SQL and stored procedures by Microsoft is called Transact SQL, or T-SQL for short. Even though both Microsoft and Oracle use temporary tables, in Microsoft SQL Server the temporary tables are not stored permanently in the application schema. Oracle, on the other hand, retains the definition of the temporary table permanently in the schema when the user manually removes and drops the temporary table after usage.

One possible option concerning temporary tables in SQL Server during a migration to Oracle 10g would be to rewrite these temporary tables as Oracle materialized views to help smooth the migration process. Keep in mind that the Microsoft SQL Server uses a conflicting naming convention for implementation of temporary tables. There are two types of temporary tables in Microsoft: local and global temporary tables. These are prefixed with a hash mark (#) for a local temporary table and a double hash mark (##) to reference a global temporary table.

These tables must be converted to the Oracle syntax for temporary tables as part of the migration. In addition, another caveat with temporary table conversions from SQL Server to Oracle lies in how temporary tables are dropped. Microsoft uses a drop table *#mytemp_table* which does not exist with the Oracle syntax for removal of temporary tables. Instead, the syntax must be replaced with a *delete mytemp_table* command for Oracle 10g.

|  | SQL Server 2000 | Oracle 10g |
|---|---|---|
| Join Syntax | ANSI-92 based | ANSI-92 based, legacy support |
| Triggers | Before, After | Before, Instead, After, Logon |
| Stored Procedures | Transact SQL | PL/SQL |
| Views | Inline views | Many types |
| Materialized Views | Not available | Yes |

**Table 1.3:** *SQL Differences for MS SQL Server 2000 and Oracle 10g*

As the migration test cases for MySQL and SQL Server to Oracle are worked through, more coverage will be presented on syntax differences and how to address these conflicts in the migration to Oracle 10g.

## Data Type Issues: MySQL and Oracle 10g

To shift gears a bit, the issue of data type differences between MySQL and Oracle 10g will be covered since this will pose a challenge during the migration process. The chart below lists a summary of the major differences in data type structure between MySQL and Oracle 10g.

| Oracle 10g Database | MySQL Server 4.x/5.x | | |
|---|---|---|---|
| Data Type | Data Type | Numeric Type | Range Values |
| NUMBER(19) | TINYINT | INTEGER | -128 to 127 |
| NUMBER(10) | SMALLINT | INTEGER | 0 to 255 |
| NUMBER(6) | MEDIUMINT | INTEGER | -32768 to 32767 or 65535 |
| NUMBER(3) | INT | INTEGER | -8388608 to 8388607 |
| NUMBER (p,s) | BIGINT | INTEGER | -2147483648 to 2147483648 |

**Table 1.4:** *Numeric Data Types MySQL and Oracle 10g*

The main issue of data type conversions from MySQL platform to Oracle 10g exists in the many versions of numerical data types that are present in MySQL and lacking in Oracle 10g. Application codes should be modified from MySQL to reflect the compatible format of Oracle numerical calculations to prevent migration errors and conflicts.

The MySQL environment has also implemented many different character data types that do not exist in Oracle 10g. These differences will need to be accounted for to successfully migrate applications to Oracle 10g from MySQL. Table 1.5 shows a chart that summarizes the main differences in how character data types are implemented in MySQL and Oracle.

| Oracle 10g Database | | MySQL Server 4.x/5.x | | |
|---|---|---|---|---|
| Data Type | Max Length (characters) | Data Type | Type | Max Length (characters) |
| CHAR | 2000 | CHAR | Fixed-length | 255 |
| VARCHAR2 | 4000 | VARCHAR | Variable-length | 255 to 65,535 (MySQL 5.03 and later release) |
| CLOB, BLOB 4,294,967,296 | | BINARY, VARBINARY, TINYBLOB, BLOB, MEDIUMBLOB, LONGBLOB | Variable-length | 0-255, up to 65,535 |
| NCHAR | 2000 | TINYTEXT | Variable-length | 255 |
| NVARCHAR2 | 4000 | TEXT | Variable-length | 65,535 |
| NCLOB | 2,147,483,648 | MEDIUMTEXT | Variable-length | 16,777,215 |
| - | | LONGTEXT | Variable-length | 4GB |
| - | | ENUM, SET | String length | 65,535, 64 |

**Table 1.5:** *Character Data Types for MySQL and Oracle 10g*

For example, if the requirements allow a simple set of standards, in terms of character data, the conversions will be a lot smoother from MySQL to Oracle 10g. Extra care must be taken to convert large applications and data types in MySQL to Oracle so that no loss in application functionality occurs after the cutover to Oracle 10g.

## Data Type Issues with Microsoft SQL Server 2000 and Oracle 10g

Among the many challenges in migrations to Oracle 10g from SQL Server are the data type model differences between these platforms. In the chart below, a list of the major features of how data types in Oracle 10g and Microsoft SQL Server 2000 is shown.

| Oracle 10g Database | Microsoft SQL Server 2000 | | |
|---|---|---|---|
| Data Type | Data Type | Numeric Type | Range Values |
| NUMBER(19) | bigint | Integer | -2^63 to 2^63 |
| NUMBER(10) | int | Integer | -2^63 to 2^31 |
| NUMBER(6) | smallint | Integer | -2^15 to 2^15 |
| NUMBER(3) | tinyint | Integer | 0-255 |
| NUMBER (p,s) | decimal | Fixed precision decimal | -10^38 to 10^38 |
| NUMBER(19,4) | money | Money | -2^63 to 2^63 |
| NUMBER(10,4) | smallmoney | Money | -214,748 to +214,748 |
| NUMBER | float | Floating point | -1.79E to -2.23E, 0 and 2.23E to 1.79E |
| NUMBER | Real | Floating point | -3.40E to -1.18E, 0 and 1.18E to 3.40E |

**Table 1.6:** *Numeric Data Types - Oracle 10g and Microsoft SQL Server*

Application codes that use the *convert* function in Microsoft SQL Server 2000 should be replaced with *cast* functions in Oracle to avoid conflicts. Other problems that can be avoided with the migration of data types include the change of Microsoft SQL Server character and date mask formats to the Oracle *to_date* and *to_char* constructs.

For example, The SQL Server expression,

```
CONVERT(datetime, expression, style)
```

should be changed to a format in Oracle similar to the following:

```
TO_DATE(expression, date_mask)
```

Below is a summary of how SQL Server and Oracle implement character data types:

| Oracle 10g Database | | Microsoft SQL Server 2000 | | |
|---|---|---|---|---|
| Data Type | Max Length (character | Data Type | Type | Max Length (characters) |

| | s) | | | |
|---|---|---|---|---|
| CHAR | 2000 | CHAR | Fixed-length | 8000 |
| VARCHAR2 | 4000 | VARCHAR | Variable-length | 8000 |
| CLOB 4,294,967,296 | | TEXT | Variable-length | 2,147,483,647 |
| NCHAR | 2000 | NCHAR | Fixed-length Unicode | 4000 |
| NVARCHAR2 | 4000 | NVARCHAR | Variable-length Unicode | 4000 |
| NCLOB 2,147,483,648 | | NTEXT | Variable-length Unicode | 1,073,741,823 |

**Table 1.7:** *Character Data Types for Oracle 10g and SQL Server*

# Stored Procedures and Oracle PL/SQL

The most difficult aspect of completing database migrations to Oracle 10g is the mapping of non-Oracle SQL and stored procedures to Oracle SQL and Oracle PL/SQL. This is due to the fundamentals of how MySQL and Microsoft SQL Server utilize SQL and application development in contrast to the model used by Oracle. In this section, the major differences between how MySQL and Microsoft SQL Server use SQL and stored procedures will be shown here.

One of the main goals for migrating stored procedures from MySQL and MS SQL Server is to simplify the migration process to Oracle as much as possible to avoid errors during the migration process. Challenges that are most difficult, in terms of migrating from MySQL and/or Microsoft SQL Server, are the conversion of data types, SQL, and stored procedure code. All three vendors provide unique additions to the ANSI-SQL standard as well as individual vendor-based programming extensions for stored procedure development.

# Microsoft Transact SQL and Oracle PL/SQL

Another challenge with migrating applications on SQL Server to Oracle 10g exists in the different uses of stored procedure development. Microsoft has implemented its custom version with Transact SQL language which was long ago closely based on Sybase. Oracle, in contrast, has implemented stored procedures using PL/SQL, which are loosely based on the Ada object oriented language. As such, there are specific constructs that need to be mapped to Oracle from Microsoft Transact SQL code in SQL Server.

For example, stored procedures in SQL Server that create result set patterns will need to be mapped to OUT REF cursors by Oracle. By default, the Oracle Migration Workbench will only create a single cursor of this type for implicit result sets generated by SQL Server procedures. An additional cursor of this type will need to be added to avoid migration errors.

# Migration Workbench: The Preferred Method for Database Migration

Earlier in the introduction various methods were introduced that perform complex database migrations from MySQL and Microsoft SQL Server to Oracle 10g. Each methodology has its merits and weaknesses. If the database and tech team has a large budget for third party tools, a nice suite of products may be purchased to ease the pain of migrating to Oracle 10g. With current IT budgets, most database professionals are forced to make do with limited budgets for additional software and hardware purchases. This forces the DBA's hand to try his or her craft using homegrown free solutions to complete a migration to Oracle 10g.

Native utilities within the MySQL and Microsoft SQL Server suite, such as BCP for Microsoft SQL Server and the MySQL load and export utilities can be used to offload the initial data loads for future use with an Oracle 10g environment. There are manual techniques to convert the application, database code, and structures to an Oracle format. However, as was shown in the beginning, these are painful at best and pose major infrastructure difficulties that pose great risk for the migration process.

Enter the best possible solution for strapped IT budgets and overworked DBAs: the Oracle 10g Migration Workbench tool. This nifty and free tool provides a great deal of relief in the migration from MySQL and Microsoft SQL Server as well as from Informix and IBM DB2 to the Oracle 10g platform. Best of all, the OMWB can be used in concert with all of the standard Oracle 10g native utilities, such as Oracle transportable tablespaces and data pump export and import, to make the entire migration process a stunning success.

The good news is that the OMWB takes 99% of the pain and suffering out of complex migrations from MySQL and Microsoft SQL Server 2000 to the Oracle 10g platform. Best of all, it is free! So senior management executives should now be easily convinced to advocate use of this powerful tool.

However, it is not a complete panacea, and experienced database professionals will be required to administer the process of migrations using this tool. In some cases, due to lack of support for migrations to Oracle 10g, another method may be required. This includes the use of a third party tool from a vendor such as GoldenGate Software or Quest Shareplex.

It really depends on the environment that is being migrated away from to Oracle 10g. With that said, when administering MySQL and Microsoft SQL Server 2000 platform migrations to Oracle 10g, the OMWB provides a handy Swiss army knife tool.

## Conclusion

In this chapter, a background necessary to perform a complex migration from MySQL and Microsoft SQL Server to Oracle 10g has been examined. An introduction to the database migration tools, including native utilities within Oracle, MySQL, and Microsoft SQL Server, were covered. Also important is the consideration that there is an option to deploy a third party commercial vendor solution such as GoldenGate or Quest SharePlex software in concert with the migration to Oracle 10g.

Second, this chapter reviewed a series of critical project planning and management planning activities which are crucial to the success of all database migration projects to Oracle 10g. Often neglected, these project review skills are an essential piece of the database migration puzzle from MySQL and Microsoft SQL Server to Oracle 10g.

Next, the differences in database architectures were illustrated to provide an overview of the major structural designs for MySQL, Microsoft SQL Server 2000, and Oracle 10g. These differences are important to understand conceptually to resolve any fundamental migration questions early in the database migration to Oracle 10g platform.

In addition to migration techniques, project method, and testing, a brief review of differences in the data types and SQL dialects was provided between MySQL, Oracle 10g, and Microsoft SQL Server. This helps users to understand how such design variations in the database environment will pose special challenges to the entire migration process. Fortunately, the OMWB provides many excellent solutions to address these application design differences, which will be covered further in future chapters.

Last but not least, the closing remark for the chapter touched upon the rationale for a decision to deploy the OMWB as the tool of choice for database migrations to the Oracle platform. The free available tool has many features and wizards to ensure a fairly smooth process for the migration to Oracle from MySQL or SQL Server. The next chapter will begin with a tour guide view of the Oracle 10g Migration Workbench. It will cover the architecture and layout design of the OMWB from an initial 50,000-foot view and then will drill down into the details on installation and configuration.

# Overview of the Oracle Migration Workbench

*"The architecture of the Migration Workbench can be rather complex"*

## Introduction to Oracle Migration Workbench

In the last chapter, a brief exploration about database migrations was presented to prepare for the use of the Oracle Migration Workbench (OMWB). In this chapter, a more detailed overview of the OMWB architecture will be provided. This will allow for all components that make up the environment to be understood, paving the way to a successful database migration from MySQL and/or Microsoft SQL Server to Oracle 10g via Oracle 10g Workbench Migration.

The OMWB is a powerful and freely available tool that is new to the Oracle 10g suite of database technology and will assist database professionals in complex database migrations. Using this tool offers a much greater chance of success than with manual techniques.

To become familiar with the tool, the architecture layout for both the OMWB environment and Oracle Application Express (APEX) Migration Workbench tools will be covered. A brief examination of the installation preparation and associated suite of tools and requirements will also be provided for both OMWB and APEX Migration Workshop utilities.

# Oracle Migration Workbench and the APEX Migration Workbench

Begin the tour of the OMWB with the big picture, and then drill down to the micro level of this new tool. Oracle 10g introduced the migration workbench tool with the main suite. This includes the workbench and additional modules called plugins that are used for various application database vendors such as MySQL, IBM DB2 Universal Database and Microsoft SQL Server. Figure 2.1 shows a diagram of the OMWB.

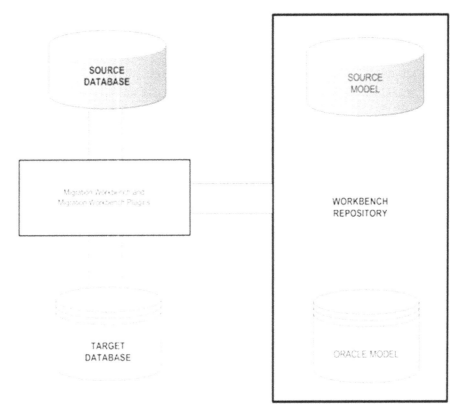

**Figure 2.1:** *Oracle 10g Migration Workbench Architecture*

## Oracle 10g Migration Workbench Components

The Migration Workbench architecture includes the following tools for the migration of non-Oracle databases including MySQL and Microsoft SQL Server to Oracle 10g:

- Capture Wizard

- Migration Wizard

- Migration Scripts for both online and offline capture

- Migration Plug-ins

- Workbench Repository

## Capture Wizard

The Capture wizard component of the OMWB is a feature-rich, easy to use tool that allows users to capture all of the source data and database definitions such as schemas and DDL from the source database in preparation for migrating to the new target Oracle 10g environment. During the migration process from MySQL or MS SQL Server, the capture wizard connects to the source database, extracts the source database definition, and populates the source model in the OMWB repository. The use and deployment of the capture wizard will be discussed in further detail in subsequent chapters.

## Migration Wizard

The Migration wizard feature within the OMWB interfaces with the Migration Workbench and the workbench repository areas. Together they move the new source model cloned database to the Oracle model database during the migration process.

## Migration Scripts: Offline and Online Capture

In addition to the capture and migration wizards, the OMWB includes numerous migration scripts for non-Oracle database platforms such as MySQL, IBM DB2, Informix, and MS SQL Server environments. These scripts are used to capture both database structures, i.e. schemas and DDL, and actual data capture scripts that enhance the migration process. For example, there are both offline and online capture scripts that interface with MS SQL Server databases. Native SQL Server commands and utilities can be used to perform a "hot" online capture, while the SQL Server database is available, with BCP scripts. On the other hand, if the migration is performed during weekend maintenance non-user hours, offline BCP scripts are provided to capture both the data structures and data from the SQL Server source database to use as part of the migration process with the OMWB.

In all, these scripts create a set of script files that describe the metadata structure and DDL of the non-Oracle database as well as provide the actual database copy scripts to perform either the online or offline data capture process.

## Migration Plugins

As part of the migration process to Oracle 10g, the workbench tool provides a comprehensive set of plugins for the majority of database vendors including MySQL, Microsoft SQL Server, IBM DB2 UDB, Informix and many other platforms. The function of these plugins is to serve as a method for the OMWB to convert these database environments to the Oracle 10g architecture and translate these non-Oracle structures into Oracle database structures. For example, migration plugins perform the following critical tasks within the migration workbench suite:

- Source model creation for a new Oracle 10g database

- Perform conversion from the source model to the Oracle model

- Initial data capture and extraction from the non-Oracle source database dictionary tables and system structures

## Workbench Repository

The Oracle Workbench Repository is a main component of the OMWB that performs many of the critical functions during a database migration from either MySQL or MS SQL Server to Oracle 10g. As part of the migration process, the workbench repository provides a set of tables. There is also the option to use a specific database schema, or separate database, to contain all of the migration details that are to be performed before, during, and after the database migration. It offers a buffer against the risk of using the source production database to perform the migration in the event that an error occurs during the migration process. With this component, the original source database in production will not be impacted, and risk can be mitigated and providing a cushion to test the migration in place.

The workbench repository has two main subcomponents: the source model and the Oracle model containers for the Oracle migration workbench environment. The workbench repository also takes a backup of the source MySQL or MS SQL Server database metadata information. As for storage methods for the repository data, Oracle recommends users use a new Oracle 9i or 10g database to store the workbench repository models. If building a new Oracle 9i or 10g database is not possible, the repository tables and schemas may be stored in the default repository that is available with the default workbench repository. This comes readily installed with the OMWB.

# The Oracle 10g Application Express (APEX) Migration Workbench

The Oracle Application Express, APEX for short, provides a useful tool for migrations of database applications which nicely complements the more robust suite of database migration tools provided with the OMWB suite. The APEX workshop enhances the suite of application and migration tools from Oracle that includes the OMWB and the new Oracle 10g SQL Developer Migration Workbench. It provides a method to migrate all of the schema definitions and data from Microsoft Access environments to that within the APEX environment. In contrast to a non-browser MS Access environment, the APEX migration workshop will allow the team to migrate these applications to a web based browser environment on the APEX platform.

## Oracle 10g APEX and the Oracle 10g APEX Migration Workshop Suite

Before perusing the details of the APEX workshop, it would be useful to first review the components of the APEX environment.

The APEX workshop was formerly known to Oracle web developers and database administrators as Oracle EnterpriseDB which served web enabled database centric applications in previous releases. Because the intranet, internet, and web enabled commercial applications are a critical feature of modern business enterprise applications and the web marketplace, the requirement to deploy web enabled database platform is paramount. Oracle has answered this urgent need with the APEX environment to port legacy Microsoft Access databases and applications to Oracle 10g web enabled environments. The Oracle 10g APEX platform is a robust Java J2EE enabled environment with many excellent tools and features for web developers to use as part of their repertoire for the enterprise infrastructure. These tools are great when developing new applications to meet the needs of the modern business environment.

The APEX provides a multitude of options to generate web-enabled reports including HTML formats, PDF format, and text based reports with Oracle 10g database environments. Besides an excellent IDE environment that is feature-rich for developing quality enterprise web enabled database content, the interface and tool suite for Oracle 10g APEX is simple to learn and deploy. This provides developers who are new to the APEX environment less of a learning curve and ramp up time than most commercial internet developer tools.

Figure 2.2 shows a snapshot of the Oracle 10g APEX environment:

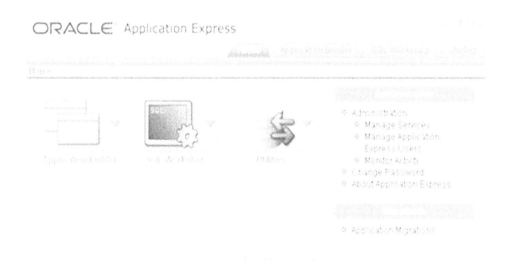

**Figure 2.2:** *The Oracle 10g APEX Environment*

In order to provide development staff with education on how to use and work with the APEX Workshop suite of internet development tools, Oracle provides a free online access to the Oracle 10g APEX 3.0 suite along with free online tutorials to get started quickly with the environment. Figure 2.3 is a sample of the tutorial suite welcome screen:

**Figure 2.3:** *Oracle 10g APEX Tutorial Online Access Provided by http://apex.oracle.com*

In order to use the online version of the APEX 3.0 workshop environment, one will need to sign up for a free online account and request a free workspace to use the online environment. A second option is to download a free developer license copy of the software available from the Oracle site listed next:

- http://www.oracle.com/technology/products/database/application_expr ess/download.html

An example of the enrollment process to access the workspace area for a new Oracle 10g APEX environment is shown in Figure 2.4:

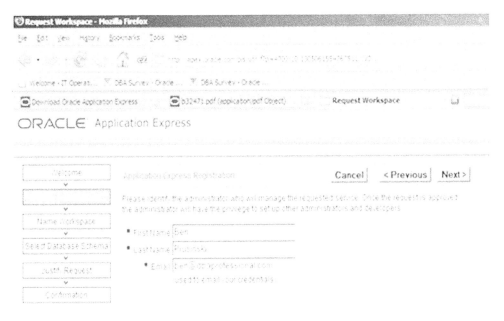

**Figure 2.4:** *Oracle 10g APEX Registration Access*

# Oracle 10g APEX Components

Next to be covered are the components of the APEX environment. The APEX environment contains the APEX migration workshop as one of its key components. The purpose of the APEX migration workshop tool is to perform migration and recovery features for Microsoft Access applications to the Oracle Application Workshop environment.

The Oracle 10g APEX environment consists of the following key components:

- Application Builder
- SQL Workshop
- Utilities
- Administration
- Migrations

## Application Builder

The application builder component of the Oracle 10g APEX environment provides a collection of wizards and tools for the creation and deployment of web enabled database centric applications and reports.

## SQL Workshop

The SQL Workshop application cluster within the APEX Workbench provides tools for the development and modification of database queries, tables, and schema objects for use with Oracle 10g applications and reports.

## Utilities

The Utilities interface within APEX web developer tools provides functions for managing the various application and database modules. This includes the export and import of data between workspaces and applications.

## Administration

The administration arena of the Oracle APEX package is where new and current user accounts are managed, created, deleted or changed for use with the Oracle APEX environment.

## Migrations

The migrations feature provides the interface for performance of application migrations from MS Access to Oracle 10g.

# A Closer Look at Oracle 10g APEX Migration Workshop

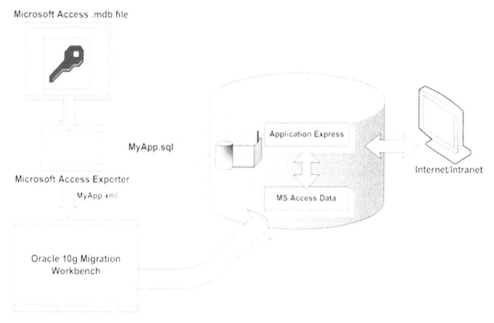

**Figure 2.5:** *Oracle 10g APEX Workshop Architecture*

A full examination of the inner workings and uses of the Oracle 10g APEX Workshop would require a substantial discussion that is beyond the scope of this guide. For further reading and discourse on the use of this tool, it is advised to review texts on the Oracle 10g APEX Workshop that are available from various publishers and online documentation. Oracle provides excellent documentation on how to use and manage an APEX environment with whitepapers and documentation freely available for download at the following site:

- http://www.oracle.com/technology/products/database/application_express/index.html

## Benefits of the Oracle 10g APEX Migration Workshop

The Oracle APEX Migration Workshop is a free new tool released with Oracle 10g that provides a powerful method to migrate Microsoft Access database applications to the Oracle APEX environment.

While it is possible to develop web enabled database applications with other methods and programming languages such as HTML, PHP, Java, C# and .NET, the APEX workshop has a unique advantage over these web developer languages. It provides a major leap in productivity for new and experienced development staff members who need to quickly develop and deploy complex web enabled database applications quickly. It also is able to generate powerful reports for business application needs. Furthermore, with the close integration between the Oracle APEX development environment and the APEX Migration Workshop, powerful applications can be migrated quickly from Microsoft Access to Oracle platform. These can then be deployed rapidly, thus saving time and cost while increasing productivity for large enterprise web applications.

For more details on the APEX Migration Workshop and the Oracle 10g APEX suite, review the following site from Oracle:

http://www.oracle.com/technology/products/database/applicatio n_express/migrations/readme/accmgrdme.htm

## Oracle 10g APEX Migration Workshop Components

The Oracle 10g APEX Migration Workshop provides the following tools and features:

- The creation of snapshots to view all of the metadata for applications that are captured from a Microsoft Access database

- Ability to identify and mark any tables that do not have a primary key (PK) or a default user interface

- Functionality which identifies all invalid Oracle views that were previously queries in MS Access database

- A verification process for all database SQL code to ensure that the SQL syntax is correct for ported Access code to Oracle APEX applications for all reports that are query related

- List of all objects in MS Access applications that are selected for migration to the Oracle APEX environment

- Ability to create or generate an application based on the APEX environment using the selection of MS Access reports and forms based on a list of selected tables and views

- Ability to develop various projects for migration using Oracle APEX workspaces

- Ability to allow migration from multiple releases of MS Access versions including MS Access 97 to MS Access 2003 to the Oracle APEX environment

# Migrating MS Access Applications

While the APEX Migration Workbench is a potent tool for the migration of MS Access reports, databases, and applications to the Oracle APEX environment, there are several steps that are required for implementation in order to use the tool for the migration of Microsoft Access databases to the new Oracle APEX environment. The first step involves the setup and configuration of the tools and applications for the Oracle APEX Migration Workshop environment.

In order to make use of the APEX Migration Workshop package of tools to port Microsoft Access applications to the Oracle APEX environment, the following tools must be downloaded and installed:

- Oracle Application Express 3.0

- Oracle 10g SQL Developer Migration Workbench

- Oracle 10g Exporter Tool

## Oracle Application Express 3.0

The Oracle APEX 3.0 workshop feature provides the facility for the migration of Microsoft Access reports and forms to the APEX environment.

The installation guide for this utility, along with free downloads, are available from the Oracle download site located at http://www.oracle.com/technology/apex.

## Oracle 10g SQL Developer Migration Workbench

The Oracle SQL Developer Migration Workbench provides the tools to migrate all of the Microsoft Access schemas and data to the Oracle 10g database platform. In addition to the Oracle 10g SQL Developer Migration Workbench, a required MS Access plugin download is required to perform migrations from MS Access to Oracle 10g.

## Oracle 10g Exporter Tool

The Exporter tool is a critical part of the Oracle 10g APEX Migration Workshop suite. It is a custom module that is written in MS Access code which provides some of the files that are generated for use with Access migrations to Oracle 10g. These files are deciphered by the OMWB and Oracle 10g APEX tools. To perform migrations from MS Access to APEX, the exporter tool will need to be installed on a computer system with access to the Microsoft Access database that will be migrated to Oracle.

# Oracle 10g SQL Developer Migration Workbench

The next generational version of the OMWB will be tightly coupled with the new database development environment, Oracle 10g SQL Developer, to provide more comprehensive toolsets for database migrations to Oracle 10g.

 More details on the future release of the Oracle 10g SQL Developer Migration Workbench, is available from: http://www.oracle.com/technology/tech/migration/ workbench/pdf/new_omwb_ds.pdf.

All technical subjects often appear to be moving targets because of constant new developments and enhancements to products. The future enhancements to the OMWB include all of the currently available tools and features for migration of most common non-Oracle databases to Oracle 10g. Features of the Oracle 10g SQL Developer Migration Workbench are as follows:

- User Interface with GUI environment from SQL Developer

- Incorporation of the developer environment from the new SQL Developer and the Oracle 10g SQL Developer Migration Workbench

- Migration with the least privileges in that it provides the ability to migrate database objects from the source environment to the target with non-DBA level access. In a sense, the workbench tools will perform the migration for objects with no requirement to have DBA elevated privileges.

- Multiple platforms which support most versions of MS Access, including Access 97 through Access 2005, as well as most MySQL database versions

- Online Parallel Data Movement allows data to be moved using multiple parallel connections for optimum performance

- Offline script generation for moving data. This involves the creation of scripts to export source data and perform import to the target database environment in an offline capacity.

- Features for language conversions and translation in which built-in support for the translation with respect to stored procedures, triggers, functions, schema level objects as defined in either the MS Access SQL or MS SQL Server Transact SQL (T-SQL) languages are provided

- Translation Scratch Editor which provides for an interactive editor to convert from either MS Access SQL or MS SQL Server Transact SQL to either Oracle PL/SQL and/or Oracle SQL code. Both complex SQL scripts and single level statement support is provided.

- Viewer for code translation changes to examine differences in SQL that is converted from Access or SQL Server to Oracle. This provides a comparison scheme to contrast and display differences between source code and new conversion related code.

>  The new changes and enhancements as well as release notes are available from the following Oracle site:
>
>  http://www.oracle.com/technology/tech/migration/workbench/files/ReleaseNotes.html.

As of March 2007, the future release of the OMWB was released for early adopter status.

# Oracle 10g Database Migration Verifier

In addition to the OMWB and the new APEX Migration Workshop, another useful and necessary tool is available to assist with complex database migrations from MS SQL Server to Oracle 10g platform. The Oracle Database Migration Verifier (DMV) provides support for either the Sybase Adaptive Server or Microsoft SQL Server database applications. The purpose and function of the new DMV is to analyze the source database system and perform a complete application and database comparison to the new target Oracle 10g database environment. The tool validates the data integrity structures of the newly migrated database from SQL Server to Oracle 10g. Afterwards, it provides a comprehensive report of all verification checks from an application, schema level, and data level perspective. This provides an effective method to test and verify that the database migration has been accurate and successful. This tool will covered in more detail in Chapter 8.

# Conclusion

In this chapter, the high-level architecture of both the Oracle 10g Migration Workbench (OMWB) and the Oracle 10g Application Express (APEX) Migration Workshop was featured. In addition to the introduction of the technical components of these tools, the required tools and environments that must be configured before the use of these migration tools for Oracle 10g were briefly touched upon.

In the next chapter, the process for installation and configuration of the OMWB and APEX Migration Workshop suite of tools will be investigated. In addition, the new tools for use with the Oracle 10g migration suite, the Oracle 10g DMV, and SQL Developer Migration tool will be covered in more detail.

As the latest members of the Oracle 10g migration toolbox, these tools perform complex application and database migrations to the Oracle 10g platform. The next chapter will also present the installation requirements and methods to install and configure these powerful application and database migration tools.

# Installation Planning and Configuration for the Oracle 10g Migration Workbench

*"Proper Installation is essential for Oracle migration success"*

## Introduction to Oracle 10g Workbench Migration Tools

The previous chapter introduced the various components that form the architecture of the Oracle 10g package of migration tools. This chapter will move forward into the more substantial implementation process. The procedures for how to install all of the Oracle 10g Workbench Migration (OMWB) tools will also be covered.

A major component of OMWB installation for Microsoft SQL Server and MySQL to Oracle 10g migration is the required software packages and associated utilities that are necessary to have a fully functional environment for the performance of the migrated database. In addition to learning about these downloads, the steps and procedures for how to install the APEX tools for migrating Microsoft Access databases and applications to the Oracle 10g APEX environment will be touched upon. Oracle has also integrated these migration tools with the new SQL Developer tools for Oracle 10g and 11g.

Finally, the future direction for software development and migration to Oracle is to use the integrated set of tools with SQL Developer and APEX Workbench for all development and migration tasks with Oracle. As such, all three tools in the Oracle migration environment will be examined.

# Prerequisites: Oracle 10g Migration Workbench Installation

This section will show support for release 10.1.0.4 of the migration workbench for MS SQL Server 2000, MySQL 3.x through 4.x. For later releases of SQL Server and MySQL, the March 2007 released SQL Developer Migration Workbench is advised to be used for migration procedures. In order to maintain a balanced approach to database migrations from MySQL and MS SQL Server, both the OMWB and SQL Developer Migration tools will be covered in terms of installation and configuration techniques.

## Preparation for Oracle Migration Workbench Installation

The first task to install the complex OMWB software is to assemble all of the software tools, libraries and packages. Since this is a confusing and unclear process, all of the steps to get the OMWB installed correctly and efficiently will be reviewed.

## Roadmap to the Installation Process - Oracle Migration Workbench

The appropriate stops on the roadmap are as follows:

1. Download all required software packages and tools

2. Check for required Java libraries and packages

3. Review installation guides and release notes

4. Perform software installation

5. Configure migration tools

# Required Software for the Oracle Migration Workbench

The latest release of the Oracle 10g and 11g SQL Developer Migration Workbench is available from the OTN download site listed here. To save on the mystery of finding a needle in a haystack, the Oracle technical site below has the link to download the workbench software binaries:

- http://www.oracle.com/technology/software/tech/migration/workbench /index.html

The following steps are helpful in preparing for installation of the OMWB. First, download and review the OMWB Release Notes from Oracle. These contain many "gotchas" and bug fixes with the most current version of the OMWB. Second, make sure to download, in the following order, the binaries for the OMWB software as they are required for a minimum OMWB installation:

- Oracle Migration Workbench software binary (version 10.1.0.4)

- Oracle Migration Workbench Plugins for Microsoft SQL Server 7.0, MS SQL Server 2000, MS SQL Server 2005 and MySQL 3/4/5.0 database versions

- Optional Software for MySQL database platform only: MySQL5 Beta Release Bundle package (includes the Workbench 10.1.0.4.3 software installer and MySQL 5 plug-in)

---

> 🔔 Note that with software releases there may be a more current release. Be sure to check the Oracle download site.

---

Lastly, download and review the documentation set for the OMWB. Many problems can be avoided by review of the latest release for the OMWB documentation set.

## Tips from the Oracle Migration Workbench Release Notes

On the journey to migration success with the OMWB, visit the tips and tricks that can be obtained from the most recent OMWB release notes from Oracle. In the release notes for the OMWB, be sure to take an especially close look at the Oracle Migration Workbench User's Guide. The User's Guide contains valuable tips and tricks for first time OMWB environment users. Reference the installation section of the User's Guide for up-to-date changes in concert with the Oracle 10g Migration Workbench Release notes before installation of the software.

# Downloading the Oracle Migration Workbench Software

The next task is to perform the download process and installation tasks associated with the OMWB software environment. For case studies, Oracle Release 10.1.0.4.0 for Microsoft Windows 98/NT/2000/XP platform will be used as one proceeds with installation and configuration of the OMWB software.

OMWB supports most database platforms. Table 3.1 shows a list of the supported database environments for the current release.

| SOURCE DATABASE | SUPPORTED OS PLATFORM/VERSION |
|---|---|
| Microsoft SQL Server 6.5, 7, 2000 | Windows |
| Microsoft Access 95, 97, 2000, 2002, XP, 2003 | Windows |
| Sybase Adaptive Server 11/12 | Linux and Windows |
| Informix Dynamic Server 7.3, 9.x | Linux and Windows |
| IBM DB2 UDB V6, V7.1, V7.2 (in Beta release) | Windows |
| MySQL 3.22, 32.23, 4.X and 5.X | Linux and Windows |
| IBM DB2/400 V4R3 and V4R5 | Windows |

**Table 3.1:** *Supported Platform List for Oracle 10g Migration Workbench*

As a caveat in order to use the OMWB, the required plugin software will need to be downloaded and installed for each specific database and platform that will be migrated to Oracle 10g. In the cases that will be examined, the plugins for MySQL and Microsoft SQL Server 2000 will need to be downloaded and installed during the installation and configuration process for the Oracle Migration Workbench.

>  Be sure to visit the Oracle software sites listed in the references section at the end of this chapter to find the most current releases as well as those available from Oracle Metalink. Since software development cycles tend to be quite rapid in the database world, it is critical to research and obtain latest release notes, patches and software versions for the migration tools.

## Download the Required Plugin Software

The next step after a successful download and installation for the OMWB is to configure the plugin software. For example, since the plan is to test migrations from MySQL and SQL Server 2000 to Oracle 10g, one will need to download and setup the plugin software for these two environments. Oracle allows installing multiple plugins at the same time if one wishes to migrate more than one third party database to Oracle 10g. This flexibility is a great asset to the complex migration process.

In addition to the database plugin software, one will also need to download and configure several types of software drivers for these third party databases that will be migrated to Oracle 10g. A review of the release notes for the OMWB, as well as the Oracle Migration Workbench User's Guide, will be a benefit here in making sure that this critical step and last minute errata involved with the installation and configuration process are not overlooked.

Table 3.2 shows the assortment of drivers and requirements in a table matrix.

| Database Platform | Supported Version(s) | Required Plug-in | Software Driver |
| --- | --- | --- | --- |

| (Migrate from) | | | |
|---|---|---|---|
| Microsoft SQL Server | 6.5 | MS SQL Server 6.5 Plug-in | MS SQL Server ODBC driver release 3.70.06.23+ |
| Microsoft SQL Server | 7.0 | MS SQL Server 7.0 Plug-in | MS SQL Server 7.0 Driver |
| Microsoft SQL Server | 2000 | MS SQL Server 2000 Plug-in | MS SQL Server 2000 Driver |
| Microsoft Access | All versions supported (95, 97, 2000, 2003) | MS Access Plug-in | MS Microsoft Data Access Component (MDAC) driver |
| Sybase | Sybase Adaptive Server 11, Sybase Adaptive Server 12 | Sybase Adaptive Server Plugin for 11 or 12. | Sybase Adaptive Server ODBC Driver Release 3.11.00.01 or later. Available with Sybase client software. |
| IBM DB2 UDB; IBM DB2/400 | IBM DB2 UDB 6.x, 7.1, 7.3 ; IBM V4R3, V4R5 | IBM DB2 UDB 6.x, 7.x Beta Plug-in | IBM DB2 UDB JDBC driver; IBM DB2 400 JDBC Driver |
| Informix Dynamic Server | 7.3, 9.x | Informix Dynamic Server 7.3, 9.x Plug-in | Informix Dynamic Server JDBC Driver, version 1.4 JAR file, ifxjdbc.jar. Informix driver is available with Informix Server software installation. |
| MySQL | 3.x, 4.x, 5.x | MySQL 3.x or MySQL 4.x Plugin | MySQL Connector/J JDBC driver release 3.0.14-production |

**Table 3.2:** *Oracle 10g Migration Workbench Plugin Matrix*

## Downloading Third Party Drivers for the OMWB Environment

Next to be reviewed are the procedures to download the required third party database drivers for the OMWB.

Download driver for MS SQL Server 2000 and save it locally as *SQLServer2K.jar*.

---

🔔 Note for MySQL Plugins and Drivers:

🔔 Download this file and save it locally as MySQL4.jar for MySQL 4.x database

🔔 Download this file and save it locally as MySQL3.jar for MySQL 3.x database

---

- For download of the above listed driver software, Microsoft has a free download of required components from the main download site at http://www.microsoft.com/downloads/

- The MySQL drivers will need to be downloaded from the MySQL download software site at: http://www.mysql.com/products/

- IBM drivers for DB2 platform are available at the IBM DB2 download software site: http://www.ibm.com/developerworks/db2/downloads/

- The Sybase Drivers are available for free download at the main Sybase download site: http://www.sybase.com/downloads

## Download Relevant Software for MySQL Platform

It is necessary to download the required plugins and beta software, if the testing environment is available, for the MySQL database platform.

Oracle provides support for MySQL 3.x through 5.1 versions. One will need to download the MySQL 5.0 Beta version software. This is available as a bundle from the Oracle download site listed previously. In addition, be sure to download the correct version of the connector/j driver software for MySQL 5.

---

The installation process is fairly straightforward in that a simple unzip of the binaries to the MySQL installation directory is required.

## Review the Oracle 10g Migration Workbench Documentation

Of the OMWB guides, these are particularly critical:

- Oracle 10g Migration Workbench Administrator's Guide
- Oracle 10g Migration Workbench User Guide

> 🔔 Both are available for free download from the Oracle technical site located at http://otn.oracle.com.

# Oracle 10g SQL Developer Migration Workbench

The next step in the migration process is to review and cover how to install and configure the Oracle 10g SQL Developer Migration Workbench. The following overview will cover the entire process from the big picture to a drilled-down step-by-step task list to configure the software.

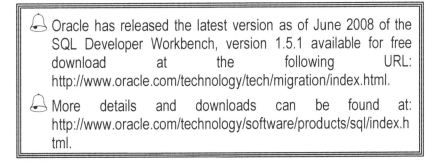

> 🔔 Oracle has released the latest version as of June 2008 of the SQL Developer Workbench, version 1.5.1 available for free download at the following URL: http://www.oracle.com/technology/tech/migration/index.html.
>
> 🔔 More details and downloads can be found at: http://www.oracle.com/technology/software/products/sql/index.html.

Oracle has released a new and improved version of the OMWB called the Oracle 10g SQL Developer Migration Workshop. In addition to the OMWB installation, it may also be necessary to download and configure the Oracle 10g SQL Developer Migration Workshop software. The beginner's guide is available from the Oracle download site below:

- http://www.oracle.com/technology/tech/migration/workbench/files/omwb_getstarted.html

## Configuration Summary

Prepare the Database Environment to Migrate to Oracle 10g:

- Installation/Setup for the new Oracle Migration Repository
- Configure MySQL/MS SQL Server 2000 Connections
  - Configure the database connection JDBC Drivers
  - Add new connections for MySQL/MS SQL Server 2000

Migration Process for MySQL and Microsoft SQL Server:

- Capture Process for MySQL and MS SQL Server 2000
- Conversion Process for database captured models
- Generate SQL scripts for MySQL/ MS SQL Server 2000
- Execute generated SQL Scripts for Database Models
- Move MySQL/MS SQL Server databases to Oracle 10g
  - Create the new connections
  - Perform data move to Oracle 10g

Note: Being that the focus of this chapter is for installation, the capture and migration tasks will be covered in subsequent chapters.

# Preparing the Database Environment to Migrate to Oracle 10g

In order to configure the MySQL and MS SQL Server 2000 databases for migration to Oracle 10g via the OMWB, there are several critical preparation steps to perform in advance. One of the prerequisites for the installation for the OMWB is to create a new database schema that will store all of the metadata objects. These will be collected during the migration process as the MySQL and Microsoft SQL Server 2000 databases are in the process of migration to the new platform.

According to Oracle documentation, the new database migration repository contains over thirty-seven new tables, views, triggers and assorted PL/SQL objects. These function to create the new metadata model which will be used by the OMWB to clone and transform the MySQL and MS SQL Server 2000 databases to an Oracle 10g database model. While it is not required to create an entirely new schema in the OMWB database repository, it is recommended so that a clean and accurate migration process is accomplished. By using a new and separate database schema for the migration process, much confusion and many potential problems will be avoided, thereby simplifying the difficult and already complex migration process.

# Required Privileges for the New Oracle 10g Migration Workbench Schema

As part of the preparation and configuration process for the new OMWB schema, there are required privileges that must be granted as a bare minimum to ensure that no database authentication errors occur as the migration process is executed.

To build out the new repository schema for containing the OMWB metadata, the following Oracle database privileges are required:

- * connect
- * resource
- * create view
- * create session

## Creating User and Schema for Oracle Migration Workbench

For example, logon to the new Oracle 10g database that will be used to perform these tasks:

### cr_miguser.sql

```
SQL> SQLPLUS /NOLOG
SQL>  connect /as sysdba
SQL> CREATE USER miguser IDENTIFIED BY miguser
default tablespace users
temporary tablespace temp;
SQL> GRANT CONNECT TO MIGUSER;
SQL> GRANT RESOURCE TO MIGUSER;
```

```
SQL> GRANT CREATE VIEW TO MIGUSER;
SQL> GRANT CREATE SESSION TO MIGUSER;
```

Figure 3.1 is an example of how to configure the user schema for the OMWB. In this case, connect to the new database called ORCL as the SYSDBA privileged account.

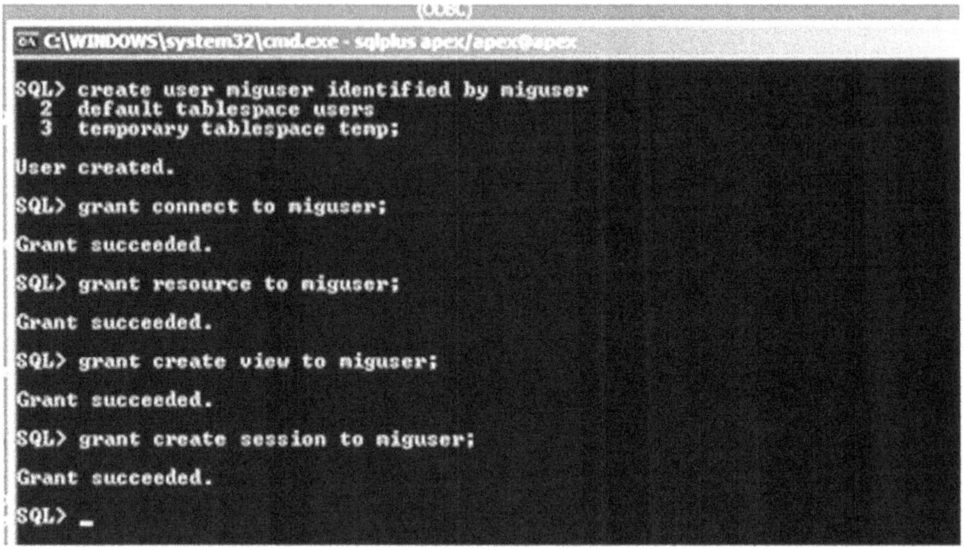

**Figure 3.1:** *Creating the OMWB Schema Account and User*

Now install a repository on this user. This task will be performed later in the chapter when the Oracle Migration Workbench software is installed.

## Install and Configure Migration Tools for SQL Developer

To install and configure migration tools for SQL Developer, the first step is to set up the connection in SQL Developer, and then assign it to act as the migration repository.

After the latest release of SQL Developer and Workbench have been downloaded, open the SQL Developer application. The first workbench screen, as shown in Figure 3.2, should appear:

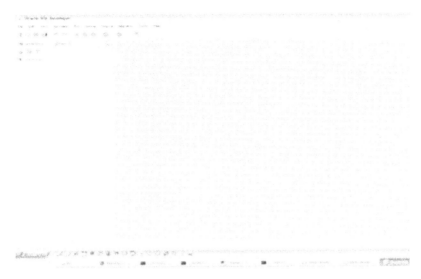

**Figure 3.2:** *SQL Developer 1.2 Installation*

# Creating a Connection with SQL Developer 1.2

The first step of working with the new version of the Oracle SQL Developer and migration workbench is to create a new connection. It is a very simple and straightforward process, as shown in Figure 3.3. Simply right click on the connections icon and click "New Connection".

**Figure 3.3:** *SQL Developer 1.2 - Create a New Connection*

The configuration screen for the creation of the new connection with SQL Developer will then appear. Enter the details for the setup with the example show in Figure 3.4:

**Figure 3.4:** *SQL Developer 1.2 New Connection*

In the New/Select Database Connection window, enter the following configuration settings:

- Connection Name: orcl

- Username : sys

- Password: oracle

Under the next section there will be several tabs for Oracle, Access, MySQL, and SQLServer settings for the new connection being created. The first step is to set up the connect string for the Oracle 10g environment. Enter the following settings for the Oracle tab:

- Role: click on sysdba

- For connection type, choose "TNS" and have the Network Alias as *listener_orcl*

After the settings are in place, click on the Test button to verify connectivity to Oracle database for the SYS account.

Keep in mind that the default setting for Basic is set to a default value. This being, when the test is performed an error will occur. For resolution, configure the default screen as shown in Figure 3.5 below to ensure connectivity is available and correct.

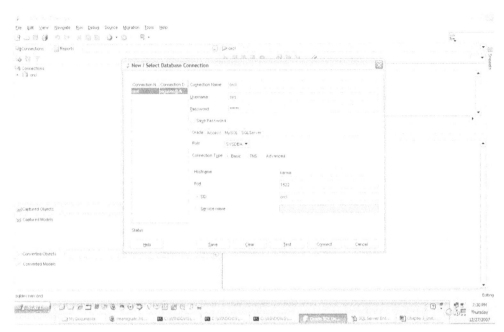

**Figure 3.5:** *SQL Developer 1.2 New Connection Settings*

Next, verify that the settings for the Basic environment, shown above, are correct for the Oracle listener port, hostname and SID.

Be sure to click the save button to save the new connection. This is a measure to avoid losing any settings. The new connection will appear on the left side of the workbench as shown in Figure 3.6.

The next step is to create a new user that will function as the migration user with SQL Developer.

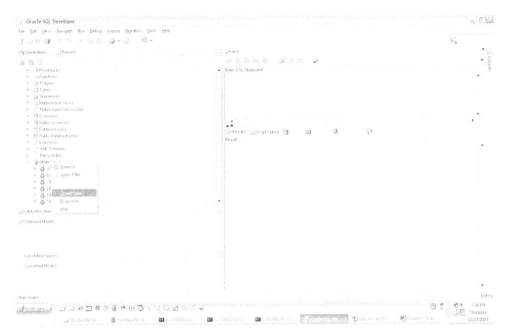

**Figure 3.6:** *SQL Developer 1.2 – Create Migration User and Schema*

Earlier, the user miguser was created. However, in order to avoid confusion when using SQL Developer, there will need to be another user and schema created. This will be used for migrations performed with SQL Developer to Oracle 10g. The other schema and user, miguser, will then be reserved to perform migrations from MySQL and MS SQL Server 2000 to Oracle 10g with the older release of the OMWB. This process will be shown later in this chapter.

Next create the migration schema called omwb as shown in Figure 3.7.

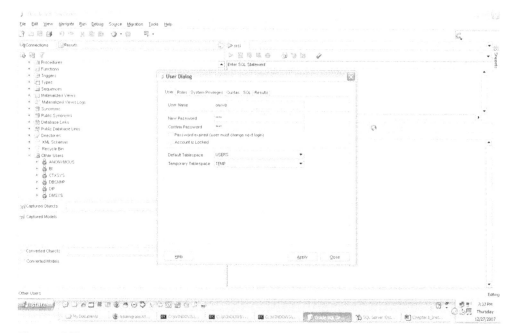

**Figure 3.7:** *SQL Developer 1.2- New User and Schema Configuration*

Next, assign the correct default tablespace, temporary tablespace and associated privileges and roles to the new migration account omwb.

- Username: omwb

- Password: omwb

- Default Tablespace: users

- Temporary Tablespace: temp

Use the drop down boxes to choose the tablespace assignments for the new schema account as shown in Figure 3.8.

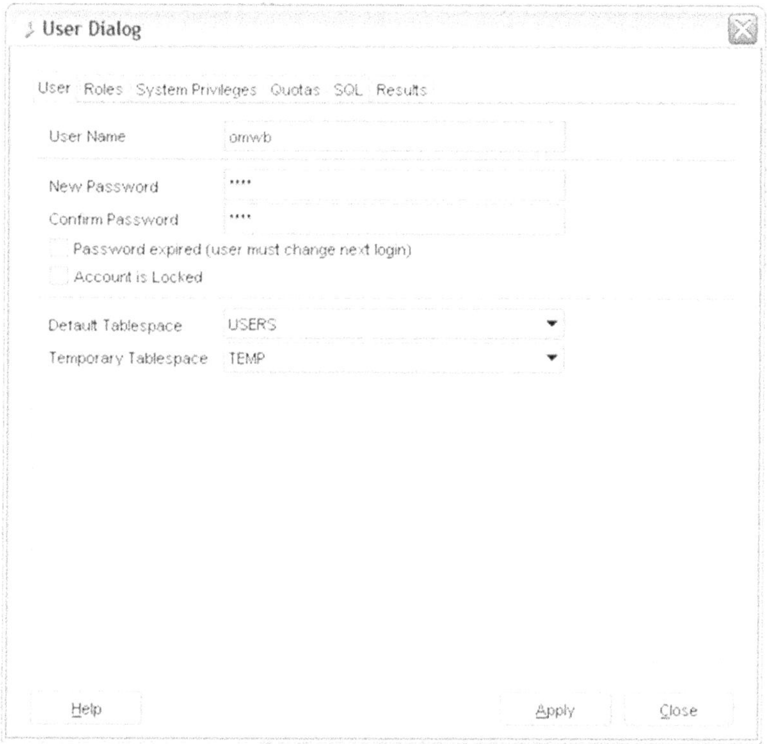

**Figure 3.8:** *SQL Developer 1.2 - New User Roles and Privileges*

Click on the tab for roles and privileges for omwb, and select the checkboxes under the Granted option for connect and resource roles as shown in Figures 3.9 and 3.10.

**Figure 3.9:** *SQL Developer 1.2 - New User and Schema Setup*

**Figure 3.10:** *SQL Developer 1.2 - New User Settings*

Choose the System Privileges tab and check the box for *create session* and *create view* as shown in Figures 3.11 and 3.12.

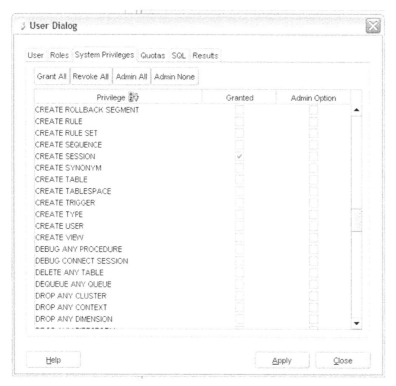

**Figure 3.11:** *SQL Developer User Configuration*

**Figure 3.12:** *SQL Developer 1.2 User Privileges*

Click the Apply button. Then, verify that the new schema user is created without errors as shown in Figure 3.13.

**Figure 3.13:** *SQL Developer 1.2- New User Schema Creation*

The new user and schema omwb should now appear in the left pane window for SQL Developer as shown in Figures 3.14 and 3.15.

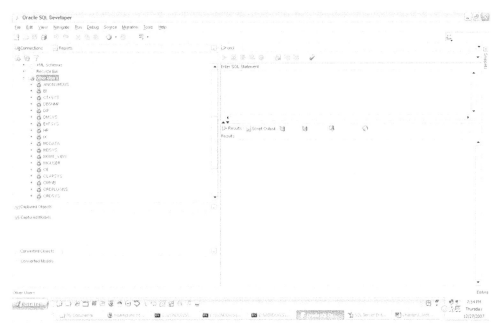

**Figure 3.14:** *SQL Developer 1.2 – New User Created*

**Figure 3.15:** *SQL Developer 1.2 - Verify User Account*

# Migration Repository Creation for SQL Developer

The next step is to create and set up a new migration repository for use with SQL Developer. For this task, a new connection similar to the one that was made earlier will have to be created. This time it will be for use with the new omwb migration user account and schema objects.

Before creating the new repository for each database environment that will be migrated to Oracle, such as Access, MS SQL Server 2000 or MySQL, one must first create a new connection for each source database. This will also be used with the omwb user account. Go ahead and get started by creating the new connection for Access to migrate to Oracle.

Right click on connections and create a new connection as shown in Figure 3.16:

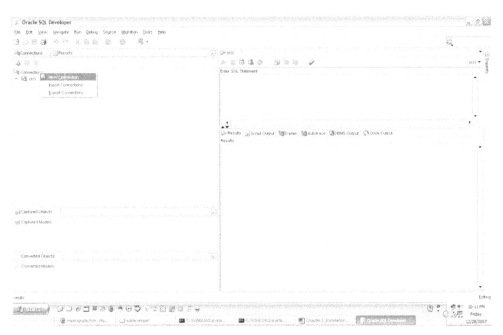

**Figure 3.16:** *Oracle SQL Developer – Create a New Connection*

Now enter the user name and password for omwb along with the *oracle_sid* (orcl) and click on connect for the new connection as shown in Figure 3.17.

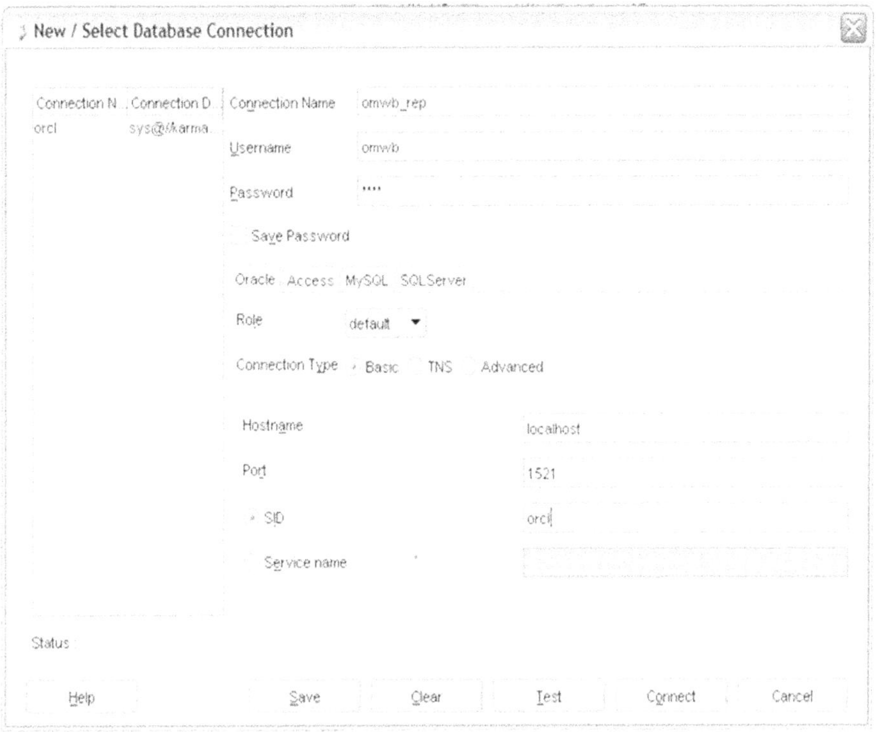

**Figure 3.17:** *Connecting with New Connection*

Once the new connection opens, it will display the contents. This is displayed in the following figure. The next step as shown in Figure 3.18 will be to associate a new repository with the omwb user and schema and create the repository objects in order to migrate Access to Oracle.

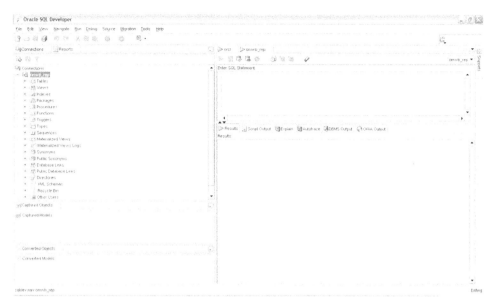

**Figure 3.18:** *Create Repository Objects*

Right click on the new *omwb_rep* connection and choose Associate Migration Repository.

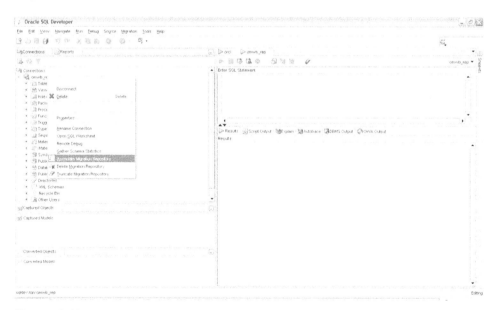

**Figure 3.19:** *Choosing Associate Migration Repository*

---

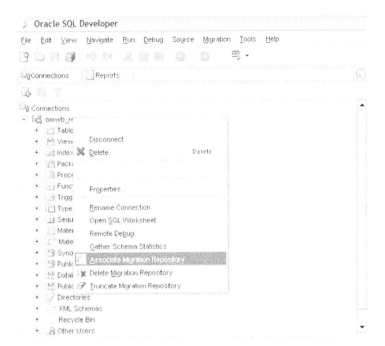

**Figure 3.20:** *Enlarged View of Associate Migration Repository Screen*

Once the Associate Migration Repository selection is clicked on, the progress window will appear. The progress window shows a progress meter as the objects are created and installed for the new *omwb_rep* repository.

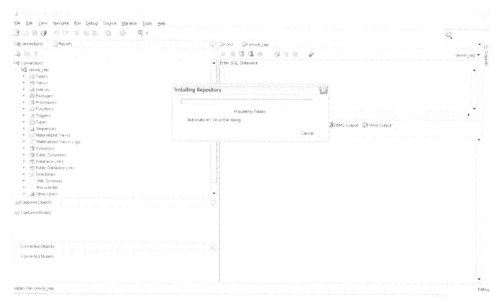

**Figure 3.21:** *Associate Migration Repository Progress Window*

Once it has successfully completed, a screen similar to the one shown next should appear.

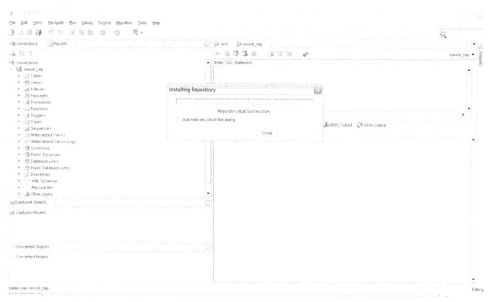

**Figure 3.22:** *Migration Repository Successfully Completed*

---

Now the repository can be used to build the premigration database model for Access to migrate to Oracle.

To do this, click on the Close button. The new repository should appear for omwb user and schema as shown in the next example.

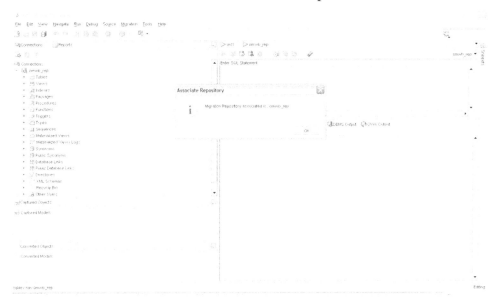

**Figure 3.23:** *New Migration Repository for OMWB User and Schema*

# Setup for MySQL, Access and SQL Server

Now that the setup for Oracle has been completed, the next task for the new connection is to configure settings for MS Access, MySQL and SQL Server environments.

Once the new connection has been made, right click on it and select "Create Repository". One can also use the main Migration Menu option, Repository Management.

An easier method to create the new migration workbench repository is to select the menu item from top of the SQL Developer toolbar called Migration-> Repository Management-> Create Repository.

**Figure 3.24:** *SQL Developer 1.2 – Create Repository*

If the Help button is clicked on, a new popup help box will appear with details on the *Create Repository* command. This can provide useful details on how to use the SQL Developer tools.

**Figure 3.25:** *SQL Developer 1.2 - Using Help*

Close the Help menu and select the Create icon to create the new migration repository for the new connection.

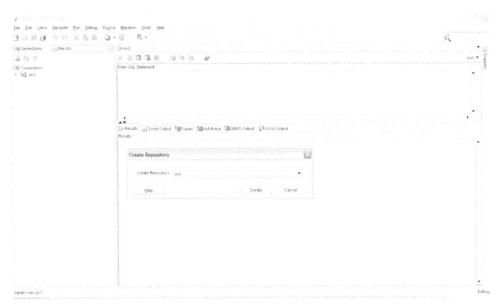

**Figure 3.26:** *SQL Developer 1.2 - Create New Repository*

The repository will now be created.

**Figure 3.27:** *SQL Developer 1.2 - Installing A New Repository*

The following error message may show up during the initial setup for the new migration repository.

**Figure 3.28:** *SQL Developer 1.2 - SQL Error During Repository Creation*

Click OK and it will have failed.

**Figure 3.29:** *Repository Installation Failure Message*

If these errors occur during the initial creation for the new repository, truncate and delete the repository objects.

To clean up a failed repository creation for the new connection, there are two choices. The first is to right click on the connection and select delete. Then perform a truncate on the repository.

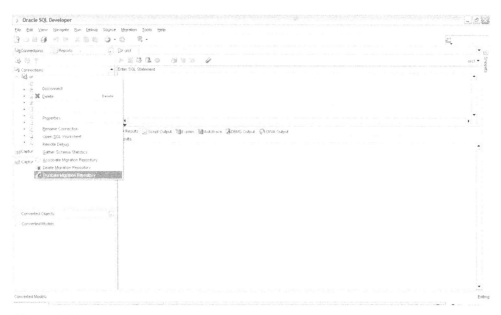

**Figure 3.30:** *Truncate Migration Repository*

This method can also be used to delete the migration repository.

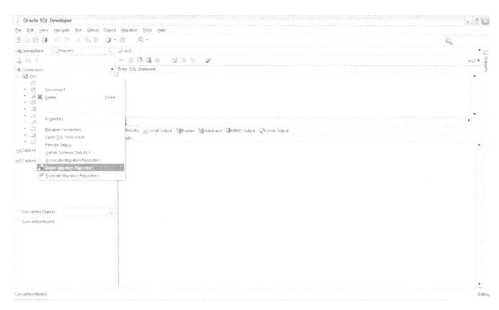

**Figure 3.31:** *Delete Migration Repository*

Migrating to Oracle

Another method is to select the repository menu from the top main toolbar as shown in Figure 3.32.

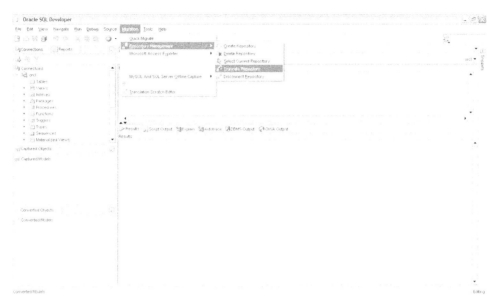

**Figure 3.32:** *Migration-> Repository Management-> Truncate Repository*

Use this method to delete the repository.

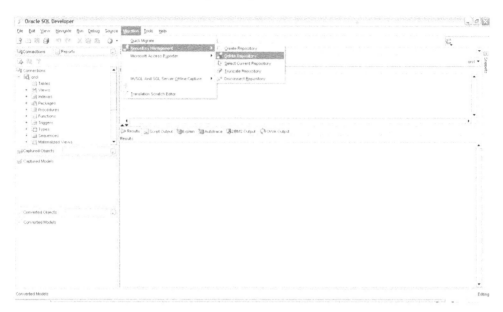

**Figure 3.33:** *Migration-> Repository Management-> Delete Repository*

Next is the screen showing the repository being deleted.

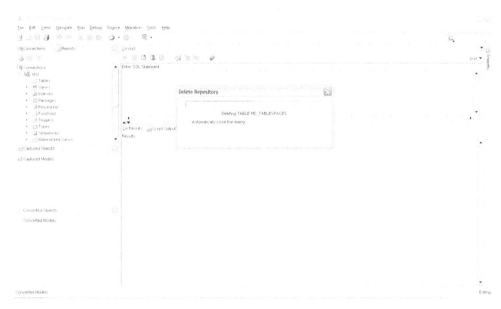

**Figure 3.34:** *Repository Deletion in Progress*

Oracle SQL Developer will perform the necessary cleanup to remove the failed repository objects.

**Figure 3.35:** *SQL Developer 1.2 - Repository Removal Completed*

**Figure 3.36:** *Final Cleanup of Repository Object Removal*

The next step is to recreate the repository, as shown in the following figure. Without errors, it should create the new migration objects.

**Figure 3.37:** *Migration-> Repository Management-> Create Repository #2*

The procedure of creating the new repository will proceed and a status progress bar will appear to show completion time.

## Migration Setup for Access

To configure the Access database for migration to Oracle 10g using the SQL Developer workbench, select the Access tab of the main connection that was created earlier. Enter the following settings for the specific Access database that will be migrated as shown in the following example.

**Figure 3.38:** *Migrating Access Database*

# Database Connections - MySQL and MS SQL Server 2000

The next step in the setup procedure for migration with both the OMWB and SQL Developer is to configure a database connection for MySQL and Microsoft SQL Server databases that will be migrated to Oracle. This is similar to the process that was performed earlier for the Access database migration to Oracle. New connections will be created with SQL Developer to migrate these environments. There are two steps to this process:

1. Configure the JDBC drivers

2. Configure the third party connection

> 🔔 Configuration of JDBC drivers needs to be carried out once per third party connection, such as MySQL and SQL Server, whereas the second step is carried out for each database one wishes to migrate.

## Configure JDBC Drivers

JDBC are the drivers for Java database connection to relational database platforms using Java interfaces.

> 🔔 More details on JDBC can be obtained from Sun at: http://java.sun.com/javase/technologies/database/.

In order to connect to databases via JDBC, the drivers must be downloaded and installed. As mentioned earlier, these are available from the database vendor, such as MySQL or Microsoft, and are free to download.

According to Oracle support, the latest versions of SQL Developer and the Oracle Migration Workbench have been tested and validated with the following JDBC drivers:

- MySQL JDBC drivers: Download the latest MySQL JDBC Driver, version 5.04, which is currently available from http://dev.mysql.com/downloads/connector/j/5.0.html

- Microsoft SQL Server JDBC drivers: The jTDS driver can be downloaded from http://jtds.sourceforge.net/. Oracle advises that version 1.2 of the JDBC driver for MS SQL Server 2000 be used.

- Microsoft Access: Fortunately for MS Access migrations, there are no additional drivers required for JDBC

## Install JDBC Driver Files for MySQL and SQL Server

Download the JDBC driver software to the installation location for the migration staging area. Next, expand the jar files in a directory structure for the staging area for each environment with MySQL and MS SQL Server 2000.

Usually the jar files are packed into separate files which are located inside the archive file structure of the download package.

MySQL has an archive file called *mysql-connector-java-5.0.4.tar.gz* for Linux, and for Windows the jar file will end in a .zip extension. There should also be another binary file inside the directory called *mysql-connector-java-5.0.4-bin.jar*.

For the MS SQL Server 2000 JDBC files inside the jtds distribution, locate the archive file called *jtds-1.2-dist.zip*. Another binary jar file called *jtds-1.2.jar* should also exist in the archive download for MS SQL Server 2000.

Extract these jar files to the migration directory for staging area. The next step is to configure SQL Developer with these jar and archive files.

## Configure JDBC for SQL Developer

Here is a summary of steps to configure JDBC for SQL Developer:

1. In SQL Developer, choose Tools -> Preferences...

2. Expand the Database option in the left hand tree

3. Click on Third Party JDBC Drivers

4. Click on Add Entry

5. Navigate to the third party driver jar file and choose OK

Download both of these JDBC drivers and install them for MS SQL Server 2000 and MySQL before setting up SQL Developer Migration tasks. Doing this will complete the installation process for SQL Developer Migration Workbench environments. Then do a walk-through to illustrate the process for configuration of the JDBC drivers for Microsoft SQL Server 2000 and MySQL.

First of all, the new drivers for MS SQL Server from the SourceForge.net website need to be downloaded as shown in Figure 3.39.

**Figure 3.39:** *Downloading the New Drivers*

After clicking on the Download section, the files for the JDBC drivers will be revealed to select from. Choose the file called *jtds-1.2.2-dist.zip* :

**Figure 3.40:** *File Name jtds-1.2.2-dist.zip*

Once the download is completed, extract and unzip the file to the staging directory for SQL Developer 1.2.

**Figure 3.41:** *Staging Directory for SQL Developer 1.2*

Extract the JDBC driver files to the SQL Developer 1.2 bin directory for JDBC so that they can be installed as shown in Figure 3.42.

Figure 3.42: *Extracting JDBC Driver Files*

Next, open a session of SQL Developer 1.2 to install the JDBC drivers for MS SQL Server 2000. At the main panel menu for SQL Developer 1.2, select Tools, then Preferences as illustrated in Figure 3.43.

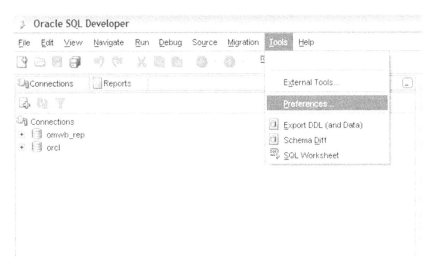

Figure 3.43: *Choosing Preferences Option in SQL Developer 1.2.2*

**Figure 3.44:** *Preference Screen for Third Party JDBC Drivers*

The key in the preferences screen for SQL Developer 1.2 is to select the left panel menu item, Database, and expand to see the selection called Third Party JDBC Drivers. After this, click Add Entry to choose the JDBC drivers for MS SQL Server 2000.

**Figure 3.45:** *Choosing JDBC Drivers for MS SQL Server 2000*

Navigate to the directory where the *jtds-1.2.2.jar* files for MS SQL Server were downloaded and extracted and choose Select. Now one should be able to see the JDBC drivers for MS SQL Server 2000. This is shown in the following example.

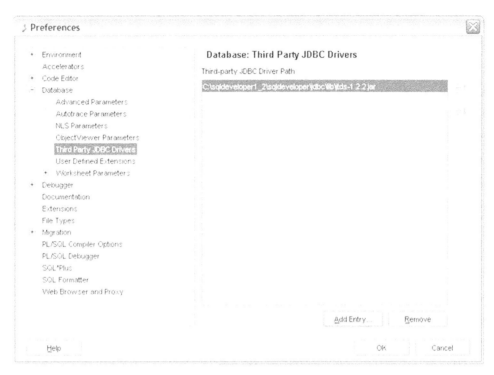

**Figure 3.46:** *JDBC Drivers Shown for MS SQL Server 2000*

Click OK to exit the menu.

## Downloading and Installing the JDBC Drivers for MySQL

The next process is to download and install the JDBC drivers for MySQL to use with SQL Developer 1.2. First, navigate to the MySQL download site to obtain the JDBC drivers.

**Figure 3.47:** *Download Site for the JDBC Drivers for MySQL*

Since the Windows platform is being used to set up the JDBC drivers with SQL Developer, click on the Source and Binaries file in .zip format. The next page will ask the user to register for a free MySQL user account. Here, one should fill out the registration screen and download the files, then choose the mirror site to download the JDBC files for MySQL.

**Figure 3.48:** *Choosing a Mirror Site for Downloading JDBC Files*

After the download is complete for the MySQL JDBC files, extract and unpack them to the staging directory for SQL Developer 1.2. It may also be favorable to choose a new directory and copy over these files to a staging directory for JDBC files for migration. These JDBC files will also be used with the OWMB for establishing JDBC connectivity to MySQL. Because they will get double duty, having a separate directory for staging will assist in keeping things clean and tidy for migrations.

**Figure 3.49:** *Staging Directory for JDBC Files*

Extract the files to the staging area as well as to the bin directory for JDBC files with SQL Developer 1.2.

**Figure 3.50:** *Extracting JDBC Files for MySQL*

Verify that the files are in place and unzipped.

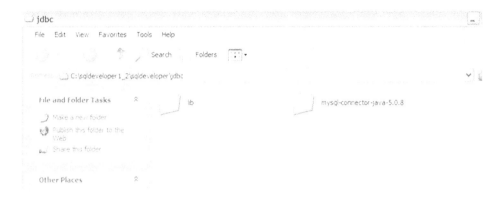

**Figure 3.51:** *Unzipped JDBC Files*

After the JDBC files have been extracted to the JDBC directory for MySQL, the next step is to install them so that SQL Developer can access the JDBC drivers for MySQL. To do this, open up a new session window for SQL Developer 1.2.

**Figure 3.52:** *Installing JDBC Files for MySQL*

Just like the example below, go to Tools, and then Preferences, to configure and install the JDBC drivers for MySQL.

**Figure 3.53:** *Preference Screen for Installing MySQL JDBC Drivers*

Now expand the Database options, on the left panel, to show Third Party JDBC Drivers option. Select Add Entry on the right panel window and navigate to the location for the MySQL JDBC drivers.

**Figure 3.54:** *Location of the MySQL JDBC Drivers*

As shown in Figure 3.54, navigate to the staging directory where the jar files for MySQL JDBC drivers were downloaded and extracted/unzipped. Choose Select to add the jar file.

If all has been installed correctly, the JDBC drivers and associated pathnames will appear in the main pane window for the Database Third Party JDBC drivers. If this is successful, the screen will look like the following figure:

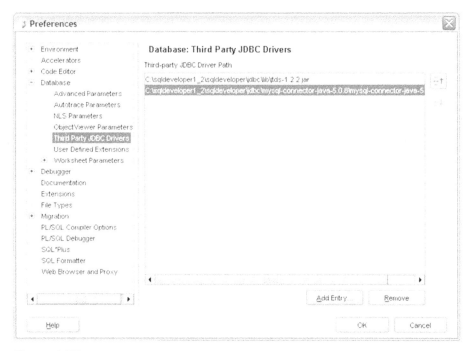

**Figure 3.55:** *JDBC Drivers Successfully Installed*

To finish this portion, click on OK to exit and save the new configuration in SQL Developer.

# Oracle 10g Application Express (APEX) Migration

With the new release of the APEX Migration 3.1 and SQL Developer 1.2, integration allows both tools to exchange data for conversions and migrations. This powerful feature will greatly enhance application development tasks during and after a complex migration. Earlier it was revealed how the SQL Developer 1.2 Migration Workbench and the OMWB can be used to migrate third party databases such as MS SQL Server 2000 and MySQL to Oracle 10g and 11g. With the APEX Migration Workbench, the MS Access databases can also be easily migrated over to the Oracle platform.

Now that the migration workbench and repository for SQL Developer 2.1 has been installed and configured, the next leg of the journey will be to install and configure the APEX Migration Workshop software.

## Installation Procedures for APEX 3.0 Migration Software

The first step is to download and extract the files for APEX 3.0 software to a stage directory. The unzipped files should be similar to this figure:

**Figure 3.56:** *View of Unzipped Files for APEX 3.0 Software*

Now expand the APEX 3.0 directories and check to ensure all files and scripts were unzipped without errors.

| Name | Size | Type | Date Modified |
|---|---|---|---|
| builder | | File Folder | 12/27/2007 6:39 PM |
| core | | File Folder | 12/27/2007 6:37 PM |
| doc | | File Folder | 12/27/2007 6:14 PM |
| images | | File Folder | 12/27/2007 6:37 PM |
| owa | | File Folder | 12/27/2007 6:37 PM |
| utilities | | File Folder | 12/27/2007 6:39 PM |
| apex_epg_config.sql | 15 KB | SQL Script File | 6/27/2007 9:59 AM |
| apexins.sql | 4 KB | SQL Script File | 5/10/2007 10:43 AM |
| apexvalidate.sql | 7 KB | SQL Script File | 3/3/2007 3:19 PM |
| apxconf.sql | 3 KB | SQL Script File | 3/3/2007 3:19 PM |
| apxdbmig.sql | 7 KB | SQL Script File | 6/27/2007 9:59 AM |
| apxe101.sql | 1 KB | SQL Script File | 6/27/2007 9:59 AM |
| apxe102.sql | 1 KB | SQL Script File | 6/27/2007 9:59 AM |
| apxldimg.sql | 5 KB | SQL Script File | 6/27/2007 9:59 AM |
| apxremov.sql | 2 KB | SQL Script File | 3/3/2007 3:19 PM |
| apxsqler.sql | 1 KB | SQL Script File | 4/26/2007 10:39 AM |
| apxxemig.sql | 6 KB | SQL Script File | 6/7/2007 11:32 PM |
| apxxepwd.sql | 2 KB | SQL Script File | 3/3/2007 3:19 PM |
| catapx.sql | 4 KB | SQL Script File | 8/17/2007 2:33 PM |
| coreins2.sql | 95 KB | SQL Script File | 5/1/2007 4:10 PM |
| coreins.sql | 93 KB | SQL Script File | 5/10/2007 10:43 AM |
| load_trans.sql | 2 KB | SQL Script File | 2/27/2007 2:35 PM |
| welcome.html | 4 KB | Firefox Document | 6/8/2007 9:57 AM |

**Figure 3.57:** *Expanded View of APEX 3.0 Directories*

The suite for APEX 3.0 tools can be called from SQL Developer 1.2, which is the preferred method to use the software for migrations of MS Access database applications to Oracle 10g and 11g. Due to the complex nature of using the APEX software, too much time cannot be spent on directives using the tool. Entire books have already been written on APEX as well as hundreds of white papers and tutorials available on the Oracle main technology site. The following website provides additional resources for Oracle APEX technology:

- http://htmldb.oracle.com/i/index.html

## Oracle 10g Database Verifier (DMV)

Oracle introduced an optional new tool called the Oracle Database Migration Verifier (DMV) to perform checks and verification for schemas and table data that is migrated from MySQL and MS SQL Server 2000 to Oracle 10g/11g platforms. It provides useful measures to compare the source database to the newly migrated Oracle database to ensure that the data and structure integrity are intact for the new migrated environments. Support is currently limited to Sybase and Microsoft SQL Server 2000. While this is an optional tool and does not support MySQL, it does provide useful checks for MS SQL Server 2000 environments.

## Features of the Database Migration Verifier Tool

The DMV tool provides the following features:

- Compare all tables, indexes, functions, views, procedures, and triggers that are within the source database against the newly migrated Oracle database

- Perform a check to verify that the database objects exist in both source (SQL Server 2000) and target Oracle databases

- Perform a check for the order of table columns

- Perform verification check that table columns exist and support NULL values

- Checks to see if the stored procedures and functions exist in the migrated Oracle target database

- Verification checks to ensure that all data types, functions and other types exist and are correct in both source and target

- Verify the argument pattern for stored procedures and functions

- Row count checks are performed for user tables to verify data integrity

- Creates a DMV report which provides a snapshot of all results for above verification checks for schema and data level

- All objects that were not successfully migrated to Oracle can be quickly identified

-  JDBC is used to perform connects to source database (MS SQL Server 2000) and target Oracle database

Requirements for the installation of the DMV tool are covered in depth in Chapter 8.

# Oracle 10g Migration Workbench (OMWB) Installation

- Download and install plugins for OMWB
- Download and install OMWB software

## Install the Plugins for the Oracle Migration Workbench

The various plugins and java files that need to be obtained for MySQL and Microsoft SQL Server 2000 in order to use the OWMB and SQL Developer Migration Workbench tools have been covered. If these plugins and associated jar files are not installed and configured correctly, all migration tools will be inoperative. If this occurs, migrating the source databases from MySQL and Microsoft SQL Server 2000 to Oracle will not be possible. Be sure to take the extra time and caution to download, install, and test everything to ensure that these plugins are working and in place before migration is attempted.

## Installation Process of Oracle 10g Migration Workbench

Next to be reviewed are the steps on installation for the OMWB as they differ from the procedures covered earlier for the SQL Developer 1.2 Migration Workbench.

The first task to cover is the downloading and installing of the plugins and binaries for the OMWB and associated third party JDBC drivers. For the MySQL migration, use the same JDBC driver that was used to configure for SQL Developer 1.2 Migration Workbench.

First, copy the *mysql-connector-java.zip* file to the following directory:

- On Windows, copy to:

*OMWB_install_dir\Omwb\drivers*

- On UNIX, copy to:

*OMWB_install_dir/Omwb/drivers*

Next, verify that the MySQL database is up and running and that one can connect and login to the database as the root user.

---

The root user for MySQL must have full DBA level privileges!

```
C:\WINDOWS\system32\cmd.exe - mysql -uroot -padmin

C:\mysql\bin>mysql -uroot -padmin
Welcome to the MySQL monitor.  Commands end with ; or \g.
Your MySQL connection id is 24 to server version: 5.0.27-community-nt

Type 'help;' or '\h' for help. Type '\c' to clear the buffer.

mysql> show databases;
+--------------------+
| Database           |
+--------------------+
| information_schema |
| mysql              |
| omwb               |
| test               |
+--------------------+
4 rows in set (0.00 sec)

mysql> _
```

**Figure 3.58:** *Logging in as Root User*

The procedure is different for setup on Linux platform:

1.  Run the *dos2unix* utility on the *omwb.sh*

2.  Update the *omwb.sh* script with the *-Dforce.plugins=true line*

It should appear as follows:

```
java -ms30m -mx256m -Dforce.plugins=true -jar ../lib/boot.jar
oracle.mtg.migrationUI.MigrationApp &
```

The following websites provide additional tutorials and resources on migration suite of tools from Oracle.

For Migration Toolkits:

▪  http://www.oracle.com/technology/tech/migration/index.html

For Oracle 10g Migration Workbench (OMWB):

▪  http://www.oracle.com/technology/tech/migration/workbench/index.html

- http://www.oracle.com/technology/software/tech/migration/workbench/index.html

- http://www.oracle.com/technology/software/tech/migration/workbench/index.html

## Verify Setup for Oracle 10g Migration Workbench

Earlier, a walk-through of the newest member of the migration tool suite from Oracle called SQL Developer 1.2 was completed. While it is newer technology and recommended strategy to use for migrations from MySQL and MS SQL Server 2000 to Oracle 10g, for environments that are not supported the original OMWB suite is still available for use with migrations from MySQL and SQL Server 2000 to Oracle 10g.

After the software for the OWMB has been installed, the next step is to verify that installation was successful. Open a new Windows shell prompt window and try to connect to the workbench schema.

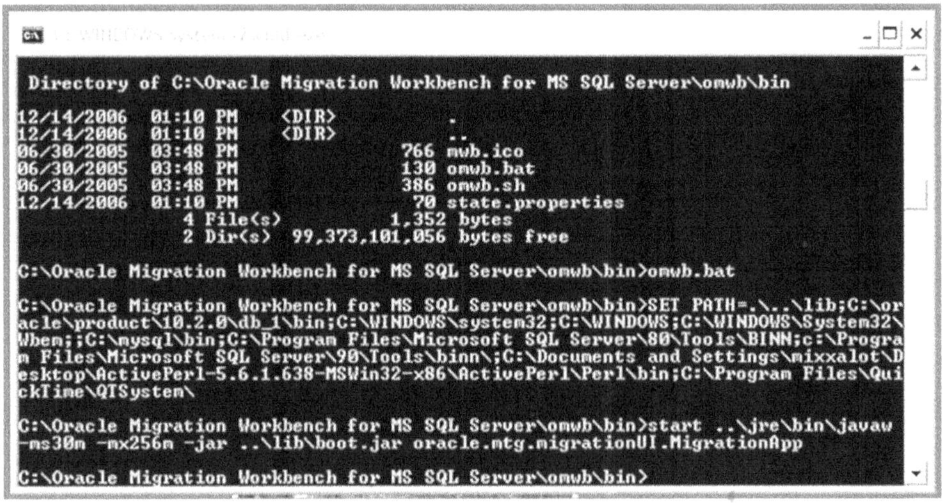

**Figure 3.59:** *Prompt Window to Connect to Workbench Schema*

On Windows, the executable to start the OWMB is located under the bin directory for the default OWMB software. Since there is both the Microsoft SQL Server 2000 and the MySQL software binaries for the OWMB, there will be two separate installation directories for the software. In the case above, test the installation for the OWMB for migration of MS SQL Server 2000 first.

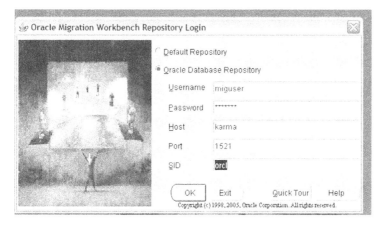

**Figure 3.60**: *OMWR Login Screen*

If the installation is correct and no errors occur, there should be a screen for the OWMB similar to the following screen:

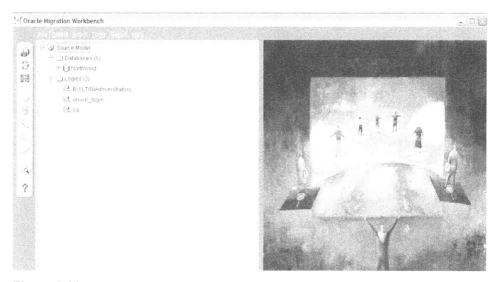

**Figure 3.61**: *Oracle Migration Workbench Screen*

# Conclusion

In this chapter, the details for installation of the OMWB assemblage were given. Due to the complex nature of installation, it is recommended to first review and download all of the software components and plugins for the OMWB software. Oracle released an updated and newer method of using the migration process in SQL Developer. The original, standalone version of the migration tools of OMWB is still available and supported. Even still, the future direction for Oracle migration is to deploy and use the new release in SQL Developer.

SQL Developer has an integrated approach for development and database administration functions to perform complex migrations from MySQL and MS SQL Server 2000 to Oracle 10g platform. The main focus of the migrations will highlight usage of SQL Developer, as this is the future supported direction granted by Oracle for all customers migrating to Oracle 10g and the new Oracle 11g release from MySQL and SQL Server 2000 and other non-Oracle platforms.

The usage of all three tools from the original and current release (10.1.0.4) of the OMWB will be covered in this book. Furthermore, the coverage of database migrations from third party databases to Oracle 10g/11g will be expanded by including a more detailed explanation of the Oracle SQL Developer Migration Workbench.

In the next few chapters, the migration tasks will be presented for using all of the tools which have been covered to perform the conversions and migrations to Oracle from MySQL and Microsoft SQL Server 2000. As mentioned earlier, it is critical that all components have been installed correctly or migrations will not be successful.

# References

Oracle Migration Workbench User's Guide
Release 10.1.0.4 for Microsoft Windows 98/2000/NT/XP
and Linux x86, Part B19134-01, July 2005

Oracle Database Application Express Installation Guide
Release 3.0, Part B32468-02, July 2007

Oracle Migration Technology Center
http://www.oracle.com/technology/tech/migration/index.html
Oracle SQL Developer Site
http://www.oracle.com/technology/products/database/sql_developer/index.html

Oracle Application Express Site
http://www.oracle.com/technology/products/database/application_express/index.html

Oracle Migration Toolkits
http://www.oracle.com/technology/tech/migration/index.html
Oracle Database Migration Verifier
http://otn.oracle.com/tech/migration/dmv

http://www.oracle.com/technology/software/tech/migration/dmv/index.html

# Configuration Tasks for the Oracle 10g Migration Workbench

*"Configuration for the OMWB can be quite a challenging battle"*

## Configuration - The Oracle Migration Workbench

In the last chapter, the complex installation requirements and procedures for the Oracle 10g migration workbench tools for MySQL and Microsoft SQL Server 2000 environments were detailed. Some of the topics for the configuration of the OMWB and SQL Developer Migration Workbench will be covered in the next several chapters. First, the basic tasks and concepts concerning the operation of the migration tools need to be explained to provide a clear understanding before moving on to the mechanics of using them.

# Building the Source and Target Models

Oracle migration tools, including both the OMWB and the new family member, Oracle SQL Developer 1.2 Migration Workbench, function on what is called source and target models. In a nutshell, Oracle requires users to pre-stage database architecture, schemas, and database objects in a template before migration. This staging area consists of a source model of the MySQL, or MS SQL Server 2000 database, and the target model environment. Think of it as a clay mold or die cast model that artisan potters and machine shops use for building production-ready crafts and automobiles. It is Oracle's method for migration preparation.

In a sense, the source model is the original third party database copy and clone that will be migrated to the Oracle platform. Both SQL Developer 1.2 and the OMWB require the source model to be captured and created before migration tasks can be performed. After the source model database has been created and set up, the target model can be configured for the new Oracle database environment. This target model database is a new cloned structure of the Oracle database that will contain the mapped copy of the newly migrated database from MySQL or MS SQL Server 2000.

# Source Database Capture

During the initial source database capture phase of using both the OMWB and SQL Developer Migration Workbench, source data is extracted for the metadata of the original third party database. Next, the source data is sent to the source data model in OMWB and SQL Developer Migration Workbench to be stored as a staging area for migration to the Oracle target model for later use in the migration process. To access the destination MySQL or MS SQL Server 2000 database, the following database level roles and privileges will need to be granted.

## Privileges Required:

- alter any role
- alter any sequence
- alter any table

- alter any tablespace

- alter any trigger

- comment any table

- create any sequence

- create any table

- create any trigger

- create view with admin option

- create public synonym with admin option

- create role

- create tablespace

- create user

- drop any sequence

- drop any table

- drop any trigger

- drop tablespace

- drop user

- drop any role

- grant any role

- insert any table

- select any table

- update any table

## Roles Required

- connect with admin option

- resource with admin option

### 🖫 omwb_user.sql

```
SPOOL ROLEPRIVS.SQL

--CREATE USER OMWB IDENTIFIED BY OMWB
```

```
--DEFAULT TABLESPACE USERS
--TEMPORARY TABLESPACE TEMP;

GRANT CONNECT TO OMWB WITH ADMIN OPTION;
GRANT RESOURCE TO OMWB WITH ADMIN OPTION;

GRANT ALTER ANY ROLE TO OMWB;
GRANT ALTER ANY SEQUENCE TO OMWB;
GRANT ALTER ANY TABLE TO OMWB;
GRANT ALTER ANY TRIGGER TO OMWB;
GRANT COMMENT ANY TABLE TO OMWB;
GRANT CREATE ANY SEQUENCE TO OMWB;
GRANT CREATE ANY TRIGGER TO OMWB;
GRANT CREATE ROLE TO OMWB;
GRANT CREATE TABLESPACE TO OMWB;
GRANT CREATE VIEW TO OMWB WITH ADMIN OPTION;
GRANT CREATE PUBLIC SYNONYM TO OMWB WITH ADMIN OPTION;
GRANT CREATE ROLE TO OMWB;
GRANT CREATE TABLESPACE TO OMWB;
GRANT CREATE USER TO OMWB;
GRANT DROP ANY SEQUENCE TO OMWB;
GRANT DROP ANY TABLE TO OMWB;
GRANT DROP ANY TRIGGER TO OMWB;
GRANT DROP TABLESPACE TO OMWB;
GRANT DROP USER TO OMWB;
GRANT DROP ANY ROLE TO OMWB;
GRANT INSERT ANY TABLE TO OMWB;
GRANT SELECT ANY TABLE TO OMWB;
GRANT INSERT ANY TABLE TO OMWB;
GRANT SELECT ANY TABLE TO OMWB;
GRANT UPDATE ANY TABLE TO OMWB;
SPOOL OFF
@ROLEPRIVS.SQL
```

# Choosing between Online and Offline Data Capture

When having to decide between online or offline data capture, the answer depends on the nature and requirements of the environment. For example, if there are non-production databases that have open maintenance windows, the offline capture option is feasible. However, if the environment is a banking or financial institution that cannot afford much downtime for maintenance, the online capture method is the best way for migrating MySQL and Microsoft SQL Server 2000 to Oracle. Offline capture can also be used for non-production development, sandbox, and test database environments. These environments usually have maintenance windows that can provide time for the busy DBA staff to perform testing and maintenance operations outside of business operations.

# Advantages and Disadvantages of Online Capture Method

The OMWB and SQL Developer Migration Workbench provide both online and offline capture techniques as methods for performing the initial database capture for the new source model database that will be migrated to Oracle 10g or 11g. The online capture of live production and test databases occurs with zero down time or impact. The DBA is now free from scheduling painful maintenance windows on weekends or evenings in today's IT world of 24x7x365 mission critical enterprise databases and applications. This is because online captures provide the robust method of live capture and extractions of database schema and objects for migration to Oracle 10g and 11g platforms. Online captures are also faster than the offline method for performing database migrations. This is key when considering that performance matters a great deal with production environments and service level agreements. In fact, next to backup and recovery and disaster recovery issues, performance is the most important process for live production high traffic sites such as banking and electronic commerce.

The main disadvantage of the online capture method is that if a failure occurs during the migration process, the availability of the source database may be affected. There is also a slight risk that if a failure occurs on the source database for MySQL or Microsoft SQL Server 2000 environments during the online capture procedure, it may cause the original site to crash or fail. Even though it is only a small risk, it is prudent for the DBA team to ensure that a full database backup has been taken before and after the capture process of both the original source database for MySQL and/or MS SQL Server 2000 and the new Oracle 10g or 11g target database to avoid data loss. This reinforces the premise that having a solid backup and recovery plan and procedure in place from the get go is the best insurance policy against potential failures.

In addition to making sure the backup is done properly, it is also wise to consider a disaster recovery hot standby site for large and complex multiple-tiered database environments. Microsoft SQL Server 2000 offers the Microsoft Cluster Services (MCS) method for disaster recovery. MySQL also has clustering standby technology to ensure against data and site loss in the event of an emergency. As such, it is recommended that users first test out all migrations in a development or non-production sandbox environment so that potential issues can be avoided. As an added bonus, this will provide the DBA team with superb practice and additional skills on how to perform complex database migrations from MySQL and MS SQL Server 2000 to Oracle using the migration workbench tools.

The last precautionary issue is that there may be a small performance impact on source production databases during the initial online data capture process. This could possibly impact currently running batch and transactional jobs and processes. To remedy this, the recommendation is to schedule the online data capture for the source database during fairly quiet times when there are no long-running transactions or large batch jobs. This is simply to avoid causing a performance impact to the current source database environments. A review of some of the performance tips to help monitor performance will be offered later on in future chapters.

## Advantages and Disadvantages of Offline Capture Method

Offline capture is an excellent method for source third party database environments that do not have 24x7x365 availability and service level requirements. It is also an excellent strategy for the initial database capture for test, development, and quality assurance (QA) environments. An additional benefit of the offline capture method for the source database capture and model creation includes the ability to take a specific snapshot of the MySQL or MS SQL Server 2000 database. This can then be compared to previously captured snapshots for detailed analysis. Oracle provides an assemblage of useful offline database capture scripts for the majority of large third party database vendors such as MySQL, MS SQL Server 2000, IBM DB2 UDB, and Informix. There will be a sneak peek at some of these offline capture scripts in the next few chapters. This information will portray how these scripts can provide a more fine-grained customization on the data capture process for the OMWB.

While the offline capture method provides a more focused process for the initial database capture for MySQL and Microsoft SQL Server 2000, there are some areas that affect the use of the offline capture procedures. First of all, since it is an offline capture of the third party original source database such as MySQL or MS SQL Server 2000, a maintenance downtime must be scheduled. This is used to obtain the snapshot and capture of the original source database to clone and produce the offline capture for the source model.

Because of these time demands, larger, critically available production sites, such as Wells Fargo and eBay, should probably stick to using the online capture method. Offline capture should only be used for those source databases that allow maintenance windows for scheduled downtime to perform the offline capture process. Most firms employ offline capture for development, test and QA source database environments.

## Conclusion

So which is the best method for the chosen environment? This chapter covered the merits and deficits of both online and offline capture methodologies for the initial database configuration with the OMWB. Online capture provides techniques to migrate live production level source databases from MySQL and MS SQL Server 2000 among third party database platforms to Oracle 10g and 11g with zero impact to availability. As such, it is advised to deploy the online capture method for sites that have 24x7x365 service availability requirements and cannot afford to take a downtime for maintenance.

For non-production environments, including most development, test, sandbox, and quality assurance database sites, the offline capture provides an excellent method to fine tune and capture the source database. This can then be used for analysis and review before migration to the new Oracle target model and Oracle platform. The next few chapters will provide a hands-on approach through performing the source data capture with both of these methods to illustrate the nuances of how these tools work with the OMWB and SQL Developer.

## References

Oracle Migration Workbench Reference Guide for MySQL 3.22, 3.23, 4.x
Migrations Release 10.1.0 for Microsoft Windows 98/2000/NT/XP
Part B13911-01

Oracle Migration Workbench Reference Guide for SQL Server and Sybase
Adaptive Server Migrations Release 9.2.0 for Microsoft Windows
98/2000/NT/XP
Part B10254-01

Oracle Migration Workbench Frequently Asked Questions (FAQ) Release 9.2.0 for Microsoft Windows 98/2000/NT/XP
Part B10258-01

# Online Capture Process for the Oracle 10g Migration Workbench

*"Capture can end up in disaster and chaos if not performed correctly"*

## Introduction to the Online Capture Process

In previous chapters, the methods for installation and basic configuration with the Oracle 10g migration tools were covered. This includes the Oracle 10g Migration Workbench, the new version called the Oracle 10g SQL Developer Migration Workbench as well as the Oracle 10g APEX Migration Workbench set of tools. The latter is aimed at the simplification of complex migrations from MySQL and Microsoft SQL Server 2000 databases to the Oracle 10g platform.

This chapter will continue with the migration process by performing the critical capture and configuration process of these data models to a format that can be cloned to the Oracle 10g and 11g environment. Next is an exploration of the methods for the online capture process for MySQL and Microsoft SQL Server 2000 with the OMWB. After completing the walk-through procedures for online capture, the automation methods and various configuration parameters for both migration tools will be reviewed. First, online capture with the OMWB will be detailed.

# Online Capture with Oracle 10g Migration Workbench

The online capture process uses the wizards from the OMWB to connect to the source database. This may be done with MySQL or Microsoft SQL Server 2000. Either way, this process extracts all of the metadata from the source database to populate the new target model which will eventually become the newly migrated Oracle database. In order for this to be effective, the source database must be available for access; if not, the offline capture method can be used if the source database is offline for maintenance. With the majority of production databases in a 24x7x365 online state, most migration tasks will need to be performed using the online capture method to not affect service availability during the migration project.

## The Automation Process for Online Capture with the Oracle 10g Migration Workbench

The first step to automate online capture for database migrations to Oracle 10g using the OMWB involves some basic groundwork to set up schema objects for the new migration repository.

In previous chapters, considerable time was spent on how to create the new migration user accounts and repositories for new database connections. The required Oracle privileges and roles for the schema account were also granted. Now it is time to begin the migration process for the online capture and automation.

In the first test case, the choice will be to migrate a current Microsoft SQL Server 2000 database to Oracle 10g with the OMWB. Then online capture procedures will be performed to migrate a MySQL database to Oracle.

## Configuration Parameters for the Oracle Migration Workbench

Before continuing, make sure that the Microsoft SQL Server 2000 database is available and accessible. Otherwise, the OMWB will be unable to continue with the online capture process.

Now it is time to get busy with some hands-on exercises! Start the first session of the OMWB since the time has been taken to install and configure the software binaries from earlier lessons. The first step is to open a session with the installed OMWB tool. Navigate to the bin directory where the OMWB tool has been installed as shown next. By default, the OMWB will have the following installation directory locations:

- Windows:

  *C:\OMWB_Install_Dir\Omwb\bin*

- Linux:

  */OMWB_Install_Dir/omwb/bin*

*OMWB_Install_Dir* is the default installation directory for the OMWB.

Next, start a new session by entering the *omwb.bat* command at either a Windows or Linux shell window to open the OMWB tool. Also, be sure to next open up the *state.properties* file and set to use the correct browser settings for the chosen environment as shown in Figure 5.1. Otherwise, the OMWB will not open and an error will result. The *state.properties* file is located under the bin directory for the OMWB. Edit the file to include the directory location for the Netscape browser to set the variable called *browser_path*. Following is an example of the *state.properties* file:

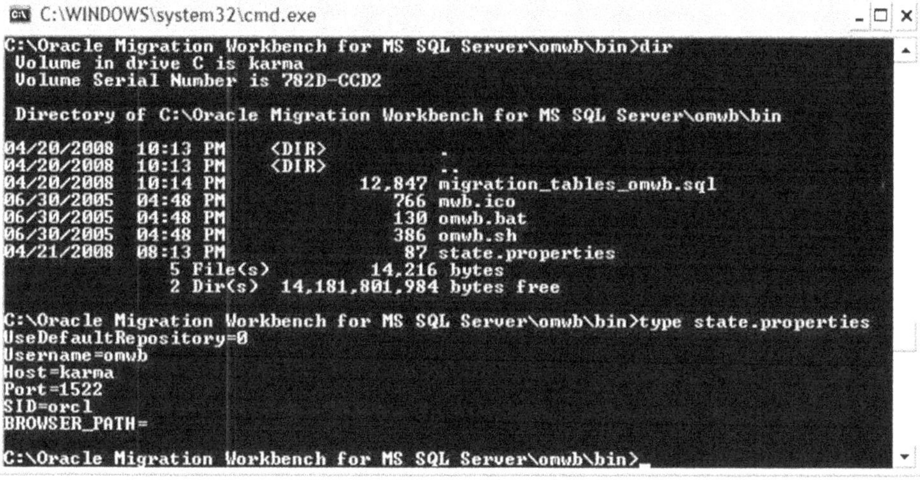

**Figure 5.1:** *Default state.properties file*

By default, the *state.properties* file will have the following parameters listed that can be modified based on a particular environment for the OMWB. Below is the sample *state.properties* file that will be used for Microsoft SQL Server 2000 to Oracle 10g or 11g migration testing.

- UseDefaultRepository=0

- Username=omwb

- Host=karma

- Port=1522

- SID=orcl

- *browser_path*=C:\ProgramFiles\Internet Explorer\iexplore.exe

Note: Newer browser versions of Netscape and Mozilla Firefox may not be compatible with the OMWB and, for this reason, it is recommended to use Internet Explorer or older versions of Netscape. Summary reports may not display correctly if newer web browsers from Mozilla Firefox are used.

To understand the *state.properties* file, take a look at Table 5.1 which summarizes the State.Properties Oracle Migration Workbench components.

| Parameter | Default Value | Purpose |
|---|---|---|
| UseDefaultRepository | 0 | repository value |
| Username | schema name | user for OMWB |
| Host | current host name | identify host |
| Port | default tns listener port | network port |
| SID | current Oracle SID name | Oracle SID |
| BROWSER_PATH | default browser executable | path to browser |

**Table 5.1:** *State.Properties Parameters for Oracle Migration Workbench*

# Beginning to Use the Migration Workbench Environment

Now that an introduction has been provided to the prerequisites for the Migration Workbench, use a case study in this chapter to provide instruction on how to use the Oracle Migration Workbench. This will show the tools and methods to use the suite of migration tools and move on to a description of how to perform online capture of the source database with several examples. The first step on the migration path is to start up the Migration Workbench as shown in Figure 5.2.

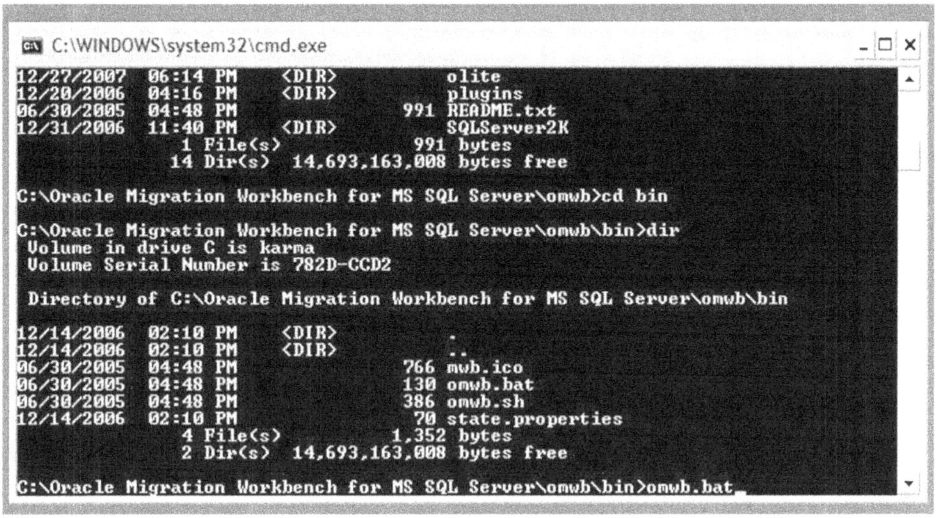

**Figure 5.2:** *Starting the Oracle 10g Migration Workbench*

There are two methods that can be used to set up an OMWB environment. The first technique involves using a default setting to store all schema objects in the default schema in the SYSAUX tablespace for Oracle 10g/11g. While this is easy to set up, it is not recommended because other Oracle utilities are stored in this tablespace. For sake of a clean migration, it is advised to create a new schema or new repository to store all of the migration objects for Oracle 10g and 11g.

In the second case, however, the OMWB requires a new database schema to store all of the metadata that it collects and transforms for the migration process. The new migration repository will contain thirty-seven tables along with associated views, triggers, and PL/SQL code to work in sync with the migration process. As a best practices guideline from Oracle, it is advised to create a new database schema, such as the test omwb schema that was created earlier, to store all of these new migration repository objects.

After learning how to set up the new migration repository for the online capture process, it will be easier to understand the intrinsic use of the repository objects for the migration database objects. It will also be easier to understand how they function in the migration process for MySQL and MS SQL Server to Oracle 10g and 11g.

The OMWB offers the choice of either using the default repository or creating a new one. To simplify the test procedures, using the new migration user account omwb that was created earlier during the installation process will be chosen. This has been exemplified with continued use of the omwb schema account for the migration procedures with online capture. Be aware that it will take a few minutes for the utility to start. Soon after, the default tool will open as shown in Figure 5.3. Be sure to check that the correct listener port and SID are specified in the logon screen or the repository will not be accessed.

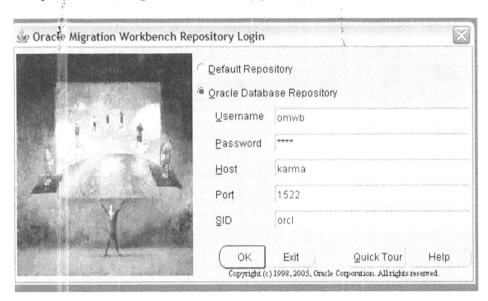

**Figure 5.3:** *OMWB Repository Login*

At this point, click OK. Since it will be the first time using the new repository schema, set up the new migration objects for the Oracle migration repository as shown in the next prompt.

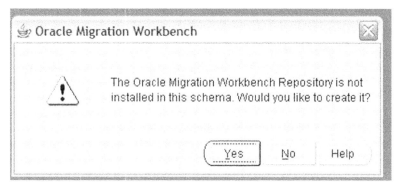

**Figure 5.4:** *Creating OMWB Repository*

Next, click on the Yes button to create the migration repository for the migration schema owmb. It will take a few minutes for the tool to create the new migration repository and install the correct plugins.  Finding plugins presents a challenge so the following link should help in locating these.

- http://www.oracle.com/technology/software/tech/migration/workbench /htdocs/utilsoft.html

If all works well without errors, the completed status report from the migration workbench tool will appear.

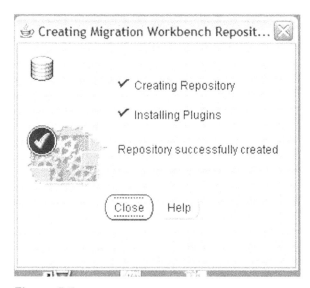

**Figure 5.5:** *Status for Newly Created Migration Workbench Repository*

Now select the Close button, at which time the Migration Workbench Repository window and a new popup window will appear. This occurs because it is the first time a database migration to Oracle using the OMWB has been performed.

In Figure 5.6, a choice of platform databases will now be shown as well as the currently installed and available plugins associated with these databases. Both a test case migration for Microsoft SQL Server 2000 and a second migration test scenario with MySQL to Oracle 10g using the OMWB will be performed.

Next, choose the option for Microsoft SQL Server 2000 Plugin and select the OK button as shown in the following example.

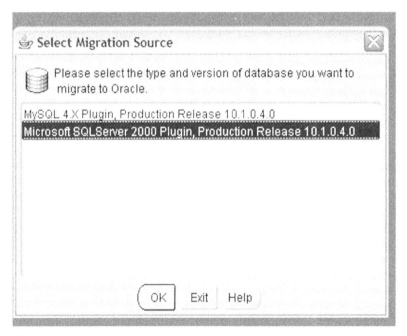

**Figure 5.6:** *Selecting Migration Source Databases*

If all of the setup configurations are correct and there are no errors with the installation for the Oracle Migration software and associated plugins, the main configuration toolbox for the OMWB will pop up like the next figure.

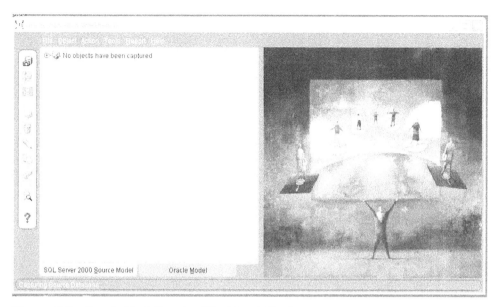

**Figure 5.7:** *Oracle 10g Migration Workbench Toolbox*

In addition, the OMWB will also open the wizard's menu to use the migration suite of wizards to perform the online or offline capture process.

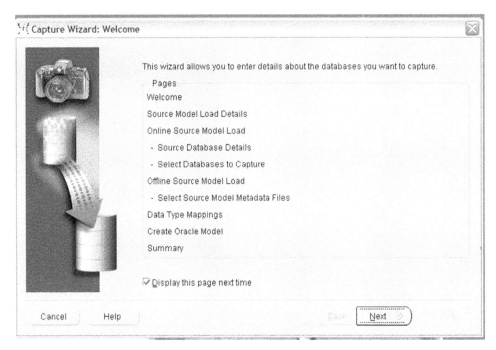

**Figure 5.8:** *Automation Wizards for OMWB*

Since the wizards are being used to automate the first test database migration for Microsoft SQL Server 2000 to Oracle 10g, choose Next and continue.

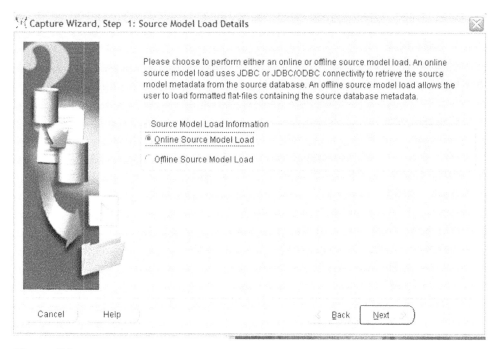

**Figure 5.9:** *Capture Wizard, Step 1: Source Model Load*

After this, the Capture Wizard tool will begin the automation process for building the source model. A choice of using either an online or offline source model load to generate the initial source model template is now present. The source model is the original non-Oracle database - Microsoft SQL Server 2000 in this case. Since an online capture process is being performed with the source MS SQL Server database up and running, the option for the Online Source Model Load and then the Next button will be chosen to continue.

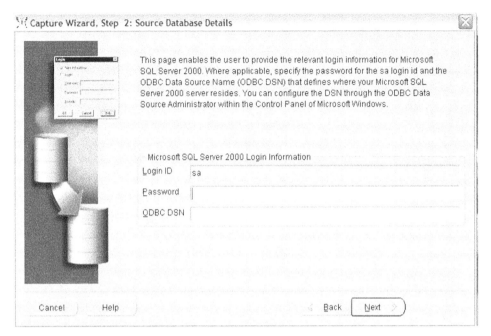

This page enables the user to provide the relevant login information for Microsoft SQL Server 2000. Where applicable, specify the password for the sa login id and the ODBC Data Source Name (ODBC DSN) that defines where your Microsoft SQL Server 2000 server resides. You can configure the DSN through the ODBC Data Source Administrator within the Control Panel of Microsoft Windows.

Microsoft SQL Server 2000 Login Information

Login ID    sa

Password

ODBC DSN

Cancel    Help    Back    Next

**Figure 5.10:** *Capture Wizard, Step 2: Source Database for SQL Server 2000*

In the above figure, the Microsoft SQL Server 2000 superuser account sa is being used to connect to the source database. Now enter the sa password for the Microsoft SQL Server 2000 source database as well as the correct ODBC DSN connection string. In order to manage the ODBC connection, open the ODBC utility from within the Administrative Tools on Windows under Control Panel as shown in the following figure.

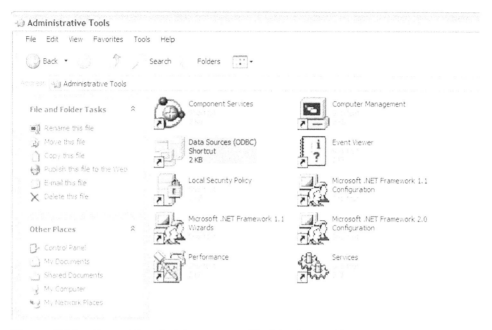

**Figure 5.11:** *Control Panel Administrative Tool for ODBC Setup*

Select the Data Sources (ODBC) icon and choose the correct DSN setup for Microsoft SQL Server 2000.

**Figure 5.12:** *ODBC Data Source Administrator*

A new ODBC connection will need to be configured to use with the migration tools. The next example can serve as an illustration on how to set up the ODBC connection to use with SQL Server 2000 and the OMWB.

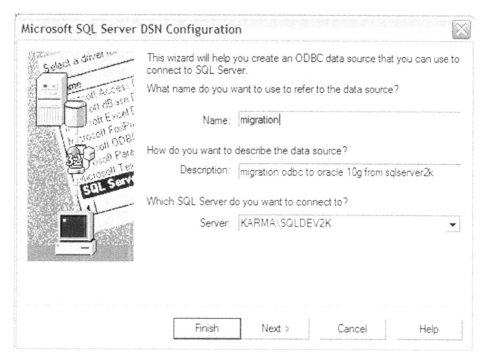

**Figure 5.13:** *Microsoft SQL Server DSN Configuration*

Enter the name and description for the data source and a fully qualified SQL Server name and click the Next button to continue with the ODBC setup configuration.

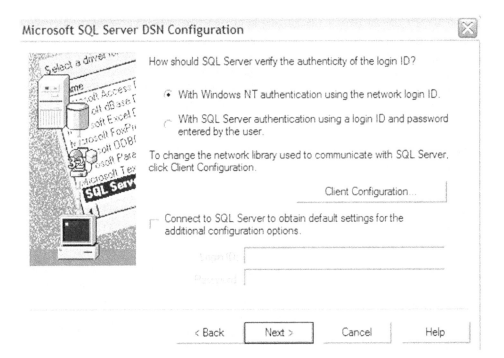

**Figure 5.14:** *Continued Microsoft SQL Server DSN Configuration*

Next, complete the final steps for the ODBC setup. Use the Northwind database in SQL Server 2000 to serve as the test bed for the migration to Oracle 10g. Northwind is a sample database that is available with every default instance of MS SQL Server 2000 and contains sample data that is useful for testing purposes.

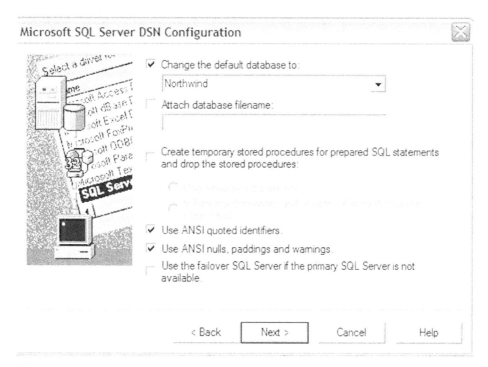

**Figure 5.15:** *Choosing Northwind as Default Database*

One final screen is required to complete the ODBC configuration setup for SQL Server.

**Figure 5.16:** *ODBC Microsoft SQL Server Setup*

Choose Test Data Source to verify that connectivity is successful to the SQL Server database. This is especially important because if there is no access to the SQL Server database from within the new ODBC connection, the migration process will fail during the online capture phase.

**Figure 5.17:** *Test ODBC Data Source Connection to SQL Server 2000*

# Using SQL*Plus for Examining New Repository Objects

Open a new Oracle SQL*Plus session window and connect to the repository database using the new repository schema. Oracle creates the following set of tables and associated new objects for the repository schema. These are used to house configuration parameters and settings for migrations from MS SQL Server 2000 and MySQL databases to Oracle.

### 🖫 Migration_Repository_Tables.sql

```
sqlplus /nolog

connect owmb/owmb

spool migration_repository_tables.sql


SQL> select table_name, status, tablespace_name
  2  from user_tables;
```

```
TABLE_NAME                      STATUS    TABLESPACE_NAME
------------------------------  --------  ---------------------------
MIGRATION_RESERVED_WORDS        VALID     USERS
MD_CONNECTIONS                  VALID     USERS
MD_PROJECTS                     VALID     USERS
MD_USERS                        VALID     USERS
MD_SCHEMAS                      VALID     USERS
MD_TABLES                       VALID     USERS
MD_VIEWS                        VALID     USERS
MD_INDEXES                      VALID     USERS
MD_COLUMNS                      VALID     USERS
MD_INDEX_DETAILS                VALID     USERS

MD_GROUPS                       VALID     USERS
MD_GROUP_MEMBERS                VALID     USERS
MD_PRIVILEGES                   VALID     USERS
MD_USER_DEFINED_DATA_TYPES      VALID     USERS
MD_TRIGGERS                     VALID     USERS
MD_STORED_PROGRAMS              VALID     USERS
MD_TABLESPACES                  VALID     USERS
MD_ADDITIONAL_PROPERTIES        VALID     USERS
MD_DERIVATIVES                  VALID     USERS
MD_SEQUENCES                    VALID     USERS

MD_PACKAGES                     VALID     USERS
MD_OTHER_OBJECTS                VALID     USERS
MD_SYNONYMS                     VALID     USERS
MD_REPOVERSIONS                 VALID     USERS
MD_CONSTRAINTS                  VALID     USERS
MD_CONSTRAINT_DETAILS           VALID     USERS
MD_CATALOGS                     VALID     USERS
MIGRLOG                         VALID     USERS
MD_GROUP_PRIVILEGES             VALID     USERS
MD_USER_PRIVILEGES              VALID     USERS

MIGR_DATATYPE_TRANSFORM_MAP     VALID     USERS
MIGR_DATATYPE_TRANSFORM_RULE    VALID     USERS


TABLE_NAME                      STATUS    TABLESPACE_NAME
------------------------------  --------  ---------------------------
MD_MIGR_PARAMETER               VALID     USERS
MD_MIGR_DEPENDENCY              VALID     USERS
MIGR_GENERATION_ORDER           VALID     USERS
MD_REGISTRY                     VALID     USERS
MD_MIGR_WEAKDEP                 VALID     USERS
MTG_VERSION                     VALID     USERS
MTG_DATABASES                   VALID     USERS
MTG_DROP_PLUGIN                 VALID     USERS

MTG_TREES                       VALID     USERS
MTG_TREE_NODES                  VALID     USERS
MTG_PROJECT_STATES              VALID     USERS
MTG_PROJECTS                    VALID     USERS
MTG_PROJECT_ATTRIBUTES          VALID     USERS
MTG_LAST_OPEN_PROJECT           VALID     USERS
MTG_COL_DEP_CHG                 VALID     USERS
MTG_DEPENDENCY                  VALID     USERS
```

```
MTG_DEPENDENCY_MESSAGES          VALID    USERS
MTG_DEPENDENCY_REL               VALID    USERS

MTG_ENTITY_DEP_CHG               VALID    USERS
MTG_SYSIDXCOL                    VALID    USERS
MTG_SYSPRIMKEY                   VALID    USERS
MTG_SOURCE_LOAD                  VALID    USERS
MTG_SOURCE_DATA_TYPE_MAP         VALID    USERS
MTG_LOG_TABLE                    VALID    USERS
MTG_SESSION_TABLE                VALID    USERS
MTG_PREF_HANDLER_TABLE           VALID    USERS
MTG_MESSAGE_TYPE_DISPLAY_PREF    VALID    USERS
MTG_LOG_COLUMN_DISPLAY_PREF      VALID    USERS

MTG_GENERAL_PREF                 VALID    USERS
MTG_LONG_TABLE                   VALID    USERS
MTG_PLUGIN_MENUITEMS             VALID    USERS
OM_USER_INFO                     VALID    USERS
OM_ALL_USER_INFO                 VALID    USERS
OM_ALL_TABLES_INFO               VALID    USERS
OM_ROLE_INFO                     VALID    USERS
OM_ROLE_USER_INFO                VALID    USERS
OM_ROLE_PRIV                     VALID    USERS
OM_USER_PRIV                     VALID    USERS

OM_OBJ_INFO                      VALID    USERS
OM_TBL_INFO                      VALID    USERS
OM_TBL_COL_INFO                  VALID    USERS
OM_DEF_INFO                      VALID    USERS
OM_CHECK_INFO                    VALID    USERS
OM_INDEX_INFO                    VALID    USERS
OM_ALL_INDEXES_INFO              VALID    USERS
OM_IDX_COL_INFO                  VALID    USERS
OM_SQLTEXT_INFO                  VALID    USERS
OM_DDLTEXT                       VALID    USERS


TABLE_NAME                       STATUS   TABLESPACE_NAME
-----------------------------    -------- ----------------------------

OM_TABLESPACE_INFO               VALID    USERS
OM_DATATYPE_INFO                 VALID    USERS
OM_ORA_RESERVED_WORDS            VALID    USERS
OM_FORN_KEY_INFO                 VALID    USERS
OM_PRIM_KEY_INFO                 VALID    USERS
OM_SYN_INFO                      VALID    USERS
OM_SEQ_INFO                      VALID    USERS
OM_FUNCTION_INFO                 VALID    USERS
OM_COMMAND_GENERATOR             VALID    USERS
OM_CONTROL_GENERATOR             VALID    USERS

OM_LIST_GENERATOR                VALID    USERS
OM_STATEMENT_GENERATOR           VALID    USERS
OM_LITE_DATABASES                VALID    USERS
OM_JAVA_TEXT                     VALID    USERS
OM_TRIGGER_INFO                  VALID    USERS
OM_GLOBAL_AREA_PKG               VALID    USERS
OM_USER_SYSTEM_PRIV              VALID    USERS
```

```
OM_ORA_SYSTEM_PRIVILEGE_MAP      VALID      USERS
OM_SRC_ORACLE_SYSPRIV_MAP        VALID      USERS
OM_PARAMETER_LIST                VALID      USERS

OM_TEMPTABLES                    VALID      USERS
OM_PRO_C_SRC_INFO                VALID      USERS
OM_TYPES_DEF                     VALID      USERS
OM_TYPE_ATTRS                    VALID      USERS
OM_SEQUENCES_DEF                 VALID      USERS
MYSQL4_DB_INFO                   VALID      USERS
MYSQL4_DATABASE                  VALID      USERS
MYSQL4_TABLE                     VALID      USERS
MYSQL4_COLUMN                    VALID      USERS
MYSQL4_INDEX_COLUMN              VALID      USERS

MYSQL4_INDEX                     VALID      USERS
MYSQL4_TABLE_PRIVILEGES          VALID      USERS
MYSQL4_DATATYPE_CONSTRAINT       VALID      USERS
MYSQL4_FOREIGNKEY_CONSTRAINT     VALID      USERS
SS2K_SYSLOGINS                   VALID      USERS
SS2K_SYSDATABASES                VALID      USERS
SS2K_SYSUSERS                    VALID      USERS
SS2K_SYSPERMISSIONS              VALID      USERS
SS2K_SYSPROTECTS                 VALID      USERS
SS2K_SYSOBJECTS                  VALID      USERS

SS2K_SYSCOLUMNS                  VALID      USERS
SS2K_SYSTYPES                    VALID      USERS
SS2K_SYSINDEXES                  VALID      USERS
SS2K_SYSINDEXKEYS                VALID      USERS
SS2K_SYSREFERENCES               VALID      USERS
SS2K_SYSCONSTRAINTS              VALID      USERS
SS2K_SYSCOMMENTS                 VALID      USERS
SS2K_SYSFILES                    VALID      USERS
SS2K_SYSMEMBERS                  VALID      USERS
SS2K_SYSFOREIGNKEYS              VALID      USERS

SS2K_SYSPARSE_OPTIONS_PREF       VALID      USERS

131 rows selected.

SQL> spool off
```

As the migration tasks are performed for both online and offline capture, these migration repository tables and schema objects will be populated to store the required metadata for migration tasks. Of particular interest in these schema objects for the migration workbench, the objects with a prefix *ss2k_* and *mysql4_* reference storage containers for the migration functions to migrate MySQL and MS SQL Server 2000 database objects to the Oracle 10g platform using the OMWB.

By logging in to the omwb schema account for the Oracle 10g/11g staging area, one can perform the SQL*PLUS *describe* command against some of these tables as one goes through the migration process to look at configuration progress.

Now that the setup of the ODBC connection is completed and has been tested to ensure that connectivity has been established with SQL Server database, return to the main OMWB environment.

## Using OMWB Capture Wizard

The OMWB provides a wizard called Capture Wizard. This gives step-by-step walk-through assistants to create the new source model database that will house the newly migrated databases within the Oracle environment.

Enter the source database details as shown in the next example using the correct entries for the MS SQL Server 2000 login, password, and DSN setting. Remember that these were created earlier for the ODBC connection to MS SQL Server 2000 environment. Then click on the Next button.

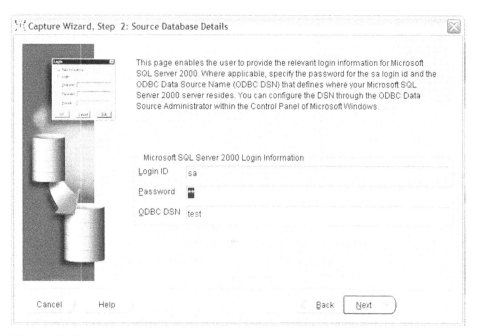

**Figure 5.18**: *Capture Wizard, Step 2: Source Database Details*

Note: It is a good idea to have a session open for MS SQL
Server 2000 Enterprise Manager to review current database
settings and schema objects.

After the OMWB has established connectivity to the source Microsoft SQL Server 2000 database using the settings in Figure 5.18, it will bring up the list of currently accessible databases that may be migrated to Oracle 10g.

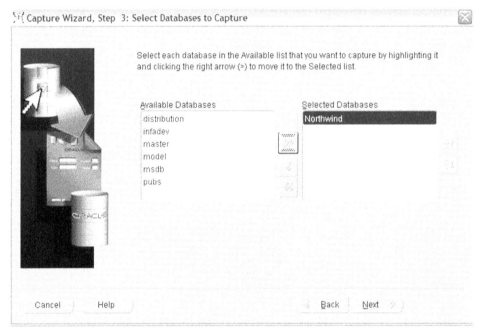

**Figure 5.19:** *Capture Wizard, Step 3: Select MS SQL Server 2000 Databases*

The benefit with the wizard for the source database creation lies in the functionality to capture either one or multiple databases for migration to Oracle. In this test case, only migrate the single database for NorthWind on Microsoft SQL Server 2000 to Oracle 10g.

Following the progress with the Capture Wizard used for creating the new source database model, the next step brings up data type mappings from MS SQL Server 2000 to Oracle 10g. The majority of errors that occur from migration to Oracle involve data type mismatch compatible errors. For now, choose the default settings that the Capture Wizard recommends and apply the tools for resolving issues around data type changes from Microsoft SQL Server 2000 to Oracle.

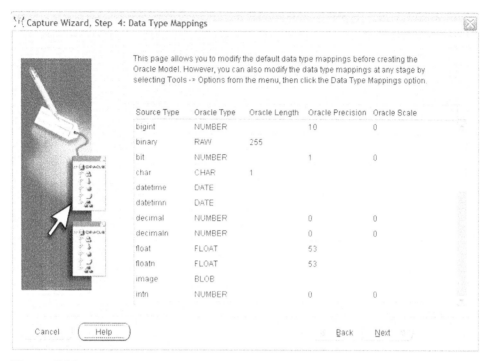

**Figure 5.20:** *Capture Wizard, Step 4: Data Type Mappings*

Next, the Capture Wizard will ask if the DBA wants to create the source model database which will be used as the template to migrate the Microsoft SQL Server 2000 Northwind database to an Oracle 10g database. The options available are to either proceed and create the new source model now or defer the procedure and make other configuration changes such as editing the data type settings or additional mapping settings. For now, proceed and create the source model database as shown in Figure 5.21.

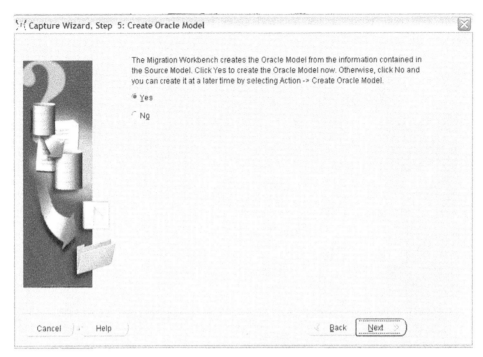

**Figure 5.21:** *Capture Wizard, Step 5: Create Oracle Model*

As an added bonus, the Capture Wizard next asks for a confirmation to proceed and then reveals the settings that have been set in place for the new source model database. This can be seen in Figure 5.22.

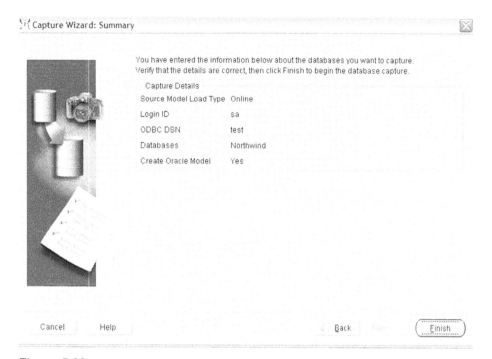

You have entered the information below about the databases you want to capture. Verify that the details are correct, then click Finish to begin the database capture.

Capture Details

| | |
|---|---|
| Source Model Load Type | Online |
| Login ID | sa |
| ODBC DSN | test |
| Databases | Northwind |
| Create Oracle Model | Yes |

Cancel      Help                        Back      Next      Finish

**Figure 5.22:** *Capture Wizard Summary*

Now that migrating the Microsoft SQL Server 2000 Northwind database to Oracle has been accomplished, choose Finish and complete the build for the new source model database.

The OMWB Capture Wizard will then proceed to build the new source model database. As the build process takes place, the conversion process will display the status monitor with all tasks completed or failed based on error messages.

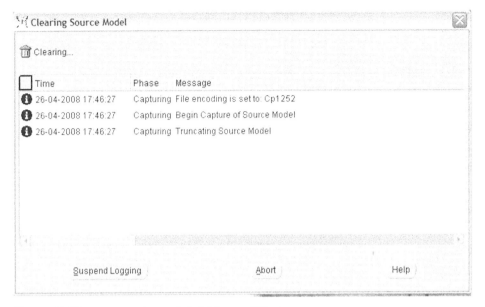

**Figure 5.23:** *Clearing Source Model Status Window*

Of particular importance are the three option buttons located at the bottom of the status display window: Suspend Logging, Abort, and Help.

- Suspend Logging provides the ability to hide the scrolling messages as the source model is being constructed.

- The Abort option allows the option to cancel and halt the build operation for the source model.

- For assistance during the source model build process, the OMWB provides a Help button for further information.

## Errors During Source Model Creation

Since all default choices for the source model creation were taken out, there are bound to be errors due to various mapping issues from MS SQL Server to Oracle as is shown in the below window. So evaluate the errors that have been received in this example case.

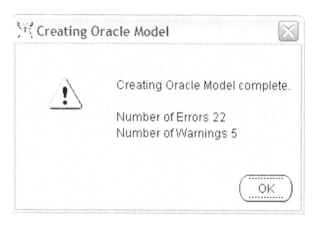

Figure 5.24: *Results from Capture Wizard Source Model Creation*

This reveals that Oracle created the source model, but there are many errors and warnings that will need to be addressed before moving forward with the Northwind database migrating successfully from MS SQL Server 2000 to Oracle 10g. The OMWB then provides further options to either continue with the migration and create the new schema objects in the source model, or cancel the migration and go back to fix the errors that occurred during the build process as shown in Figure 5.25.

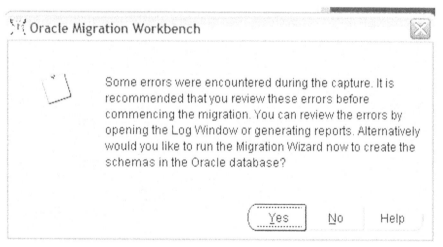

Figure 5.25: *OMWB Error Resolution*

For now, it is best to delay migrating the Northwind schema and database to Oracle with the migration workbench to address these concerns.

After deciding to halt the migration process to Oracle for the MS SQL Server 2000 database, Northwind, the default window opens for the OMWB. As shown in the next figure, there are template source models for both the Microsoft SQL Server 2000 environment and the future Oracle 10g environment.

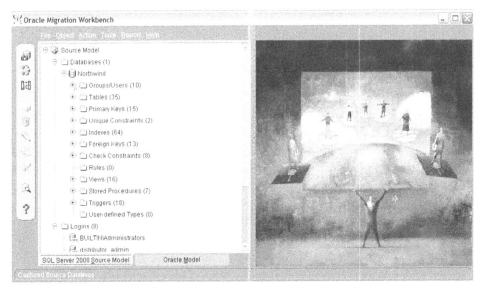

**Figure 5.26:** *OMWB Source Model*

In spite of the conversion factors, which will be addressed in the next few chapters, the majority of the build was successfully completed for the new source model databases to migrate from MS SQL Server 2000 to Oracle 10g using the Online Capture Wizard assistants. In the example above, it is particularly important to note that the OMWB provides a tab to examine both the SQL Server 2000 Source Model database, which is the Northwind database in the example, as well as an additional tab for the future Oracle 10g database under the Oracle Model tab.

This was just a dry run to show the features available for performing the online capture using the built-in wizards with the OMWB. In future chapters, these issues will be revisited and solutions will be found to errors that occur as a result of mapping data from MS SQL Server 2000 to Oracle 10g.

Next, a test migration procedure will be performed using the OMWB to build a new source database model for MySQL to utilize for migration of MySQL database environments to Oracle 10g.

# Online Capture for MySQL Database to Oracle 10g/11g

As was shown earlier, the OMWB provides a variety of excellent tools to migrate databases to Oracle right out of the box with feature-rich wizards in which to customize the migration process. The following case example begins the online capture process for a test MySQL database to migrate to Oracle 10g and 11g.

In order to prevent confusion and maintain simplicity in the migration for MySQL to Oracle, create a new migration user called mysqlmig. This will be used for the test bed schema account and to maintain the MySQL database environment aside from the previous Microsoft SQL Server account used earlier for omwb. There are a few setup steps that will need to be followed before proceeding with the online capture for MySQL.

## Prepare the MySQL Test Environment

When preparing the MySQL test environment, the first step is to create a new database schema for MySQL called mysqlmig. The following code sample script can be used to setup the MySQL test environment.

### ⊟ Mysqlformigration.sql

```
-- create new database for MySQL migration setup
DROP DATABASE IF EXISTS mysqltooracle;
CREATE DATABASE mysqltooracle;

-- create migration user for MySQL to Oracle
GRANT CREATE, DELETE, INDEX, INSERT, SELECT, UPDATE
ON mysqltooracle.*
TO mysqlmig IDENTIFIED BY 'mysqlmig';

-- Create the test migration tables for MySQL
create table dept
(
  deptno decimal(2) not null primary key,
  dname varchar(14),
  loc varchar(13)
) type=InnoDB;
```

```
create table emp
(
  empno int not null auto_increment primary key,
  ename varchar(10),
  job varchar(9),
  mgr int,
  hiredate date not null,
  sal decimal(7,2),
  comm decimal(7,2),
  deptno int not null references msdept(deptno)
) type=InnoDB;

create table bonus
(
  ename varchar(10),
  job varchar(9),
  sal int,
  comm int
) type=InnoDB;

create table salgrade
(
  grade int,
  losal int,
  hisal int
) type=InnoDB

-- Load test data into these tables
delete from dept;
insert into dept
values (1,'Finance','San Diego');
commit;

insert into dept
values (2,'Technology','Los Angeles');
commit;

insert into dept
values (3,'Marketing','New York');
commit;


delete from bonus;
insert into bonus values
('Dan','Engineer',55000,1200);
commit;

insert into bonus values
('Seth','Temp',85000,100);
commit;

insert into bonus values
('Mike','VP',155000,5200);
commit;


delete from emp;
insert into emp
values (1,'Smith','Manager',12,'2008-02-01',1200,1200,55);
```

```
commit;

insert into emp
values (2,'Jones','CPA',11,'2007-11-11',2200,4200,15);
commit;

insert into emp
values (3,'Ira','VP',21,'2001-12-21',92000,200,25);
commit;

insert into emp
values (4,'Kin','DBA',31,'2003-10-14',61200,400,35);
commit;

insert into emp
values (5,'Penny','MGR',41,'2006-10-11',2200,4200,15);
commit;

insert into emp
values (6,'Jones','CPA',51,'2003-11-11',2200,4200,15);
commit;

insert into emp
values (7,'Masters','CEO',61,'2000-09-11',93200,6200,95);
commit;

insert into emp
values (8,'Bert','LAW',71,'2002-10-13',22200,8200,75);
commit;
```

Check the status of the new database environment for MySQL by using the *status* command as shown below:

```
Mysql -u mysqlmig -p
```

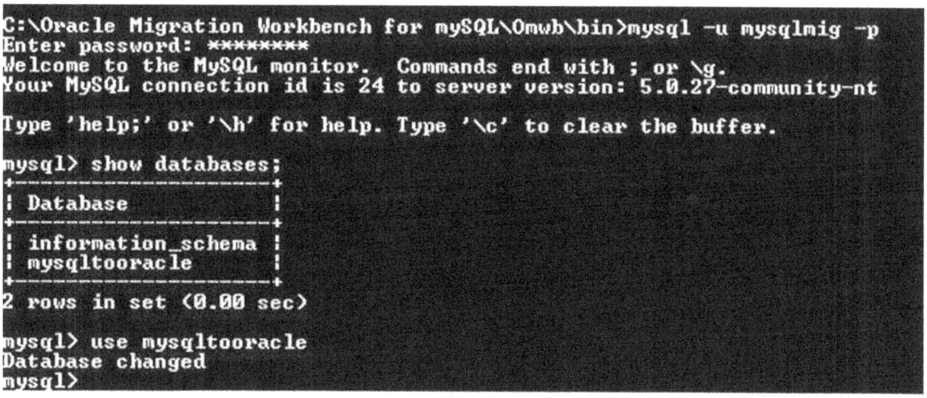

**Figure 5.27:** *Check MySQL User and Database*

Mysql> status:

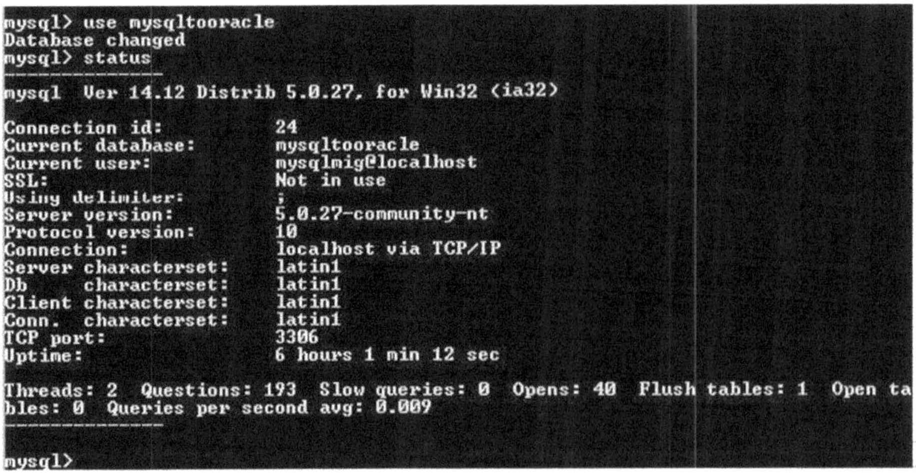

**Figure 5.28:** *Status for New MySQL Database*

Verify that the new user and database are available and tables have been fully populated. This is shown in the following example commands:

```
Mysql> show databases;

Mysql> use mysqltooracle;
Mysql> select count(*) from emp;
```

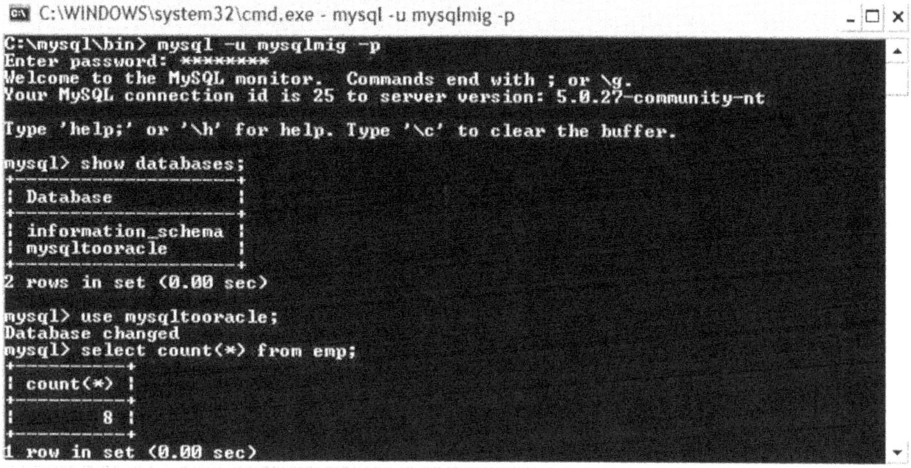

**Figure 5.29:** *Verify Environment for MySQL*

Now that the setup is completed and the MySQL test database user and environment have been configured, perform an online capture process for MySQL to Oracle 10g using the OMWB.

# Automation Process and Configuration Parameters for MySQL

First, create a new schema account in the target Oracle 10g database environment that will contain the MySQL repository objects. The following code depot script will be used to create the new Oracle account in the target Oracle database instance.

### Mysql2oracle.sql

```
-- Mysql2oracle.sql
--
-- SETUP SCRIPT FOR ORACLE 10G FOR MYSQL SCHEMA ACCOUNT
-- Purpose: to create schema in target Oracle 10g Database
--          for MySQL migration objects
--
SPOOL setupmysqlmig.log
/

CREATE USER mysqlmig IDENTIFIED BY mysqlmig
DEFAULT TABLESPACE USERS
TEMPORARY TABLESPACE TEMP;
/
```

```
-- GRANT THE PRIVILEGES TO NEW MYSQL ACCOUNT IN ORACLE
GRANT CONNECT, RESOURCE TO mysqlmig;
/

-- GRANT ADDITIONAL MINIMUM PRIVILEGES AND ROLES TO MYSQL ACCOUNT
GRANT ALTER ANY ROLE, ALTER ANY SEQUENCE, ALTER ANY TABLE,
ALTER TABLESPACE, ALTER ANY TRIGGER, COMMENT ANY TABLE,
CREATE ANY SEQUENCE, CREATE ANY TABLE, CREATE ANY TRIGGER,
CREATE ROLE, CREATE TABLESPACE, CREATE USER, DROP ANY SEQUENCE,
DROP ANY TABLE, DROP ANY TRIGGER, DROP TABLESPACE, DROP USER,
DROP ANY ROLE, GRANT ANY ROLE, INSERT ANY TABLE, SELECT ANY TABLE,
UPDATE ANY TABLE TO mysqlmig;
/

SPOOL OFF
/
EXIT
```

The next step is to edit the *state.properties configuration* file for MySQL to reflect the correct settings. Otherwise, the OMWB will fail to connect to the source MySQL database environment.

Since the MySQL to Oracle 10g migration is being tested on Windows, the *configuration* file in the test bed environment is located under the following directory:

```
Cd C:\OMWB\omwb\bin
```

Edit the file to update the correct MySQL settings as shown in Figure 5.30.

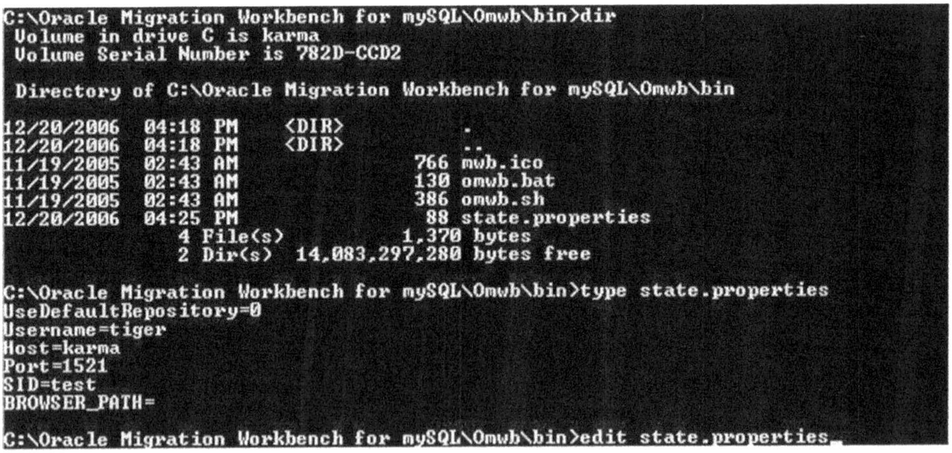

**Figure 5.30:** *Configuration Parameters for MySQL*

After setting the correct parameters for the *state.properties configuration* file for MySQL, the environment will be ready to use the OMWB as shown in the next figure.

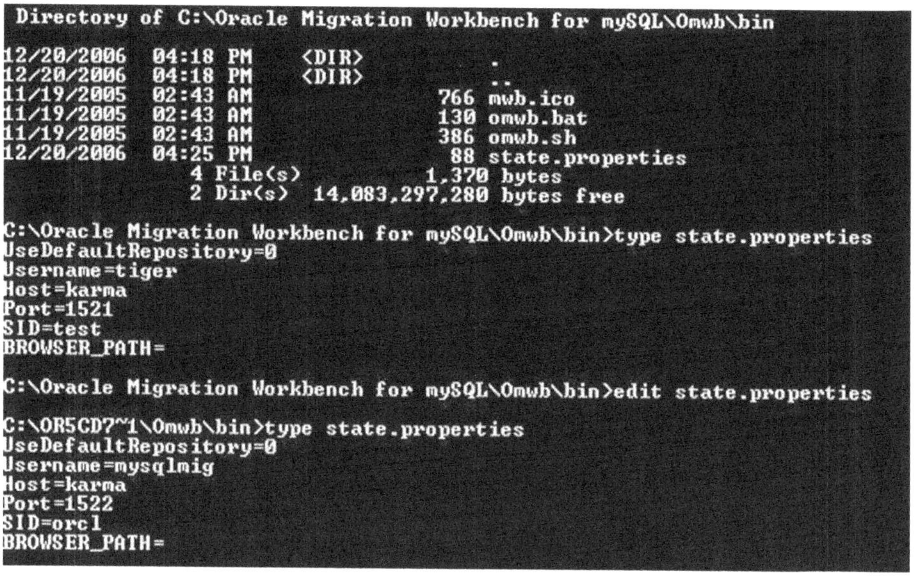

```
Directory of C:\Oracle Migration Workbench for mySQL\Omwb\bin

12/20/2006   04:18 PM    <DIR>            .
12/20/2006   04:18 PM    <DIR>            ..
11/19/2005   02:43 AM              766 mwb.ico
11/19/2005   02:43 AM              130 omwb.bat
11/19/2005   02:43 AM              386 omwb.sh
12/20/2006   04:25 PM               88 state.properties
             4 File(s)            1,370 bytes
             2 Dir(s)  14,083,297,280 bytes free

C:\Oracle Migration Workbench for mySQL\Omwb\bin>type state.properties
UseDefaultRepository=0
Username=tiger
Host=karma
Port=1521
SID=test
BROWSER_PATH=

C:\Oracle Migration Workbench for mySQL\Omwb\bin>edit state.properties

C:\OR5CD7~1\Omwb\bin>type state.properties
UseDefaultRepository=0
Username=mysqlmig
Host=karma
Port=1522
SID=orcl
BROWSER_PATH=
```

**Figure 5.31:** *MySQL Configuration Parameter Settings*

Now that the configuration preparation for MySQL has been completed, perform the online capture process. First, start a new session for MySQL with the OMWB.

Navigate to the *Omwb\bin* directory for the migration workbench and start the application by entering *omwb.bat* at a new Windows or Linux command prompt.

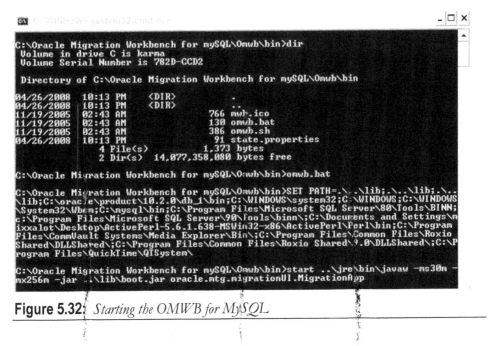

**Figure 5.32:** *Starting the OMWB for MySQL*

At the logon window for the OMWB, enter the account information that was used earlier to create the new mysqlmig schema account in the Oracle 10g target database.

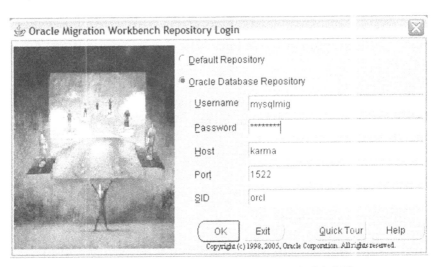

**Figure 5.33:** *Oracle 10g Migration Repository Login for MySQL*

Oracle will then ask if creating a new repository schema for MySQL is desired. Since the plan is to maintain a new schema for MySQL to Oracle 10g migrations, create this new repository to maintain only MySQL objects for the migration to Oracle.

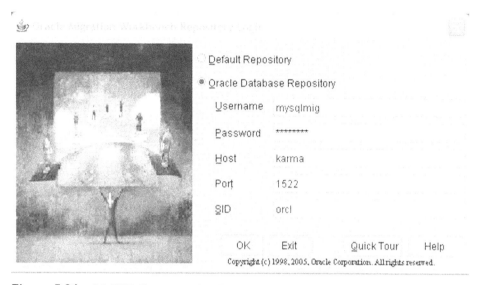

**Figure 5.34:** *OMWB Repository MySQL Login*

After selecting OK and logging in to the new schema account, the OMWB will ask if the user would like to create the new repository for MySQL. Choose Yes and continue.

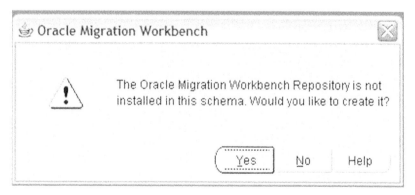

**Figure 5.35:** *Create New Repository for MySQL*

Once the decision to create the new repository is confirmed, Oracle will create the MySQL migration schema and objects.

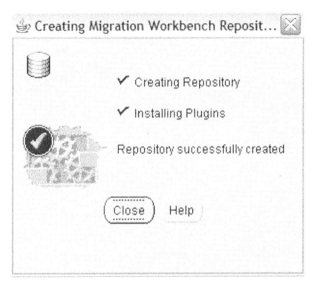

**Figure 5.36:** *Complete Migration Repository Creation for MySQL*

The next step involves a prompt for the migration source and the choice of which plugin will be needed for the migration. Recall that earlier, based on the output of the MySQL *status* command, it was possible to obtain the version information for the MySQL database environment. In addition, the port number that MySQL uses for network communication was also acquired. These will be important in the following configuration steps.

Since the database release for MySQL is version 5.x, choose the plugin for MySQL 5.x as shown in Figure 5.37.

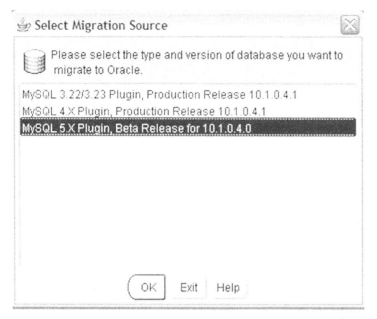

**Figure 5.37:** *Migration Source for MySQL*

As seen earlier during the test online capture process for MS SQL Server, a similar screen appears next.

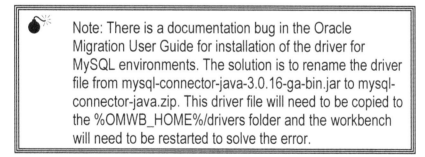

Note: There is a documentation bug in the Oracle Migration User Guide for installation of the driver for MySQL environments. The solution is to rename the driver file from mysql-connector-java-3.0.16-ga-bin.jar to mysql-connector-java.zip. This driver file will need to be copied to the %OMWB_HOME%/drivers folder and the workbench will need to be restarted to solve the error.

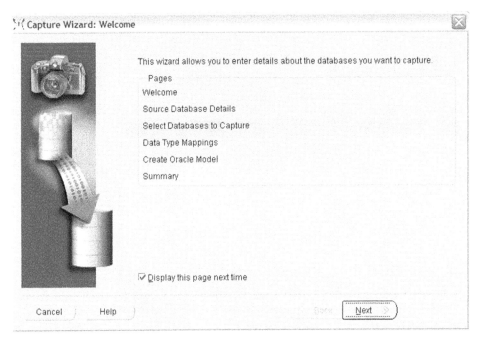

**Figure 5.38:** *Capture Wizard Welcome Screen for MySQL*

At this point, choose Next to continue. Then the Online Capture Wizard will ask for connection login details for the MySQL source database. After the correct details are provided for the MySQL source database user account, password, and port information, a list of available databases for MySQL will be shown to select for the online capture and migration.

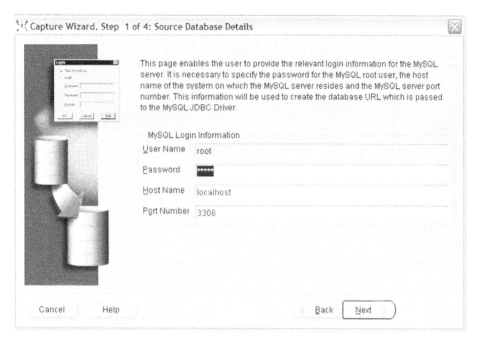

This page enables the user to provide the relevant login information for the MySQL server. It is necessary to specify the password for the MySQL root user, the host name of the system on which the MySQL server resides and the MySQL server port number. This information will be used to create the database URL which is passed to the MySQL JDBC Driver.

MySQL Login Information

User Name: root

Password: ****

Host Name: localhost

Port Number: 3306

Cancel    Help    Back    Next

**Figure 5.39:** *Capture Wizard: Source Database for MySQL Details*

The output of the MySQL *status* command will verify the MySQL database server settings. For the test case, migrate the new MySQL mysqltooracle database that was created earlier as an example.

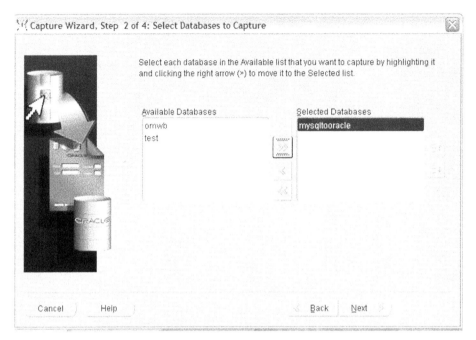

**Figure 5.40:** *Capture Wizard, Select MySQL Database for Online Capture*

As was done earlier with the Microsoft SQL Server 2000 online capture process, the Online Capture Wizard for MySQL will next display the data type mapping editor.

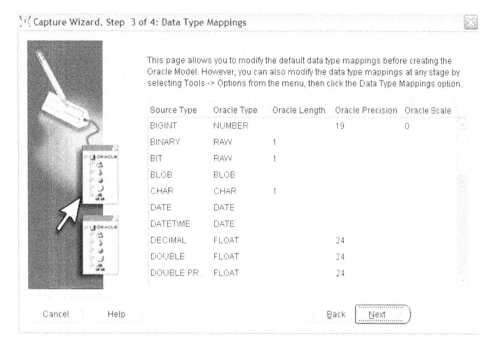

This page allows you to modify the default data type mappings before creating the Oracle Model. However, you can also modify the data type mappings at any stage by selecting Tools -> Options from the menu, then click the Data Type Mappings option.

| Source Type | Oracle Type | Oracle Length | Oracle Precision | Oracle Scale |
| --- | --- | --- | --- | --- |
| BIGINT | NUMBER | | 19 | 0 |
| BINARY | RAW | 1 | | |
| BIT | RAW | 1 | | |
| BLOB | BLOB | | | |
| CHAR | CHAR | 1 | | |
| DATE | DATE | | | |
| DATETIME | DATE | | | |
| DECIMAL | FLOAT | | 24 | |
| DOUBLE | FLOAT | | 24 | |
| DOUBLE PR... | FLOAT | | 24 | |

Cancel     Help                                        Back     Next

**Figure 5.41:** *Capture Wizard: Data Type Mappings for MySQL to Oracle*

In the meantime, since this is only a test case, choose the defaults without making any changes. Then visit the editing functions of the data mapper in future chapters.

Since immediately creating the new source model database for the MySQL to Oracle migration is not in order, defer the build step for now.

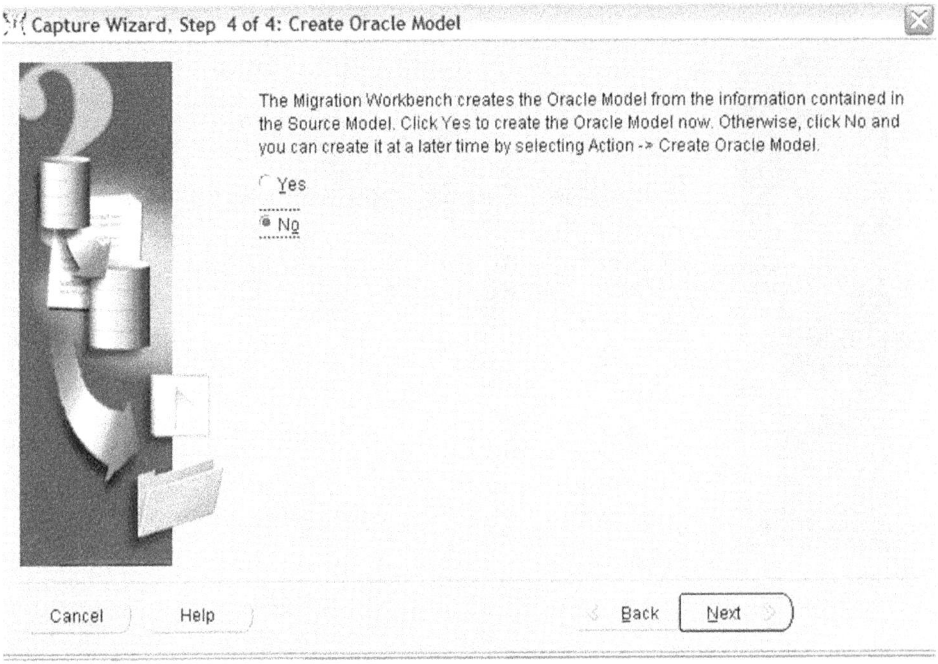
Capture Wizard, Step 4 of 4: Create Oracle Model
The Migration Workbench creates the Oracle Model from the information contained in the Source Model. Click Yes to create the Oracle Model now. Otherwise, click No and you can create it at a later time by selecting Action -> Create Oracle Model.
Yes
No
Cancel
Help
Back
Next

**Figure 5.42:** *Capture Wizard: Create Oracle Model for MySQL*

The online capture wizard will present the confirmation screen before it performs the capture process for MySQL to Oracle.

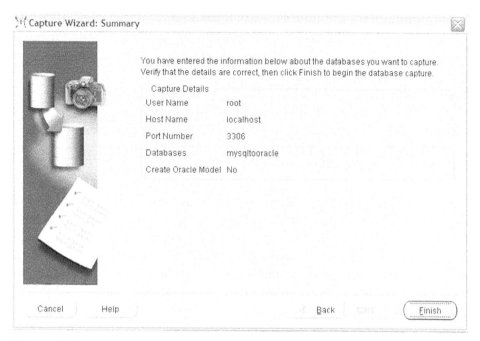

**Figure 5.43:** *Capture Wizard Summary for MySQL to Oracle*

The output for the source model is completed and with errors. However, how to resolve the errors will be further examined in upcoming chapters.

# Oracle SQL Developer Migration Workbench

As of late 2007, the Oracle Corporation recommends database professionals use the newer version of its database migration tools by development and enhancements of the Oracle SQL Developer suite of tools for migration tasks. Now that SQL Developer Migration Workbench is the current and future stated direction from Oracle for database migration tools to Oracle, support for the OMWB will end in a few years. The focus here will regard deploying and using the migration toolkit within the new versions of SQL Developer to migrate MySQL and Microsoft SQL Server 2000 database environments to

> 🔔 Oracle provides the free software download available online at the following website URL:
> http://www.oracle.com/technology/software/products/database/index.html.

Oracle 10g and 11g releases. This will begin with covering the online capture procedures. Then, in subsequent chapters, how to use offline scripts to perform database migrations to Oracle 10g and 11g will be outlined.

The first procedure to accomplish is checking the installation for SQL Developer which ensures that all settings are correct and up to date. As of December 8, 2008, the latest release for SQL Developer is version 1.5.3.57.83 with migration enhancements for third party database migrations to Oracle 10g and 11g support included.

Since the SQL Developer migration tools are new releases of the robust OMWB software, it may be appropriate to test them in a non-production environment first. If this is successful, then launch any critical production related migrations. In earlier chapters, SQL Developer 1.x release was installed and configured, so the procedure for the 1.5 release of SQL Developer should be about the same with the exception of an updated version of the JDK libraries and SQL Developer binaries.

For the purposes here, use the new release of SQL Developer 1.5 for testing the migrations from MySQL and MS SQL Server 2000 to Oracle 10g. If the earlier release of SQL Developer 1.x has been installed as was covered in previous chapters, the process to upgrade to 1.5 is simple and takes only a few minutes.

Next to be covered are some test online capture examples for Microsoft SQL Server 2000 to Oracle 10g using SQL Developer 1.5.

## Online Capture for MS SQL Server 2000 to Oracle 10g/11g with the SQL Developer Workbench

Starting with version 1.2 of the Oracle SQL Developer software, Oracle has provided migration tools to perform migrations from third party databases including MySQL and Microsoft SQL Server 2000 environments to Oracle 10g. The current, and future, strategy from Oracle appears to be harnessing the power of software development and migration tools with a one-stop shop in the Oracle 10g SQL Developer tools available from Oracle. As such, this book places a great deal of focus on how to deploy these tools in addition to explorations of database migrations using the OMWB. The next task will be to review the new options available with the current and latest release of the

Oracle SQL Developer migration tools. Now it is time to get started by opening a new session of SQL Developer.

Here is an overview of various tools offered with the latest version of the SQL Developer environment. These can be seen in Figure 5.44.

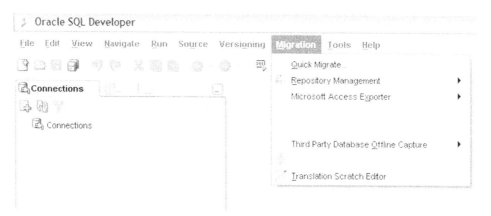

**Figure 5.44**: *Migration Options in Oracle SQL Developer 1.5 Environment*

A radical departure from the OMWB, this SQL Developer interface provides new options for performing database migrations and managing existing migration repositories that have been created in the past. This is especially useful because it provides backward compatibility in addition to robust new features to make the database migration process less complex.

## Quick Migrate with SQL Developer

The new quick migrate option located under the Migration toolbar menu section for SQL Developer 1.5 provides a new feature to complete a quick and dirty test migration from MySQL and Microsoft SQL Server 2000 databases to Oracle 10g and 11g. Up next is a look at the new quick migrate feature in SQL Developer.

The first step for using the quick migrate wizard requires that a new source database connection be set up for the third party database that should be migrated from to Oracle. In the following example, a quick migrate for MySQL to Oracle 10g will be performed.

## Quick Migration from MySQL to Oracle 10g

Once the quick migrate option is called, SQL Developer prompts the DBA to enter the new source connection as shown in the example below. As was covered in earlier chapters for SQL Developer, the correct JDBC and jar files will need to be installed for SQL Developer to migrate MS SQL Server 2000 and MySQL to Oracle.

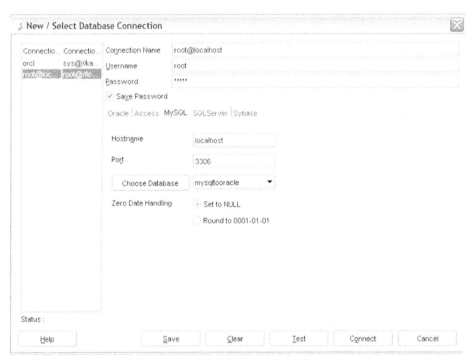

**Figure 5.45:** *Quick Migration Wizard - New Connection*

Follow the step in Figure 5.45 to set up the new source connection from MySQL to Oracle 10g. The Test button will verify that the connection to the MySQL database is accessible before proceeding.

Now that the source connection to the MySQL database has been set up, configure the target Oracle 10g environment as shown in the next example.

---

**Figure 5.46:** *Quick Migration Wizard - Step 2, Target Connection*

In the target connection step of the Quick Migration Wizard, Oracle presents the required minimum privileges and roles that must be granted to the target migration schema user for Oracle 10g. These privileges and roles should have already been granted from earlier exercises.

The following step in the Quick Migration Wizard will give a prompt to either use an existing migration repository or to create a new one if SQL Developer cannot locate one. Since it cannot find one in this example, create a new migration repository for SQL Developer.

**Figure 5.47:** *Quick Migration Wizard - Step 3, Repository Creation*

The following step of the Quick Migration Wizard for the SQL Developer tool provides a useful verification check to ensure that all prerequisites have been satisfied before the migration is performed. Fortunately, the environments for both the source MySQL and target Oracle 10g have been configured correctly and so it is okay to proceed as the results display for the verification process (Figure 5.48).

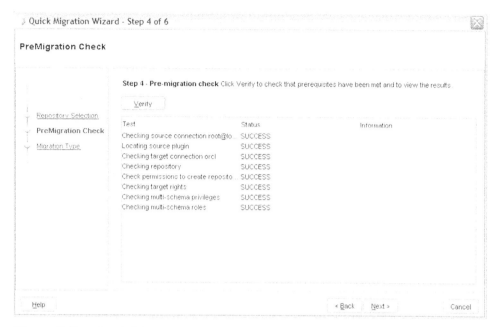

**Figure 5.48:** *Quick Migration Wizard: Step 4, Pre Migration Check*

After the verification check comes back clean, the next step is to select the objects for the MySQL database to be migrated to Oracle. There is the choice to migrate everything, tables only, or tables and data for the MySQL database environment to Oracle. Since the object is to see how the Quick Migrate function performs for a comprehensive MySQL database migration, choose everything to be migrated for the test.

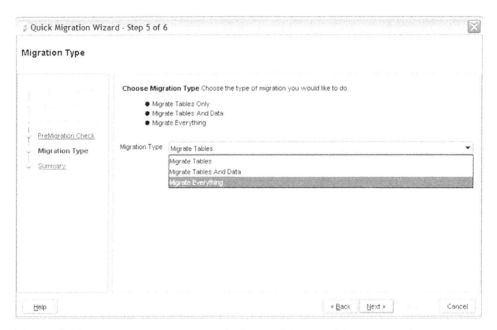

**Figure 5.49:** *Quick Migration Wizard - Step 5, Migration Type*

Once Migrate Everything has been selected from the drop down menu bar, choose Next to continue.

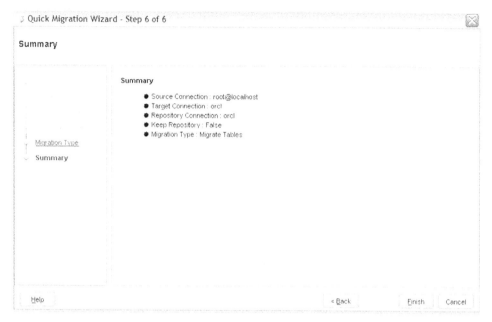

**Figure 5.50:** *Quick Migration Wizard - Step 6, Summary*

Oracle is kind enough to offer a reminder that everything is lined up, and that the correct settings for both source and target databases are established before it performs the quick migration from MySQL to Oracle.

During the Quick Migration process, the status will be displayed for objects migrated to Oracle from MySQL.

**Figure 5.51:** *Quick Migration Status Window*

There is now the option to automatically close the dialog window once the Quick Migrate completes or to leave it open for monitoring the migration process log files. After the migration completes, the test MySQL database tables migrated to Oracle 10g/11g are now available unless errors have occurred due to various factors that will be examined in the next few chapters as well as solutions on how to resolve these errors in database migration to Oracle.

# Conclusion

This chapter covered the methodologies for taking the online capture of MySQL and Microsoft SQL Server 2000 databases as part of the first step for migration to Oracle 10g. This was done using both the OMWB tools and the new version of the Oracle SQL Developer Workbench. Next to be described are illustrations on how to perform offline capture procedures for "lights out" administration database migrations. Database administrators can schedule maintenance windows for this to migrate these production environments to Oracle 10g.

# References

OMWB Reference Guide for MySQL 3.22, 3.23, 4.x
Migrations Release 10.1.0 for Microsoft Windows 98/2000/NT/XP
Part B13911-01, Oracle Corporation

OMWB Reference Guide for SQL Server and Sybase
Adaptive Server Migrations Release 9.2.0 for Microsoft Windows
98/2000/NT/XP, Part B10254-01

OMWB Frequently Asked Questions (FAQ) Release
9.2.0 for Microsoft Windows 98/2000/NT/XP, Part B10258-01

Oracle Database SQL Developer Installation Guide, Release 1.5, Part E12153-02

Oracle Database SQL Developer User's Guide, Release 1.5, Part E12152-03

Oracle Database SQL Developer Supplementary Information for MySQL Migrations, Release 1.5, Part E12155-01

Oracle Database SQL Developer Supplementary Information for Microsoft SQL Server and Sybase Adaptive Server Migrations, Release 1.5, Part E12156-01

Oracle Metalink Support References
Note 470977.1- Difference Between OMWB and SQL Developer
Note 357052.1- OMWB Repository User Privileges
Note 375380.1: OMWB Reports No Plugins Installed
Note: 397828.1- Exception with OMWB
Bug No: 5160644- ORA-1461 Creating Tablespace Using Oracle RDBMS as Repository

# Performing Offline Capture for the Oracle 10g Migration Workbench

*"Offline Capture can save lots of time for database migrations"*

## The Offline Capture Process

In the last chapter, methods for database migration from MySQL and Microsoft SQL Server to Oracle 10g using online capture within the Oracle 10g Migration Workbench were detailed. Also covered was the newer migration suite of tools for online capture process with Oracle 10g SQL Developer.

The online capture process allows busy database administrators to perform database migrations to Oracle 10g and 11g with minimal downtime to live database systems. Online capture can be especially useful for mission critical production database servers that cannot afford to take an outage or scheduled downtime for the migration process.

In this chapter, a new path will be taken illustrating the migration procedures from MySQL and Microsoft SQL Server to Oracle 10g and 11g using offline capture scripts that are provided with the OMWB and also with Oracle 10g SQL Developer.

# Offline Capture with Oracle 10g Migration Workbench

The offline capture process uses a collection of wizards in the OMWB to connect to a source database. This may be MySQL or Microsoft SQL Server 2000. There are a series of wizards that the online capture method provides for the migration of MySQL and Microsoft SQL Server 2000 platforms to Oracle 10g and 11g.

The OMWB and the SQL Developer tools use a variety of canned, off-the-shelf, batch-type scripts. These scripts are customizable for third party database platforms to create the source database model for migration to Oracle. The offline scripts are also formatted to communicate directly with the operating system (OS) and database API layer so as to extract the database definition, thereby creating the new source model. This new source model will then eventually become the new Oracle 10g or 11g database.

Although coverage of other third party database platforms such as IBM DB2 Universal Database (UDB), Informix, and Sybase Adaptive Server are beyond the scope of this text, the scripts available for offline database migration from these platforms to Oracle will be briefly mentioned. First on the agenda is the operation of offline capture scripts within the MySQL and Microsoft SQL Server environments.

## Scripts for Use with Microsoft SQL Server

Both the OMWB and new migration tools in SQL Developer from Oracle provide offline capture scripts for migrating Microsoft SQL Server 2000 and 2005 databases to Oracle 10g and 11g environments. These offline capture scripts provide a series of customizable templates that can be used to migrate Microsoft SQL Server databases to Oracle using *API level* commands and *bcp* command options. First, take a look at how the OMWB operates with offline capture scripts for SQL Server and then examine how to integrate these scripts with SQL Developer.

Part of the challenge is to find out where these offline capture scripts can be located. Since the Oracle documentation is not clear on offline capture procedures, the offline capture scripts can be found located under the following directory for Microsoft SQL Server as shown in Figure 6.1. Additionally, the default directory for these scripts is in the following directory structure on Windows:

```
C:\OMWB_install_directory\Omwb\offline_capture\SQLServer2K
```

**Figure 6.1:** *Default Location for Offline Capture Scripts*

In the following examples and test cases, navigate to the default offline capture script directory for Microsoft SQL Server 2000 as follows:

```
cd \O*SQL*\Omwb\offline_capture\SQLServer2K
```

# Microsoft SQL Server BCP Scripts - Offline Capture

First of all, below are the default offline capture scripts available for Microsoft SQL Server 2000 to Oracle. These offline capture scripts are shown in the default directory for Microsoft SQL Server 2000:

- omwb_offline_capture.bat

- properties.sql
- ss2k_bcp_script.bat

The main offline capture script for Microsoft SQL Server 2000 is *omwb_offline_capture.bat*.

The *omwb_offline_capture.bat* script provides all of the prime directives to connect to the Microsoft SQL Server 2000 database environment using a series of database level API calls to collect the database schema and architecture information. These will be used as the raw input to feed into the creation of the new source database to be migrated to Oracle.

Here is a sample code which can be used as an example of the default template structure for the *omwb_offline_capture.bat* file:

### 💾 omwb_offline_capture.bat (partial)

```
@echo off

rem ** SET THE VALUE FOR THE OFFLINE_CAPTURE_COLUMN_DELIMITER
rem ** THIS VALUE SHOULD MATCH THE VALUE SET FOR THE SAME VARIABLE IN
OMWB_INSTALL_DIR\bin\omwb.properties
set OFFLINE_CAPTURE_COLUMN_DELIMITER=§

rem ** SET THE VALUE FOR THE OFFLINE_CAPTURE_ROW_DELIMITER
rem ** THIS VALUE SHOULD MATCH THE VALUE SET FOR THE SAME VARIABLE IN
OMWB_INSTALL_DIR\bin\omwb.properties
set OFFLINE_CAPTURE_ROW_DELIMITER=¤

rem ** SET THE SCRIPT VERSION ENVIRONMENT VARIABLE
set OMWB_SCRIPT_VERSION=10104

rem ** SET THE VALUE FOR THE OMWB FILE ENVIRONMENT VARIABLE
set OMWB_SCRIPT_FILE=%3\%3_INFO.TXT

rem ** DISPLAY THE HELP PAGE IF THE USER REQUESTS IT

if "%1"=="-h"   goto help
if "%1"=="help" goto help
if "%1"=="?"    goto help
if "%1"=="-?"   goto help


rem *** DISPLAY THE SCRIPT VERSION IF THE USER REQUESTS IT

if "%1"=="-ver" goto version
if "%1"=="version" goto version

rem *** CHECK THAT THREE PARAMETERS HAVE BEEN ENTERED
rem *** THE PASSWORD CAN BE "", SO WE DON'T DO THE SAME CHECK FOR THAT
```

```
if "%1"=="" goto input_error
if "%3"=="" goto input_error
if "%4"=="" goto input_error

rem *** START THE EXECUTION OF THE SCRIPT INSTRUCTIONS

goto start

:start

rem ** CREATE THE OUTPUT DIRECTORIES

mkdir master
mkdir %3

rem *** CALL THE BCP SCRIPT TO CREATE THE METADATA FILES

call SS2K_BCP_SCRIPT.BAT %1 %2 %3 %4 %OFFLINE_CAPTURE_COLUMN_DELIMITER%
%OFFLINE_CAPTURE_ROW_DELIMITER%

rem *** CHECK THAT ALL OF THE OUTPUT FILES HAVE BEEN CREATED

goto checkoutput

:help
echo --------------------------------------------------------------
echo -------------------- OMWB --------------------
echo --------------------          Release %OMWB_SCRIPT_VERSION%        -----
---------------
echo --------------------------------------------------------------
echo ---- This script will generate delimited flat files containing
echo ---- schema metadata from the database you wish to migrate. This echo -
--- script will invoke the Bulk Copy Program (BCP) that should be ----
echo ---- part of your SQL Server install base.
echo ---- Please ensure that your path points to the version of BCP
echo ---- that is installed with the SQL Server from which you wish
echo ---- to migrate. Your current path setting is listed below:
echo ----
PATH
echo ----
echo ----
echo ---- To run this script, enter the following command at the prompt ----
echo ----
echo ---- OMWB_OFFLINE_CAPTURE dba_login_id password database_name
server_name
echo ---- where,
echo ---- dba_login_id is a login id with DBA privileges (for example, sa)
echo ---- password is the password for the login id
echo ---- database_name is the name of the database you wish to capture
echo ---- server_name is the name of the server on which the database
resides
echo ---- For example,
echo ---- OMWB_OFFLINE_CAPTURE sa sapwd employeeDB DEPT1_SERVER
echo ----
echo --------------------------------------------------------------

goto exit
```

Now create a new temporary directory and copy the offline capture files over from the OMWB plugins directory for Microsoft SQL Server 2000.

To perform the offline capture process for Microsoft SQL Server 2000, use database and server parameters to execute the *omwb_offline_capture.bat* file. To maintain a good standard build for the offline capture procedures, it is a good idea to create a new directory for the offline capture staging files.

First, copy the plugin offline capture files for Microsoft SQL Server 2000 to the new offline capture directory and folder that will be created next.

```
cd c:\OMWB*SQL*\omwb mkdir capture_files
```

Using Windows Explorer, navigate to the offline capture script directory and copy the offline script files over to the *capture_files* directory that was just created.

**Figure 6.2:** *Offline Capture Scripts for SQL Server 2000*

Next, be sure to check and verify the correct path for the Microsoft SQL Server 2000 BCP utility. Execute the following command as shown below for the correct version:

```
bcp -v
```

The right version will be displayed if all of the system variables and settings are correct, like the example below.

```
C:\Oracle Migration Workbench for MS SQL Server\omwb\capture_files>bcp -v
BCP - Bulk Copy Program for Microsoft SQL Server.
Copyright (c) 1991-1998, Microsoft Corp. All Rights Reserved.
Version: 8.00.194
```

**Figure 6.3:** *Verify Microsoft SQL Server 2000 BCP Version*

To perform the offline capture process for Microsoft SQL Server 2000, execute the offline capture scripts using the Microsoft SQL Server username, password, and database connection string. The syntax to perform offline capture is shown as follows:

- On Windows:

```
Prompt> OMWB_OFFLINE_CAPTURE.bat login_id password database_name server_name
```

- On Linux:

```
prompt> OMWB_OFFLINE_CAPTURE.sh
```

The correct *login_id*, *password*, *source database name*, and *source server name* must be provided as parameters for the offline capture script. It is very important to remember that the *login_id* must have DBA level privileges to execute the offline capture script against the Microsoft SQL Server 2000 database. In the event that there is no associated password for the *login_id*, enter "" for the default password entry. Be sure to verify that the user login account to the Microsoft SQL Server 2000 database and connectivity to the source database and server is available. If this is not done, the offline capture script will fail with errors.

Now that all of the required offline capture scripts are copied to the new offline migration staging area, and there is verified connectivity to the source database for MS SQL Server 2000, it is now time to perform the first offline capture for SQL Server 2000, starting with Figure 6.4:

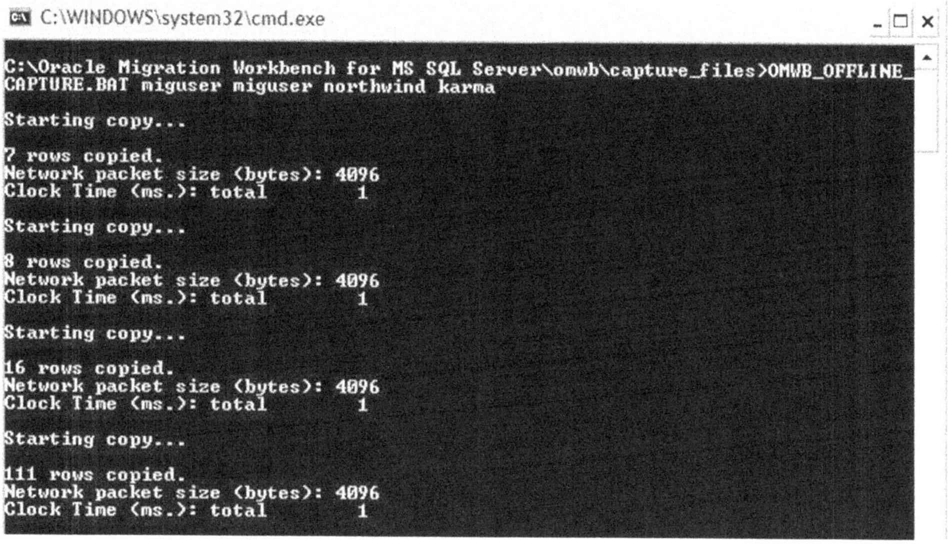

**Figure 6.4:** *Perform the Offline Capture for MS SQL Server 2000*

In this example, there is the username, miguser, for the test Microsoft SQL Server 2000 environment that has DBA level access and privileges to the Northwind database, described in Chapter 5, on the test database source server, karma.

Run the offline capture script with the required parameters. As a batch file, the script performs a login to the database through a series of API layer calls to collect the database information and creates a new directory structure with all of the data files for migration from Microsoft SQL Server 2000 to Oracle 10g and 11g. The output from the script, when completed successfully, will look like Figure 6.5.

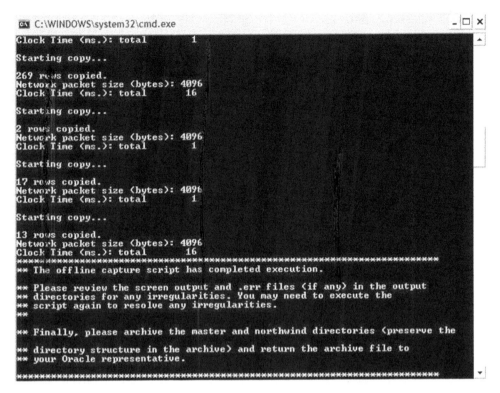

**Figure 6.5:** *Completion for Offline Capture Microsoft SQL Server 2000*

Keep in mind that offline capture scripts operate with the OMWB and may prove useful.

As soon as the offline capture script for SQL Server is kicked off, a status window appears as the database becomes captured by the offline script. Network performance statistics are also provided to gauge progress. There are new offline capture subdirectories that have been created by the OMWB to provide the creation scripts for the source database as part of the migration process to Oracle 10g and 11g. Next to be explored are these newly created and migrated files for a deeper understanding of the offline capture process.

# Files Created By Offline Capture for MS SQL Server

There are three new types of files that are created as a result of the offline capture scripts for the Microsoft SQL Server 2000 environment. These are used to build the new source model which will migrate to Oracle.

The files are as follows:

- *Dat* files

- *Err* files

- *Txt* files

In the following figure is an example listing of these files. The shot was taken after a test offline capture process was performed.

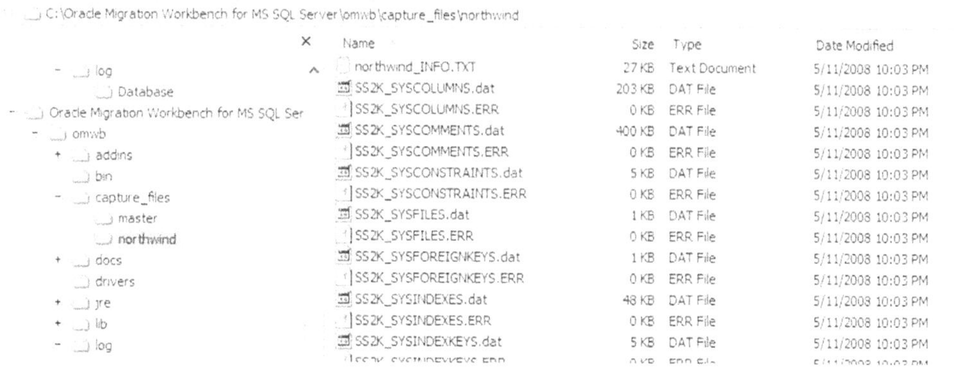

**Figure 6.6:** *Files Created by Offline Capture for MS SQL Server 2000*

The files that contain the *.dat* suffix are the data files. These contain all of the raw data, associated database definitions for the schemas, database architecture components, and database security. This content will be mapped to the source model to migrate to Oracle from SQL Server 2000. The next file type, generated after the offline capture script has run successfully, are error code files which end with an *.err* suffix. If no errors occurred during the offline capture phase, these will be zero sized files. However, if an error occurred during the offline capture script execution, these files will need to be examined to resolve the errors. Otherwise, the migration will fail.

The third file type generated after the offline capture scripts have run against the Microsoft SQL Server 2000 environment are information files, which end in a *.txt* suffix. One of these information files is created for each database which will be migrated via the offline capture process.

In the example below, a new text file has been created called *northwind_info.txt* that contains a log file of the offline capture process.

### 💾 Northwind_info.text script (partial)

```
OMWB REPORT FOR northwind
_____
* SCRIPT EXECUTION DATE AND TIME:
Sun 05/11/2008
10:35 PM
-
SYSTEM PROPERTIES
.
.
.
SOURCE DATABASE SERVER PROPERTIES
_____
* BCP VERSION:
BCP - Bulk Copy Program for Microsoft SQL Server.
Copyright (c) 1991-1998, Microsoft Corp. All Rights Reserved.
Version: 8.00.194


DIRECTORY LISTING for northwind
_____
 Volume in drive C is karma
 Volume Serial Number is 782D-CCD2

 Directory of C:\OMWB for MS SQL Server\omwb\capture_files\northwind

05/11/2008  10:35 PM    <DIR>          .
05/11/2008  10:35 PM    <DIR>          ..
05/11/2008  10:35 PM             1,558 northwind_INFO.TXT
05/11/2008  10:35 PM           207,021 SS2K_SYSCOLUMNS.dat
05/11/2008  10:35 PM                 0 SS2K_SYSCOLUMNS.ERR
05/11/2008  10:35 PM           409,064 SS2K_SYSCOMMENTS.dat
-
-
-
DIRECTORY LISTING FOR MASTER
_____
 Volume in drive C is karma
 Volume Serial Number is 782D-CCD2

 Directory of C:\OMWB for MS SQL Server\omwb\capture_files\master

05/11/2008  10:35 PM    <DIR>          .
05/11/2008  10:35 PM    <DIR>          ..
05/11/2008  10:35 PM             1,258 SS2K_SYSDATABASES.dat
05/11/2008  10:35 PM                 0 SS2K_SYSDATABASES.ERR
```

```
05/11/2008  10:35 PM              2,338 SS2K_SYSLOGINS.dat
05/11/2008  10:35 PM                  0 SS2K_SYSLOGINS.ERR
               4 File(s)          3,596 bytes
               2 Dir(s)   9,309,237,248 bytes free
-

-

-

ATTRIBUTES OF SCRIPT:
_____
-

-

CONTENTS OF EXECUTED SCRIPT
_____
@echo off

rem ** SET THE VALUE FOR THE OFFLINE_CAPTURE_COLUMN_DELIMITER
rem ** THIS VALUE SHOULD MATCH THE VALUE SET FOR THE SAME VARIABLE IN
OMWB_INSTALL_DIR\bin\omwb.properties
set OFFLINE_CAPTURE_COLUMN_DELIMITER=§

rem ** SET THE VALUE FOR THE OFFLINE_CAPTURE_ROW_DELIMITER
rem ** THIS VALUE SHOULD MATCH THE VALUE SET FOR THE SAME VARIABLE IN
OMWB_INSTALL_DIR\bin\omwb.properties
set OFFLINE_CAPTURE_ROW_DELIMITER=¤

rem ** SET THE SCRIPT VERSION ENVIRONMENT VARIABLE
set OMWB_SCRIPT_VERSION=10104

rem ** SET THE VALUE FOR THE OMWB FILE ENVIRONMENT VARIABLE
set OMWB_SCRIPT_FILE=%3\%3_INFO.TXT

rem ** DISPLAY THE HELP PAGE IF THE USER REQUESTS IT

if "%1"=="-h"    goto help
if "%1"=="help"  goto help
if "%1"=="?"     goto help
if "%1"=="-?"    goto help
```

It is important to review all of the output files with special regard to the text formatted log file for SQL Server in order to ensure no error messages occur during the offline script execution process. These directories and associated files will need to be copied to the system where the OMWB software has been installed. It is also wise to archive these files to a directory for safekeeping. This will protect against data loss.

Next is a brief mention of the offline capture scripts that are available for the Sybase database platform to perform migrations to Oracle.

## Scripts for Use with Sybase Adaptive Server

The Sybase database platform has many similarities to the Microsoft SQL Server database in terms of architecture and utilities. In fact, at one time in the history of database development, Microsoft and Sybase worked together in a partnership to create new database platforms and technologies. In any case, Sybase uses many of the same database utilities as Microsoft SQL Server, including BCP, to perform database copies as part of the offline capture process. OMWB currently provides offline capture scripts for Sybase 11 and 12 releases on Windows and Linux.

The default offline capture scripts for Sybase environments can be found in the same offline capture subdirectory as those shown below for either Windows or Linux platforms:

```
C:\OMWB_install_directory\Omwb\offline_capture\Sybase11
```

```
C:\OMWB_install_directory\Omwb\offline_capture\Sybase12
```

The two main offline capture scripts have the same names as those for the Microsoft SQL Server 2000 environments:

- Windows:

```
OMWB_OFFLINE_CAPTURE.BAT
```

- Linux:

```
OMWB_OFFLINE_CAPTURE.SH
```

To perform the offline capture for Sybase, the same database login username, password, source database name, and source server hostname need to be provided as input parameters to the offline capture script with the same syntax used for Microsoft SQL Server offline capture script execution. To avoid errors during the script execution for offline capture with Sybase, it is important to verify that the correct version of the BCP utility is installed and configured for Sybase prior to running the offline capture script.

To verify that the Sybase database has the correct version of BCP installed, run the following command in a shell prompt:

```
bcp -v
```

Once this has been verified, the offline capture script may be executed for the Sybase environments that will be migrated to Oracle. Archive the newly created files to the OMWB directory staging area that will be used on the source server after the offline capture process has completed.

The new version of the migration tools provided in Oracle SQL Developer provides offline capture functionality for Sybase. These tools are easy to use and provide options to generate the output scripts for Windows or Linux platforms in the form of either a Windows *.bat* (batch) file or Linux shell script file. How these offline capture scripts are deployed from the SQL Developer migration tools will be examined later.

To transition into the next topic on offline capture scripts for IBM DB2 UDB and Informix, it should be noted that the new migration capture functionality for offline scripts is unfortunately not available with the SQL Developer migration tools at this time. Oracle development may plan to provide the offline capture scripts in future releases past 1.5 of the SQL Developer software for Informix and IBM DB2 UDB databases.

However, as of now, offline capture scripts are provided with SQL Developer only for Sybase, MySQL, SQL Server 2000/2005, and Microsoft Access platforms.

There has been recent dialogue with the Oracle development staff on Oracle Metalink notes and forum discussions that the OMWB will eventually be decommissioned and no longer supported in future releases of SQL Developer. In the meantime, users still have to use the OMWB instead of the SQL Developer tools to migrate away from Informix or IBM DB2 UDB environments to Oracle 10g and 11g.

## Scripts for Use with IBM DB2 Universal Database (UDB)

As stated before, offline capture scripts are currently not available for IBM DB2 UDB environments and OMWB at this time. Perhaps with future releases of the Oracle SQL Developer migration tools and enhancement requests from Oracle Corporation, there eventually may be the option to create offline capture scripts for migration of IBM DB2 databases to Oracle 10g and 11g.

Until then, online capture wizards are the limit with the OMWB, and preferably, the newer tools for migration will be available with the SQL Developer migration workbench environments.

# Scripts for Use with MySQL- Offline Capture

Currently, the OMWB only provides online capture methods of the MySQL database platform to migrate to Oracle 10g and 11g.

However, there is an upside to this lack of offline capture tools in the OMWB for MySQL. In the latest release of Oracle SQL Developer, offline capture scripts are finally able to be created for MySQL database platforms. Oracle Corporation has mentioned in forums and in Metalink Support notes that future migration support for MySQL to Oracle 10g and 11g will be advocated in use of the new version of migration tools now available in the Oracle SQL Developer 1.5 release.

Since the ability to perform offline capture is a new feature within the Oracle SQL Developer migration tools, some basic techniques on how to generate the offline capture scripts with SQL Developer will be covered. Fortunately, the SQL Developer environment is a graphical interface which provides simplified methods to generate offline capture scripts for third party database platforms to migrate to Oracle.

## Offline Capture with MySQL with SQL Developer

Oracle has created the offline capture ability with the newest generation of migration tools in the Oracle SQL Developer 1.5 release.
Using menu options from within the Migration toolbar in SQL Developer, there are options for third party database platforms to create offline migration scripts including support for MySQL environments.

**Figure 6.7:** *Offline Capture for MySQL with Oracle SQL Developer 1.5*

There are two choices for third party database offline capture which allow the user to either create the database capture scripts for MySQL and other environments or to load the database capture script output. Focus will be on generating the offline capture scripts in the following example with MySQL using SQL Developer migration tools.

To access the offline capture scripts, select the following option in the SQL Developer Migration menu:

- Migration-> Third Party Database Offline Capture-> Create Database Capture Scripts

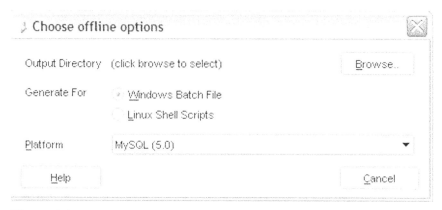

**Figure 6.8:** *Offline Capture Options for MySQL with Oracle SQL Developer*

Under the appropriate platform, select the MySQL (5.0) option and then OK.

After this, the choice will be given to generate the MySQL offline capture scripts for Windows or Linux platforms. Either way, the platform choice will be used with the Oracle SQL Developer migration process for offline capture with MySQL to Oracle. For example, if the choice is Windows, the result set of offline capture scripts will be generated as Windows batch, i.e. *bat* files. For Linux, the output will create Linux UNIX based shell scripts for MySQL to Oracle migration with offline capture.

After choosing the appropriate directory to store offline capture scripts for MySQL, choose the MySQL database version and click on the OK button. This will generate the new offline database capture scripts as shown in the following example.

**Figure 6.9:** *Offline Capture Script Generation for MySQL*

Now take a look at how these offline scripts look for MySQL. This will give one a chance to better understand the offline capture process with SQL Developer for MySQL to Oracle migrations as well as help verify that all of the offline capture completed without errors.

Of particular interest here are the scripts that are generated by SQL Developer after the offline capture process has completed:

- get_col_table_5.bat
- get_constraint_5.bat
- get_max_col_5.bat
- get_stored_proc_5.bat

- get_table_5.bat

- master_5.bat

- mysql5.ocp

The most important script that can be used to evaluate MySQL, in terms of the offline capture process, would be the *master_5.bat* script. The *master_5.bat* script contains all of the operating system and database level commands to create the source model for the MySQL conversion to Oracle.

In the code depot sample listed below, the commands that will be executed against the MySQL 5.x database to extract everything are shown. With this, metadata can create a new source model to use with migration from MySQL to Oracle 10g or 11g.

### master_5.bat offline capture file

```
mysql -u%user% -p%password% -h%host% <
routines_name%SEED%.sql>temp_routines%SEED%.txt

FOR /F "tokens=1,2,3,4" %%A in (temp_routines%SEED%.txt) DO IF NOT
%%A==ROUTINE_SCHEMA  CALL get_stored_proc_5.bat %%A %%B %%C %%D

ECHO table_info=all_tabs%SEED%.txt>> mysql5.ocp

ECHO column_table_info=all_col_data_tabs%SEED%.txt>> mysql5.ocp

ECHO constraint_table_info=all_constraints_tabs%SEED%.txt>> mysql5.ocp

ECHO max_column_info=all_cols_tabs%SEED%.txt>> mysql5.ocp

ECHO index_info=all_index_data_tabs%SEED%.txt>> mysql5.ocp

ECHO views_info=views%SEED%.txt>> mysql5.ocp

ECHO routines_info=routines%SEED%.txt>> mysql5.ocp

ECHO version_info=version%SEED%.txt>> mysql5.ocp

GOTO :CAPTURE_DONE

:ERROR_CONDITION
ECHO You need to enter either user or host or password at the beginning of
script.
GOTO DONE

:CAPTURE_DONE
ECHO Processing completed - files generated for MySQL Offline
:DONE
pause
```

Notice that in the previous code sample *master_5.bat* file, there are instructions about the username and password that should be given as parameters to execute the script correctly. In a sense, this script is quite similar in function to the *txt logger* script generated for the Microsoft SQL Server 2000 *callout* script created by the offline capture process.

The other scripts that are generated by the SQL Developer migration tool for offline capture with MySQL contain the definitions required to extract the data definitions and architecture for MySQL schema level objects. This includes tables, indices and stored procedures which will be used by the offline capture process to generate a new source model for migration from MySQL to Oracle. Future chapters will cover how to deploy offline and online capture scripts and tools with SQL Developer.

Now that the offline capture process for MySQL with the Oracle migration tools has been reviewed, how offline capture scripts work with the Informix database environment will be examined.

## Scripts for Offline Capture- Informix Database

The OMWB provides offline capture scripts for Informix database versions 7.x through 9.x on Windows and Linux platforms with the offline capture process. The offline capture scripts for Informix environments can be found in the same offline capture subdirectory as shown below for either Windows or Linux platforms:

```
C:\OMWB_install_directory\Omwb\offline_capture\Informix7
```

```
C:\OMWB_install_directory\Omwb\offline_capture\Informix9
```

The main offline capture scripts are listed below for Informix 7.

- Windows:

```
IDS7_DSML_SCRIPT.BAT
```

- Linux:

```
IDS7_DSML_SCRIPT.BAT
```

The main offline capture scripts are listed below for Informix 9.

- Windows:

```
IDS94_DSML_SCRIPT.bat
```

```
IDS9_DSML_SCRIPT.bat
```

- Linux:

```
IDS9_DSML_SCRIPT.sh
```

The offline capture scripts for Informix use the native Informix utilities to perform the offline capture process. The syntax for the offline capture process with Informix is as follows.

- Informix 7 on Windows:

```
prompt> IDS7_DSML_SCRIPT.bat database_name server_name
```

- Informix 9 on Windows:

```
prompt> IDS7_DSML_SCRIPT.bat database_name server_name
```

- Informix 7 on UNIX:

```
prompt> IDS7_DSML_SCRIPT.sh database_name server_name
```

- Informix 9 on UNIX:

```
prompt> IDS9_DSML_SCRIPT.sh database_name server_name
```

 In the offline capture script for Informix, the server_name is the value for DBSERVERNAME or the DBSERVERALIAS for the Informix environment on the source Informix host.

The offline capture scripts also make use of the Informix UNLOAD SQL statement to create a new sysmaster directory along with the associated capture files for the Informix sysmaster database that will be migrated over to Oracle.

For the Linux platform, when the offline capture is performed for Informix, it is required to convert the Informix files to UNIX using commands similar to

 After conversion of the Informix files to UNIX, these cannot be used afterwards to create offline capture files to Windows.

the following:

- dos2unix *
- chmod 755 *.sh

# Conclusion

In this chapter, a wide variety of database migration methods have been covered for the offline capture of third party databases to Oracle 10g and 11g. This chapter described using both the OMWB as well as the new tools for migration to Oracle in the latest release of SQL Developer. The methods to generate the offline capture scripts for these database platforms and the limitations for each platform in terms of offline capture process were also detailed.

In the following chapters, there will be a more comprehensive analysis of the completion of third party database migrations to Oracle. To offer as much variety as possible, the analysis will cover a wide array of migration tools and utilities in the OMWB and the latest versions of Oracle SQL Developer.

# References

OMWB User's Guide, Release 10.1.0.4 for Microsoft
Windows 98/2000/NT/XP and Linux x86, Part B19134-01, June 2005

OMWB Reference Guide for MySQL 3.22, 3.23, 4.x
Migrations Release 10.1.0 for Microsoft Windows 98/2000/NT/XP, Part B13911-01, Oracle Corporation

OMWB Reference Guide for SQL Server and Sybase
Adaptive Server Migrations Release 9.2.0 for Microsoft Windows 98/2000/NT/XP, Part B10254-01

OMWB Frequently Asked Questions (FAQ) Release
9.2.0 for Microsoft Windows 98/2000/NT/XP, Part B10258-01
Oracle Database SQL Developer Installation Guide, Release 1.5, Part E12153-02

Oracle Database SQL Developer User's Guide, Release 1.5, Part E12152-03

Oracle Database SQL Developer Supplementary Information for MySQL Migrations, Release 1.5, Part E12155-01

Oracle Database SQL Developer Supplementary Information for Microsoft SQL Server and Sybase Adaptive Server Migrations, Release 1.5, Part E12156-01

Oracle Metalink References:
Difference between OMWB (OMWB) and SQL Developer
Metalink Note 470977.1

OMWB - What is it and Who supports it?
Metalink Note:96990.1

# Mapping the Source
# Model to Target Database

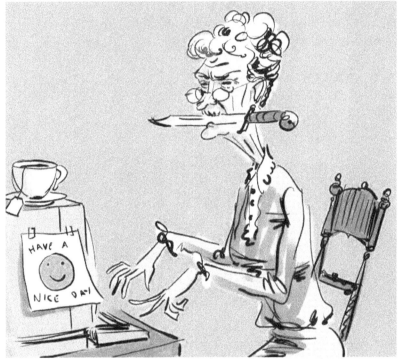

*"Mapping the Source Model to the new Oracle target database
demands total concentration and razor sharp precision."*

## Introduction

In previous chapters, the methods for database migration from MySQL and
Microsoft SQL Server to Oracle 10g were covered. The two available
methods of online and offline capture methods within the Oracle 10g
Migration Workbench and Oracle SQL Developer were detailed. In this
chapter, attention will be given to the intricate details of how to convert the
new source model database template from MySQL and Microsoft SQL Server
to the new target Oracle 10g and 11g database environments.

Both the OMWB and Oracle SQL Developer provide a plethora of useful tools to perform these tasks. As they are complex and offer a multitude of options, this chapter will provide some excellent examples to function as a step-by-step tutorial. These walk-throughs will build the foundation of understanding that is required to complete migrations to Oracle with ease.

# Building the Source Model Oracle 10g Migration Workbench

The offline capture process uses OMWB wizards to connect to the source database, whether it is MySQL or Microsoft SQL Server 2000. In order to migrate third party databases from MySQL and Microsoft SQL Server to Oracle 10g and 11g, build the source model using the OMWB or SQL Developer Migration Workbench.

The first step is to illustrate this process using the OMWB. The source model will contain all of the database objects and schemas that will be migrated to Oracle. A walk-through on how to create a new source model for Microsoft SQL Server 2000 using the online capture method for extracting the database source data definitions with the OMWB will be done.

## Capturing the Source Database for Microsoft SQL Server

First, start a new session of the OMWB by executing the omwb executable program from the installation directory under the base bin directory, as shown below, for Windows.

```
cd c:\omwb_installation_dir\omw\bin\
omwb.bat
```

From the OMWB main toolbar menu, select the option to Capture Source Database as shown in the following figure.

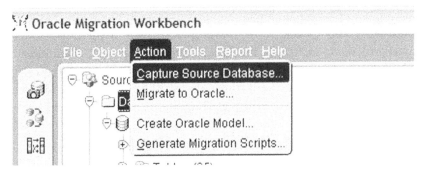

**Figure 7.1:** *Capture Source Database for MS SQL Server 2000*

Taking the default settings, choose the online capture method option presented by the wizard and select Next. This can be seen in Figure 7.2.

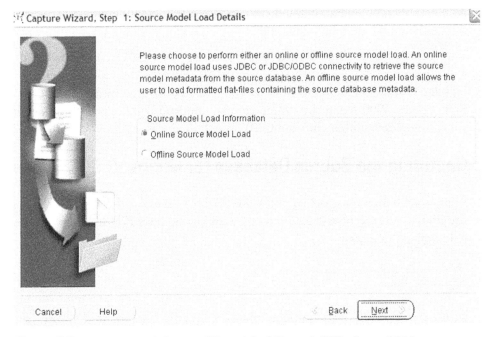

**Figure 7.2:** *Source Model Capture Wizard for Microsoft SQL Server 2000*

When the online capture wizard gives a prompt, enter the correct username and password for the ODBC connection string.

---

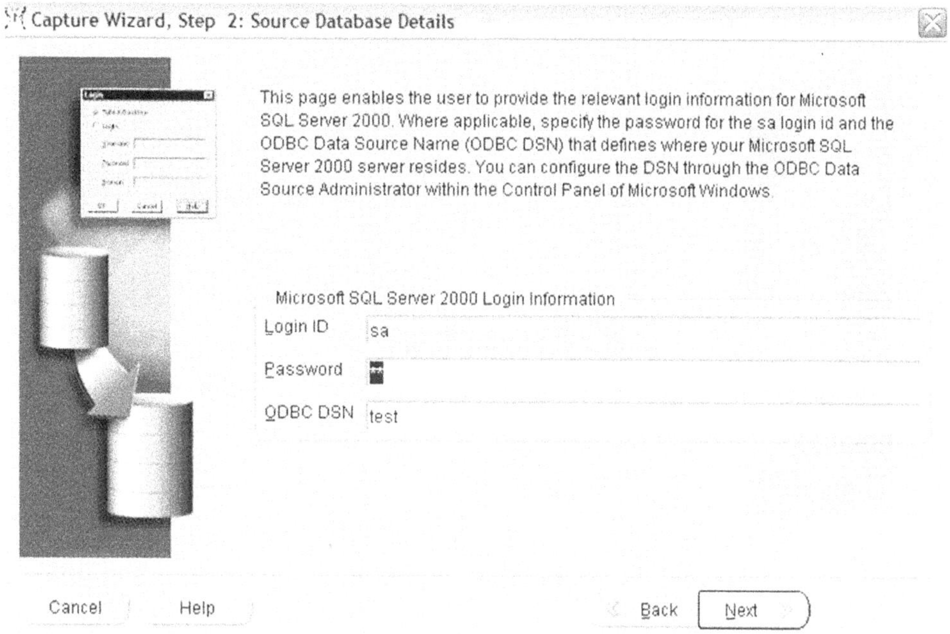

This page enables the user to provide the relevant login information for Microsoft SQL Server 2000. Where applicable, specify the password for the sa login id and the ODBC Data Source Name (ODBC DSN) that defines where your Microsoft SQL Server 2000 server resides. You can configure the DSN through the ODBC Data Source Administrator within the Control Panel of Microsoft Windows.

Microsoft SQL Server 2000 Login Information

Login ID      sa

Password      **

ODBC DSN      test

Cancel    Help                                      Back    Next

**Figure 7.3:** *Source Database Details for Microsoft SQL Server 2000*

Step 3 will present the currently available list of databases that can be migrated from Microsoft SQL Server 2000 to Oracle. In the last chapter, the Northwind database was used. In this test case, build the source model for Microsoft SQL Server 2000 using the pubs database. Multiple databases could be used to build a new source model, but for the sake of simplicity, use a single database to build the source model.

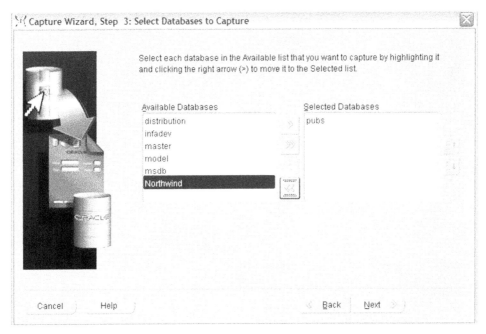

**Figure 7.4:** *Select Databases to Capture for Source Model SQL Server 2000*

After choosing Next to continue, the data type mappings will be presented for the source model. Choose the defaults to continue. Any data type errors will be corrected later in the data type mappings screen which provides the opportunity to change configurations and settings for data types between Microsoft SQL Server 2000 and Oracle 10g.

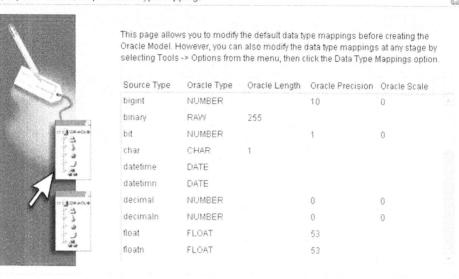

**Figure 7.5:** *Data Type Mappings for SQL Server to Oracle*

In the next screen, there is the choice to immediately create the new source model for SQL Server to Oracle based on previous inputs or to create the model at a later point in time. Choose the default option to create the new source model on the spot as shown in the following figure.

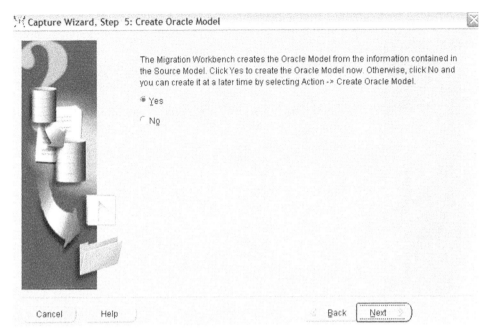

The Migration Workbench creates the Oracle Model from the information contained in the Source Model. Click Yes to create the Oracle Model now. Otherwise, click No and you can create it at a later time by selecting Action -> Create Oracle Model.

⦿ Yes

◯ No

Cancel        Help                                    Back      Next

**Figure 7.6:** *Create the Source Model SQL Server to Oracle*

In the next online capture wizard screen there will be summary details for the online capture process before the source model creation process begins.

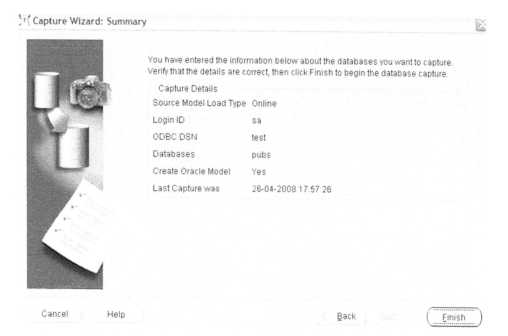

You have entered the information below about the databases you want to capture.
Verify that the details are correct, then click Finish to begin the database capture.

Capture Details

| | |
|---|---|
| Source Model Load Type | Online |
| Login ID | sa |
| ODBC DSN | test |
| Databases | pubs |
| Create Oracle Model | Yes |
| Last Capture was | 26-04-2008 17:57:26 |

Cancel    Help                    Back    Next    Finish

**Figure 7.7:** *Summary for Capture Wizard*

Click the Finish button to start the source model creation process.

Oracle will then perform the source model creation tasks and provide a logging status window for the source model build. The first step is a preparation and cleanup task that truncates the data model so that no data errors occur as the new build takes place.

**Figure 7.8:** *Logging Window for the Source Model Build Process*

As shown in the status window above, the OMWB provides options to suspend logging, abort the build process for the new source model and obtain help for reference tips on creating the new source model. When Oracle first creates this new source model from the Microsoft SQL Server database as part of the capture process, the OMWB collects the specific file encoding details and truncate processes before the data structures are inserted into the new source model. The next figure shows a successful status for the new source model build process.

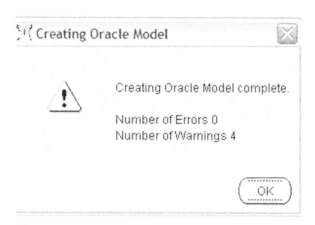

**Figure 7.9:** *Completion of the Source Model Build Process for SQL Server*

Fortunately, there were no errors in the new source model build, but OMWB has logged several warnings. These will be examined later on when exploring the resolution of any potential conflicts that could prevent a successful migration from Microsoft SQL Server to Oracle.

There are a few different options on how to migrate the schemas and associated objects from the Microsoft SQL Server 2000 environment with the pubs database as shown in the next figure.

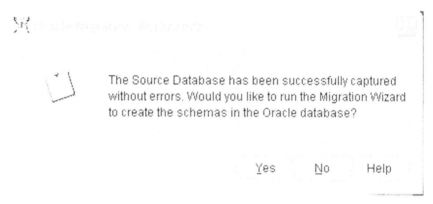

**Figure 7.10:** *Source Database Migrate Schemas Options*

At this point, either choose to do a one-off migration immediately or defer the process until a later point in time. If choosing to migrate the schemas from SQL Server to Oracle immediately, the wizard will open the Migration Wizard to complete the schema migration to Oracle. If no errors occurred during the build of the new source data model, the choice would most likely be to complete the migration quickly. However, if errors were generated during the source model creation process, it would be wise to take the time to review the errors and take corrective action before continuing migration. In this case where there are no errors, take the direct route and run the Migration Wizard to create the schemas for the new target Oracle database.

**Figure 7.11:** *Migrating Schemas Using the Migration Wizard*

The Migration Wizard kicks off with a welcome splash screen. From here, simply click the Next button to proceed.

This step requires username and database information for the Oracle 10g target database that will be used to migrate the SQL Server 2000 database to Oracle 10g. In this example, ORCL will be used as the target database to contain the newly migrated schema objects for the source Microsoft SQL Server 2000 database to Oracle 10g.

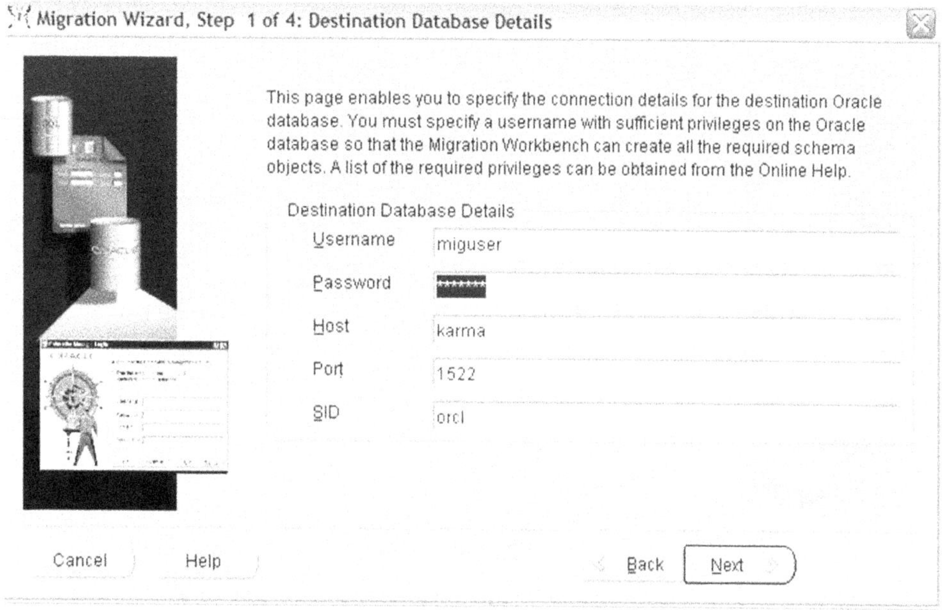

This page enables you to specify the connection details for the destination Oracle database. You must specify a username with sufficient privileges on the Oracle database so that the Migration Workbench can create all the required schema objects. A list of the required privileges can be obtained from the Online Help.

Destination Database Details

| | |
|---|---|
| Username | miguser |
| Password | ****** |
| Host | karma |
| Port | 1522 |
| SID | orcl |

Cancel    Help                                    Back    Next

**Figure 7.12:** *Migration Wizard for Destination Database Details*

Of particular importance here is to verify that all of the connection settings for the target Oracle database are correct. Otherwise, the migration process will fail. Next to show up is a summary, and the Migration Wizard will ask if the user wants to proceed with the migration for creating new tablespaces and other objects within the new target Oracle 10g database.

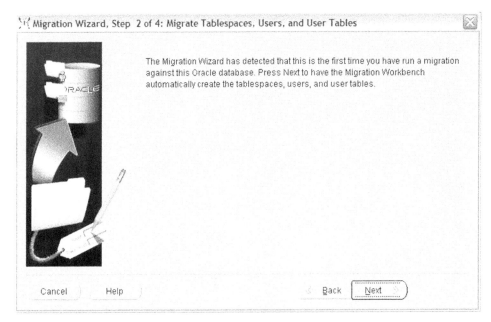

The Migration Wizard has detected that this is the first time you have run a migration against this Oracle database. Press Next to have the Migration Workbench automatically create the tablespaces, users, and user tables.

Cancel    Help                                    Back    Next

**Figure 7.13:** *Migration Wizard Creates New Tablespaces and Users*

Choose to accept and continue with the migration by selecting the Next button. After these objects have been created in the newly migrated Oracle database, it is time to explore many of the useful tools and editors for modifying settings and definitions for the newly migrated database.

In the next screen in the Migration Wizard, the OMWB gives a prompt to migrate or not migrate the actual data from the source Microsoft SQL Server 2000 pubs database. If the choice is to only migrate the database structures, user schemas and table definitions, use Oracle 10g utilities at a later point to load the data from SQL Server 2000 to Oracle 10g. This uses both SQL Server 2000 native BCP utilities to export the table data and either Oracle 10g Data Pump or SQL*Loader utilities to import the table data into the new Oracle 10g database.

For now, migrate the table data in addition to the schema objects.

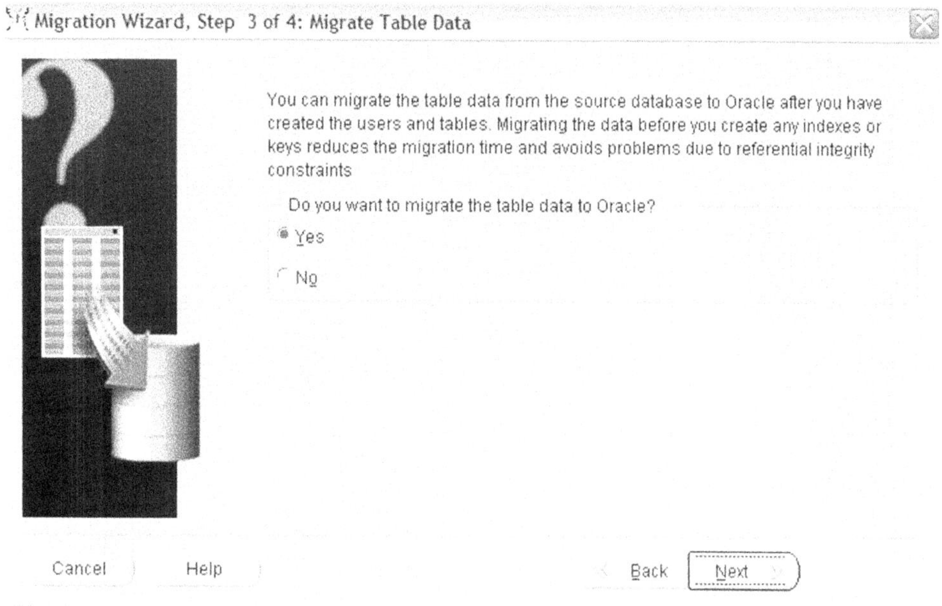
Migration Wizard, Step 3 of 4: Migrate Table Data
You can migrate the table data from the source database to Oracle after you have created the users and tables. Migrating the data before you create any indexes or keys reduces the migration time and avoids problems due to referential integrity constraints
Do you want to migrate the table data to Oracle?
Yes
No
Cancel
Help
Back
Next

**Figure 7.14:** *Migration Wizard - Migrate Table Data*

The final step in the Migration Wizard with OMWB is choosing the schema objects to migrate from Microsoft SQL Server 2000 to Oracle 10g. Either choose some schema objects or select all of the schema objects as shown in Figure 7.15.

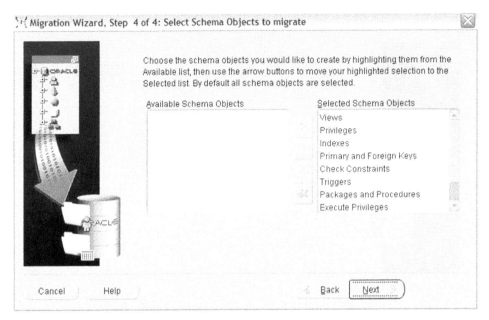

Choose the schema objects you would like to create by highlighting them from the Available list, then use the arrow buttons to move your highlighted selection to the Selected list. By default all schema objects are selected.

Available Schema Objects

Selected Schema Objects

Views
Privileges
Indexes
Primary and Foreign Keys
Check Constraints
Triggers
Packages and Procedures
Execute Privileges

Cancel    Help                    Back    Next

**Figure 7.15:** *Migration Wizard - Select Schema Objects to Migrate*

In this case, perform a complete database migration from Microsoft SQL Server 2000 to Oracle 10g. To do this, select all objects just like the action in the right hand window in the figure above.

The final screen in the Migration Wizard is the summary of database objects that will be migrated from Microsoft SQL Server 2000 pubs database to Oracle 10g target database.

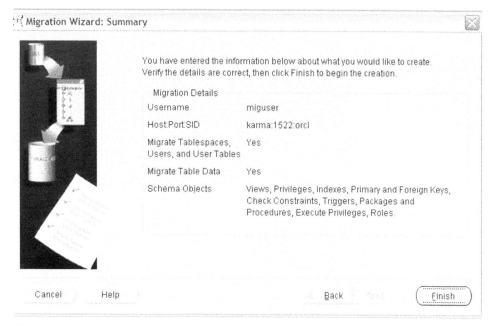

**Figure 7.16:** *Migration Wizard Summary*

Choose Finish and the Migration Wizard will kick off the migration process from the source Microsoft SQL Server 2000 database to the new target Oracle 10g database. As the migration processes, the status window will show the various migration steps performed and any error or warning conditions in the logging window.

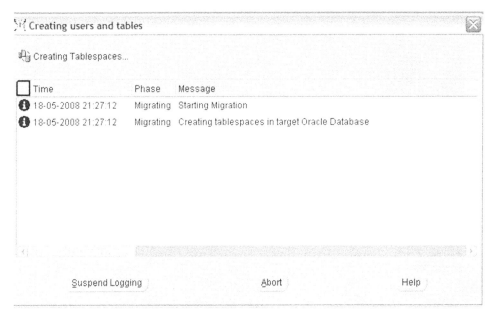

**Figure 7.17:** *Creating Users and Tables*

There may be some cleanup along the way. There are the same three options, as presented earlier, with this migration process. If an error condition occurs, choose to abort the migration to resolve the issue or ignore the errors and continue the migration process.

After the process has completed, the wizard will show the result screen, which will look like Figure 7.18.

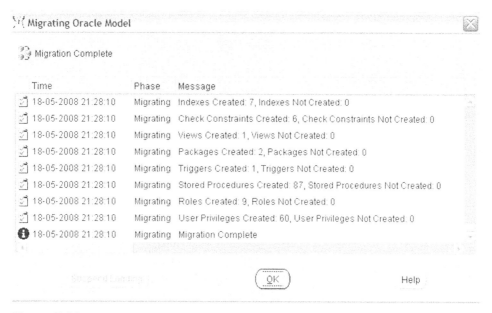

**Figure 7.18:** *Migrating Oracle Model Completion*

## Cleanup After the Migration Process

The new source model has been built for SQL Server 2000 and the new Oracle model that will be used as the template to migrate to Oracle 10g.

However, there is still a need to review both the source model for Microsoft SQL Server 2000 and the Oracle model. In the main screen for the OMWB, there are two main sections that show both the Microsoft SQL Server 2000 model and the Oracle model.

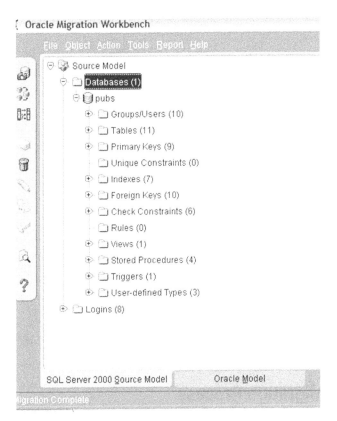

**Figure 7.19:** *SQL Server 2000 Source Model*

The left tab contains the information and definitions for the source Microsoft SQL Server 2000 pubs database that will be migrated to the Oracle 10g database. The right tab in the main OMWB window contains the newly created Oracle 10g source database model that will be migrated to the target Oracle 10g database.

At the top heading for the Microsoft SQL Server 2000 source model, there is the information on the database as well as groups and users.

**Figure 7.20:** *Source Model for SQL Server 2000 Groups/Users*

There are also sections for the other database objects and schemas that will be migrated. If the user drills down on each section, the details for the schema objects will be revealed. This allows one to crosscheck the source model for MS SQL Server 2000 with the new Oracle source model to verify that everything is correct.

**Figure 7.21:** *Source Model for SQL Server 2000 - Tables*

In Figure 7.20, the users were successfully migrated from the SQL Server 2000 source model to the Oracle 10g model in the figures listed for the SQL Server 2000 source model and in the Oracle source model. SQL Server uses the concept of logins, which would be users in an Oracle 10g database. The logins from the pubs database for the SQL Server 2000 model in the OMWB are shown here:

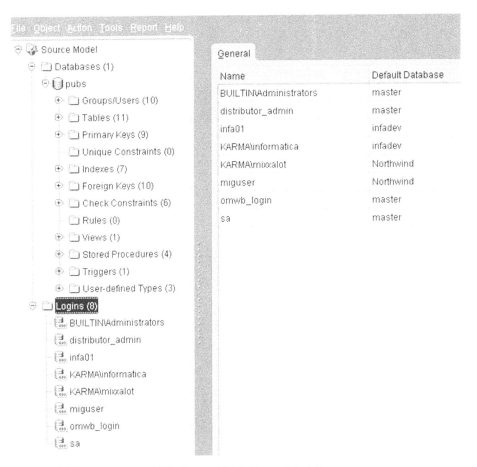

**Figure 7.22:** *Logins for SQL Server 2000 Source Model*

Now compare these to the Oracle source model users to verify that everything migrated completely to the Oracle 10g source model.

**Figure 7.23:** *Oracle Source Model - Users*

As can be seen, all went well except for miguser. Luckily, this will not be used in the source model for SQL Server 2000 since this user schema has already been reserved for migration tasks.

The tables were successfully captured from the source pubs database in Microsoft SQL Server 2000 to new the Oracle 10g source model. The source tables from the Microsoft SQL Server pubs database that are being migrated to Oracle were owned by the sa account. This being, these tables were correctly migrated to Oracle 10g by viewing the new Oracle source model database as shown in the following figure.

**Figure 7.24:** *Oracle 10g Source Model Database Tables Migrated*

Now that the new source model has been finished from Microsoft SQL Server 2000 to Oracle 10g, use the migration tools in the latest version of Oracle SQL Developer to build the new Oracle source model and perform a test migration from the MySQL database to Oracle 10g.

# Building the Source Model for MySQL and SQL Developer

Earlier, the build process was completed for the new source database models as part of the procedures to migrate a Microsoft SQL Server 2000 database to Oracle 10g using the OMWB. Now that Oracle has invested recent development in the latest generation of migration tools within SQL Developer, creating the source model for MySQL to migrate to Oracle using the migration tools in SQL Developer will be explored. Since offline and online capture has been performed in previous examples, proceed from the last step and continue with the completion of the online capture process to create the new source model for MySQL.

To begin, start the SQL Developer version that was installed and configured from the earlier examples. Using the Quick Migration Wizard, configure the source MySQL database options if it has not already been done, and proceed by specifying the target Oracle 10g database that will be migrated from MySQL to Oracle.

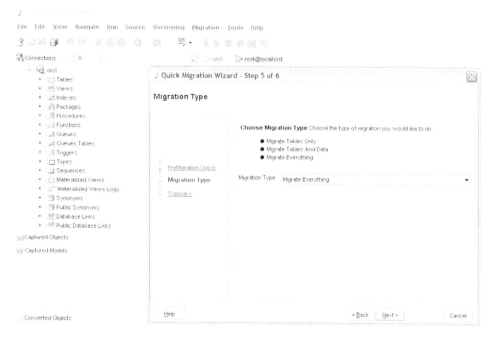

**Figure 7.25:** *SQL Developer 1.5 Quick Migration Build Source Model*

Even though SQL Developer provides the option to migrate only table definitions or raw data, choose to migrate the complete database environment for MySQL. After this, the summary screen will appear that shows the options and migration tasks needing to be performed with SQL Developer for creating the new source models for MySQL and Oracle.

**Figure 7.26:** *Quick Migration Summary for MySQL*

> 🔔 Note: There is an issue in SQL Developer 1.5 release with the Quick Migrate feature for MySQL to Oracle migrations. The workaround solution will be covered later in the troubleshooting and problem resolution section of this chapter.

Once the Finish button is clicked, the migration process will begin for MySQL to Oracle. SQL Developer uses a logging mechanism similar to the logging windows that show the status of the migration tasks in the OMWB. These log windows can be viewed as part of monitoring during the migration process to resolve errors that may occur while the migration is performed.

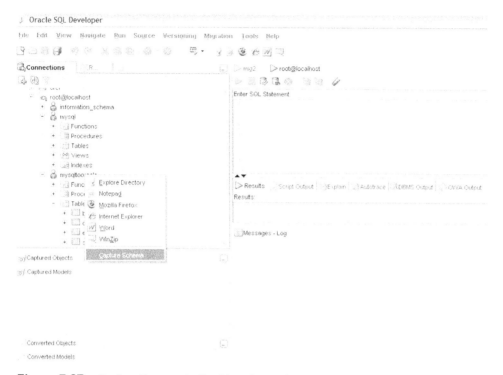

**Figure 7.27:** *Online Capture for Building Source Model with SQL Developer*

As mentioned earlier, the Quick Migrate feature in SQL Developer 1.5 may fail during the capture process for MySQL environments. If this occurs, it is recommended that the manual capture online method be performed. The previous figure highlights how to take the capture for the MySQL environment. By right clicking the mouse on the source MySQL database, the Capture Schema function will take an online snapshot for MySQL to generate the new source model.

After the online capture process has completed without incident, the SQL Developer migration wizard will present the output status windows as shown in Figure 7.28.

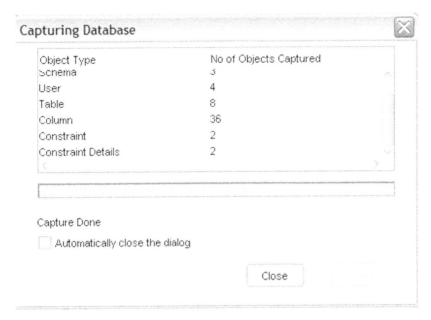

**Figure 7.28:** *Capturing the MySQL Source Database with SQL Developer*

Now that the new source model capture process is completed for the MySQL databases, next explore the features of the source model before the migration process and build of the new Oracle source model with SQL Developer.

In the following figure, SQL Developer displays the source model for the MySQL databases that have been captured by the Migration Wizard.

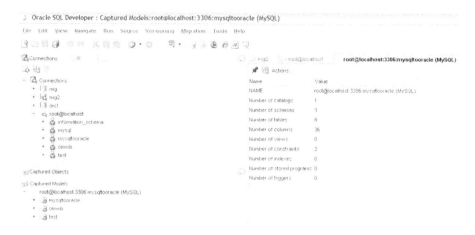

**Figure 7.29:** *Example of SQL Developer Captured Objects for MySQL Databases*

In a similar display technique to the original OMWB panels, SQL Developer shows all of the captured third party databases in the bottom left corner of the application environment under Captured Objects.

Under the following figure for the Captured Objects pane, examine the various schema objects that have been captured from MySQL 5.x databases.

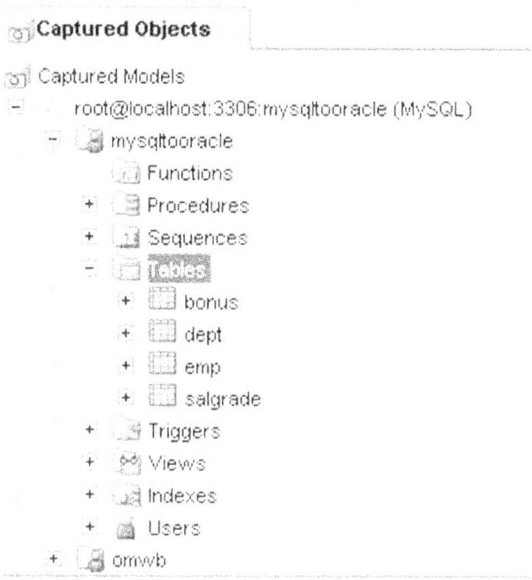

**Captured Objects**

Captured Models
- root@localhost:3306:mysqltooracle (MySQL)
  - mysqltooracle
    - Functions
    - + Procedures
    - + Sequences
    - − Tables
      - + bonus
      - + dept
      - + emp
      - + salgrade
    - + Triggers
    - + Views
    - + Indexes
    - + Users
  - + omwb

**Figure 7.30:** *Captured Objects for MySQL with SQL Developer*

The primary candidate that was captured is the MySQL database, mysqltooracle. All of the functions, procedures, tables, users and other related database objects are readily displayed for review and analysis.

Next to be detailed are the captured source definitions for the MySQL source model to verify that the data capture and objects are consistent with the source MySQL environments before creating the new Oracle source model. In the right top pane of SQL Developer, the output characteristics for MySQL source database are displayed, just like those in Figure 7.31.

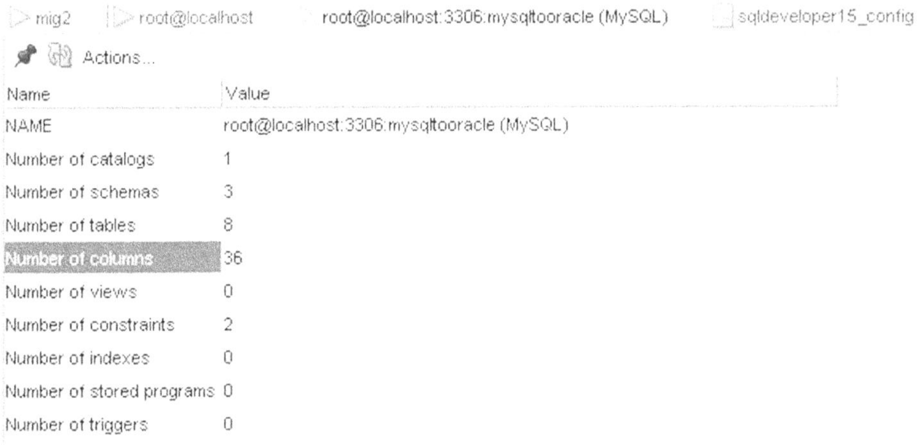

| Name | Value |
|------|-------|
| NAME | root@localhost:3306:mysqltooracle (MySQL) |
| Number of catalogs | 1 |
| Number of schemas | 3 |
| Number of tables | 8 |
| Number of columns | 36 |
| Number of views | 0 |
| Number of constraints | 2 |
| Number of indexes | 0 |
| Number of stored programs | 0 |
| Number of triggers | 0 |

**Figure 7.31:** *MySQL Source Model Characteristics in SQL Developer*

In the figure above for the MySQL source model, SQL Developer shows the connection string name for the MySQL source model, which is root@localhost:3306:mysqltooracle (MySQL) in the NAME field. The panel also shows the total number of schemas, tables, and other database objects that exist in the new source model for MySQL.

In addition to server and database level configuration details, the right panel display contains details on tables and other schema for the MySQL bonus table that was captured as part of the new source model build.

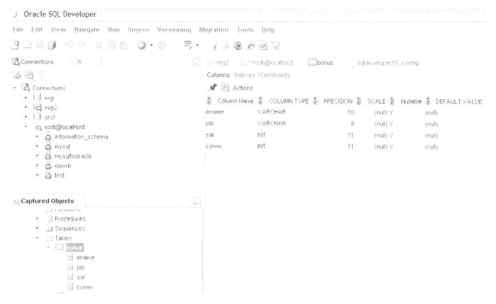

**Figure 7.32:** *Table Display for MySQL Source Model in SQL Developer*

From this window, many functions can be performed to massage and modify the source model data for MySQL before migration to Oracle. These many features and add-ons will be covered later in the chapter.

Next, the conversion tasks and migration of the MySQL 5.x source model will be performed to migrate the MySQL database to Oracle.

# Migrating the MySQL Source Model to Oracle Using SQL Developer

Two methods exist to convert and migrate the source MySQL model to Oracle using SQL Developer Migration tools. The conversion can be performed in the left pane of the source model for MySQL database captured objects or from within the right database information panel.

**Figure 7.33:** *Actions Menu for SQL Developer*

Right-click on the Actions toolbar menu to bring up the migration choices shown in Figure 7.34.

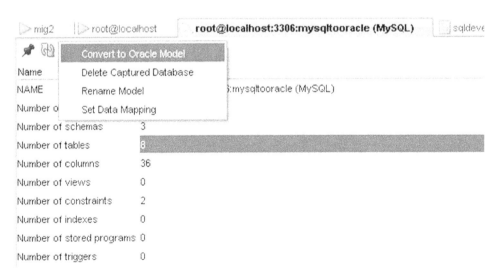

**Figure 7.34:** *Convert to Oracle Model Option in SQL Developer for MySQL*

In the Actions menu, several options exist in the drop down list: Convert to Oracle Model, Delete Captured Database, Rename Model and Set Data Mapping. These provide quite a bit of flexibility in performing both pre- and post-migration tasks for migrations from MySQL and other third party databases to Oracle.

The second method of converting from the MySQL source model available with SQL Developer migration tools is available from the menus in the Captured Source Model section as shown in Figure 7.35.

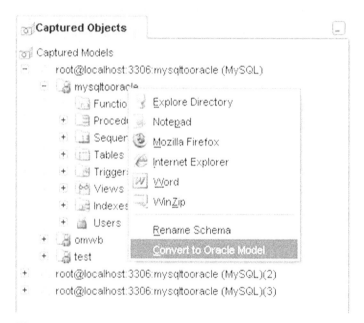

**Figure 7.35:** *Convert to Oracle Model Option from SQL Developer*

The menu options vary depending on whether or not the database server instance is selected, as opposed to if the database and schema are selected. Besides migration tasks, SQL Developer provides a wealth of supplemental options such as opening web browsers and other applications. In addition to the migration tasks, SQL Developer also allows for renaming the schema for MySQL in the menu list of options.

In the following example, convert the MySQL database to the new Oracle model as part of the migration process from MySQL to Oracle.

Once the option to create the new source Oracle model from MySQL is selected, SQL Developer will open a new window to provide data type mappings as shown in the next figure.

**Figure 7.36:** *Set Data Map for MySQL to Oracle in SQL Developer*

The Set Data Map screen in SQL Developer presents choices on how to map the data types from MySQL to Oracle. In addition, new rules can be created to map data correctly on demand to Oracle from MySQL environment. For example, if the user wants to change a default setting from VARCHAR in MySQL to map to a VARCHAR2 data type in Oracle as part of the migration, choose to edit or create a new rule as shown in the following example.

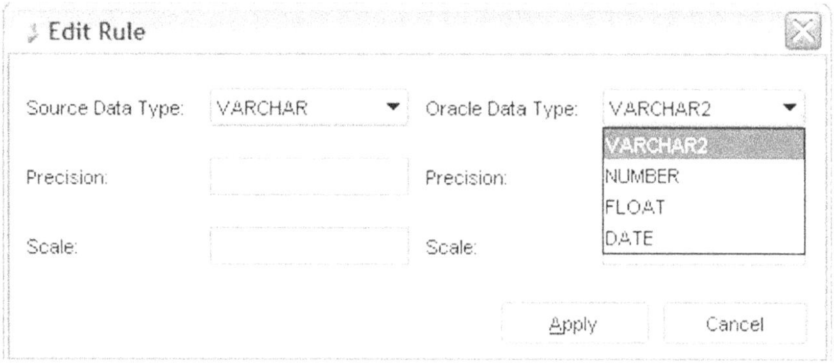

**Figure 7.37:** *Edit Rule for MySQL to Oracle Data in SQL Developer*

Once the rules have been edited to completion, the final step in the conversion process for SQL Developer is to select the Apply button. If everything has been successfully set, the conversion process will finish as shown in the following figure:

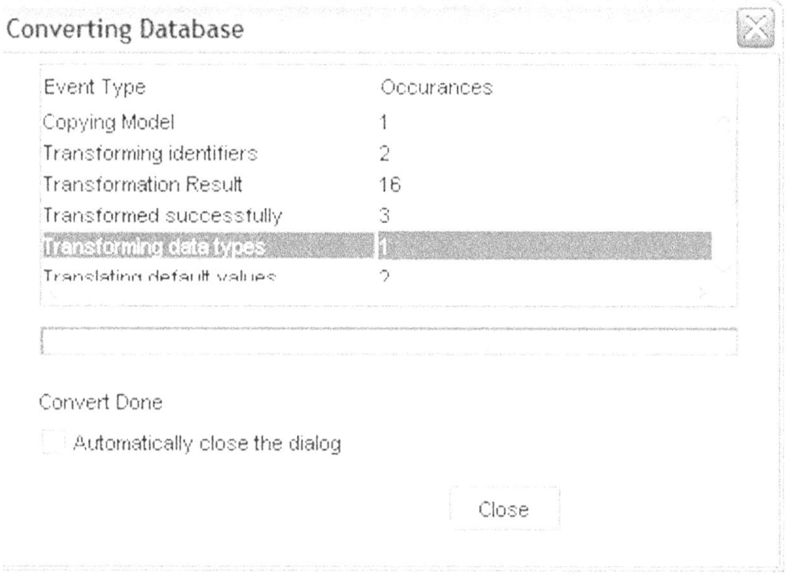

**Figure 7.38:** *Converting Database MySQL to Oracle in SQL Developer*

In the previous figure, the database conversion status is displayed as the new Oracle model is constructed from the source MySQL database. When the model build process and migration from MySQL to Oracle has completed, the new detail pane will become available in the bottom corner of the SQL Developer environment.

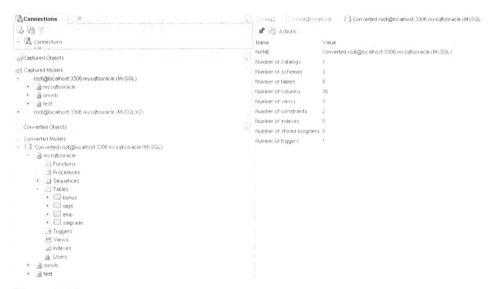

**Figure 7.39:** *Converted Objects Window for SQL Developer*

The right window panel shows details about the new schema objects for the Oracle source model that have been migrated from MySQL to Oracle. Now that the new Oracle source data model has been created from the MySQL database, the next step is to generate the database creation scripts for the schema objects and to move the data to the new target Oracle 10g and 11g databases from the source models in MySQL. Completion of the migration from MySQL to Oracle using these scripts and additional tools within SQL Developer will be shown towards the end of the chapter.

## Overview of OMWB Tools: The Editors

Here is a review of the important tools and utilities within the OMWB and SQL Developer for customizing the database migration tasks.

The OMWB provides many essential tools for customizing migrations to Oracle from MySQL and Microsoft SQL Server platforms. There are also supplemental development tools used to resolve code changes and errors that may occur as non-Oracle SQL code and stored procedures which are migrated to Oracle. First, examine the editors and utilities in the OMWB and then the editors and tools will be explained for the newer migration tools in SQL Developer.

## Tablespace Discovery Editor

The Tablespace Discoverer is a tool within the OMWB that provides the ability to use a specific set of tablespaces in an existing Oracle database environment. The useful characteristic of the Tablespace Discovery editor is that different tablespaces can be used for the new target Oracle database, and in turn, the newly migrated database. As shall soon be seen in the following examples, using the Tablespace Discoverer is quite simple.

In the OMWB, the Tablespace Discovery editor allows the user to select the default tablespace, index tablespace, and temporary tablespace for a complete database migration. All of the new user schemas and the related database objects inherit these new settings by default. The new Oracle Model schema containing all schema objects, i.e. users, indexes, and tables, can use the editor to make use of any currently available tablespaces.

Now an example will be given of how to use Tablespace Discoverer. First, map the requested tablespaces to the Oracle model by accessing the tool from within the OMWB main tools menu as shown in the next figure.

**Figure 7.40:** *Tablespace Discoverer in OMWB*

To access this tool, select the Tablespace Discoverer from the Tools menu in the OMWB. The Main screen of the Tablespace Discoverer will appear next, as shown in Figure 7.41.

**Figure 7.41:** *Tablespace Discoverer Logon and Database Connection*

Now enter the username and connection details for the schema and database that will be used for the tablespace details with the newly migrated Oracle database. The omwb, or user, that was created earlier must have connect and resource roles granted in the destination database or the Tablespace Discoverer editor will complain and not work.

To continue, enter the details and click the Connect button. Now the available tablespaces will appear in the drop down menus of the Tablespace Discoverer editor because the connection is made to the new target database, as shown below.

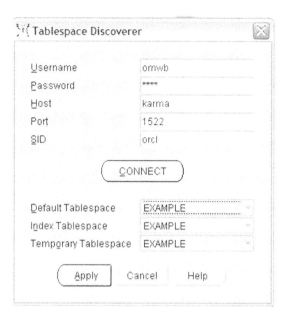

**Figure 7.42:** *Tablespace Discoverer Available Tablespaces*

Choose the default, index, and temporary tablespaces that are needed by manipulating the drop down menus as listed in Figure 7.43.

**Figure 7.43:** *Selecting Tablespaces with Tablespace Discoverer*

After selecting the choices for the default, index, and temporary tablespaces to complete the tablespace mapping to the new Oracle source model process, choose the Apply button.

Now the completed tablespace configuration will be displayed in the Oracle source model panels for the OMWB.

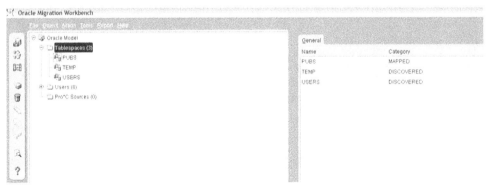

**Figure 7.44:** *Tablespace Configuration after Using Tablespace Discoverer*

The OMWB provides three different status conditions for the tablespaces with the newly migrated Oracle 10g or 11g database: Mapped, Discovered, or Generated.

Mapped tablespaces are the new tablespaces that have been created by the OMWB automatically. This occurred when the new Oracle Model was created for the Oracle database that is migrated from Microsoft SQL Server or MySQL database environments.

Discovered tablespaces are tablespaces that have been imported from the destination database using the Tablespace Discoverer editor. These tablespaces cannot be edited or renamed by the OMWB.

Generated tablespaces are tablespaces that have been created within the OMWB by using the Objects menu to create these new tablespaces. The following figure illustrates how to create this type of tablespace within the OMWB.

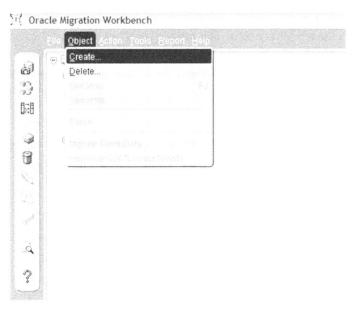

**Figure 7.45:** *How to Create a Generated Tablespace*

Creating a newly generated tablespace with the OMWB is quite useful and simple. From the Objects menu, select Create.

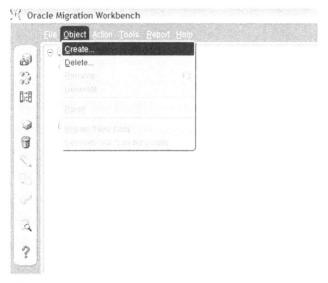

**Figure 7.46:** *Object Menu for Generated Tablespaces*

Generated tablespaces are quite useful for adding new storage to the target Oracle database that will house the newly migrated schemas and objects. For instance, if an additional tablespace is needed for a large number of index objects, a new generated tablespace can be added to house the new index objects.

Another way to create a new custom tablespace, which will appear as a generated tablespace, is to right click on the Tablespaces top menu in the Oracle Source model.

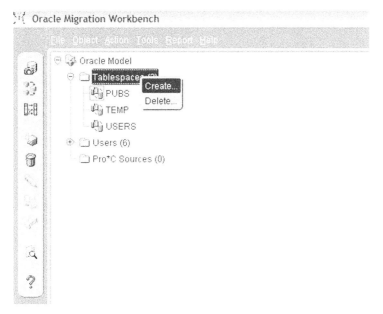

**Figure 7.47:** *Generated Tablespace Creation*

Now create a newly generated tablespace to house the large indexes that are migrated to Oracle from Microsoft SQL Server.

**Figure 7.48:** *Create New Tablespace in OMWB*

From the object menu in the OMWB, select Create. The popup window will appear. Enter INDEX01 for the new index tablespace and choose OK. The new index tablespace will appear as a Generated tablespace in the Oracle Source Model panel for the OMWB as shown in Figure 7.49.

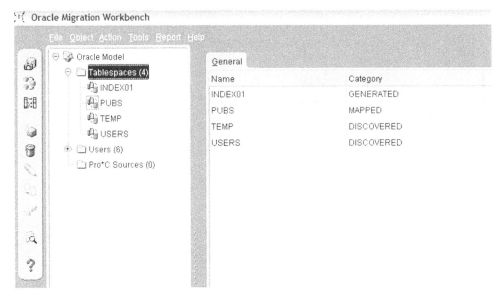

**Figure 7.49:** *New Generated Tablespace in OMWB*

To view configuration details and apply the changes, select the INDEX01 tablespace. After this, the right panel will display the DDL for the tablespace to be created.

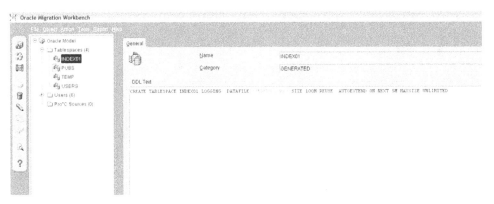

**Figure 7.50:** *Options for Generated Tablespace with Oracle Source Model*

If the generated tablespace configuration satisfies the user, then select the Apply button on the right panel bottom of the configuration. If the settings need to be cancelled, the Revert option will go back to the default setting.

There is also an option to delete any of the tablespaces in the Oracle Source Model configuration.

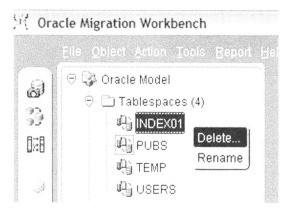

**Figure 7.51:** *Delete and Rename Options for Tablespaces*

This provides the option to delete tablespaces or perform a rename option if desired from within the OMWB. Now take a look at the Options toolbar in the OMWB. To access the Options section, from the main OMWB menu choose Tools-> Options as shown in Figure 7.52.

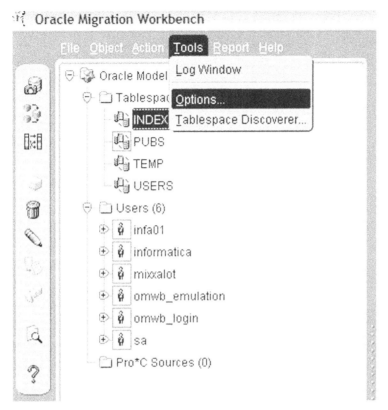

**Figure 7.52:** *Options Menu in the OMWB*

The Options menu provides many features for migrating third party databases that have been captured by the OMWB. The main section of the Options menu has the following setup as that shown in Figure 7.53.

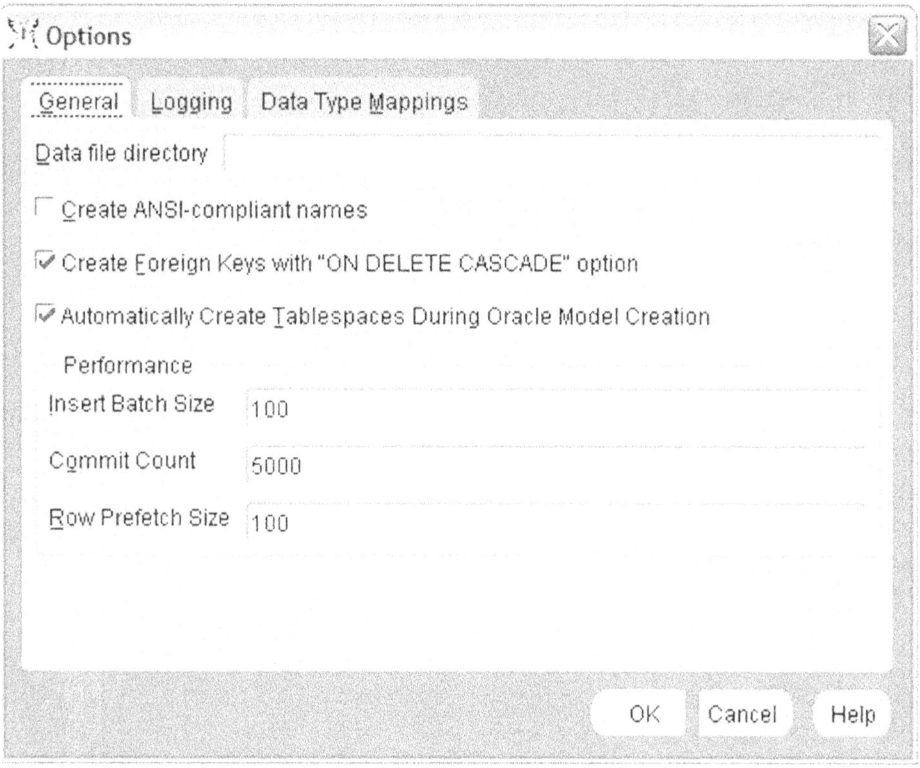

**Figure 7.53:** *Options for OMWB*

The three tabs include General, Logging, and Data Type Mappings. Each section for the OMWB Options will now be reviewed.

The General tab in the Options menu provides configuration choices about output for the data file directory, ANSI compliance naming for new schema options, the ability to automatically create new tablespaces during the Oracle Source Model creation, and the creation of foreign keys with the *on delete cascade* option along with performance settings. The data file directory section in the Options menu tells the OMWB where to create the Oracle data files associated with the tablespaces for the newly migrated Oracle 10g or 11g database.

The Automatically Create tablespace instructs the OMWB to automatically create a new tablespace in the Oracle Model to hold all of the migrated data. If this option is not selected, then create a tablespace in the Oracle Model by using the Tablespace Discoverer or selecting the tablespaces container in the Oracle Model tree and using the option from the Object menu to create the new tablespace.

Among the performance options, the Insert Batch Size shows the number of rows that the OMWB will batch up before migrating table data to the destination database.

Commit Count displays the total number of rows after which the OMWB issues a commit when migrating table data to the destination database.

The Row Prefetch Size shows the number of rows prefetched by the OMWB when reading data from the Workbench repository.

The next tab in the Options menu, Logging, covers various settings for logging status outputs for the OMWB operations.

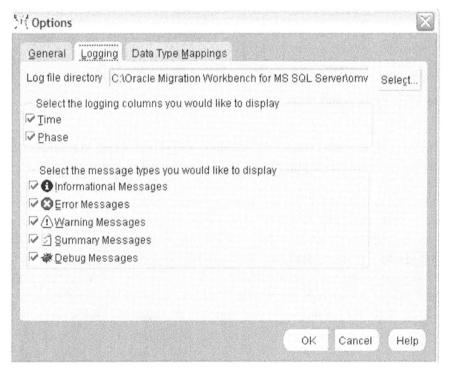

**Figure 7.54**: *Logging Options for OMWB*

The Logging tab of the Options Menu provides the ability to customize the directory where log files are stored. It also allows this function concerning which columns, phase status windows, and messages are logged to the report files during OMWB operations.

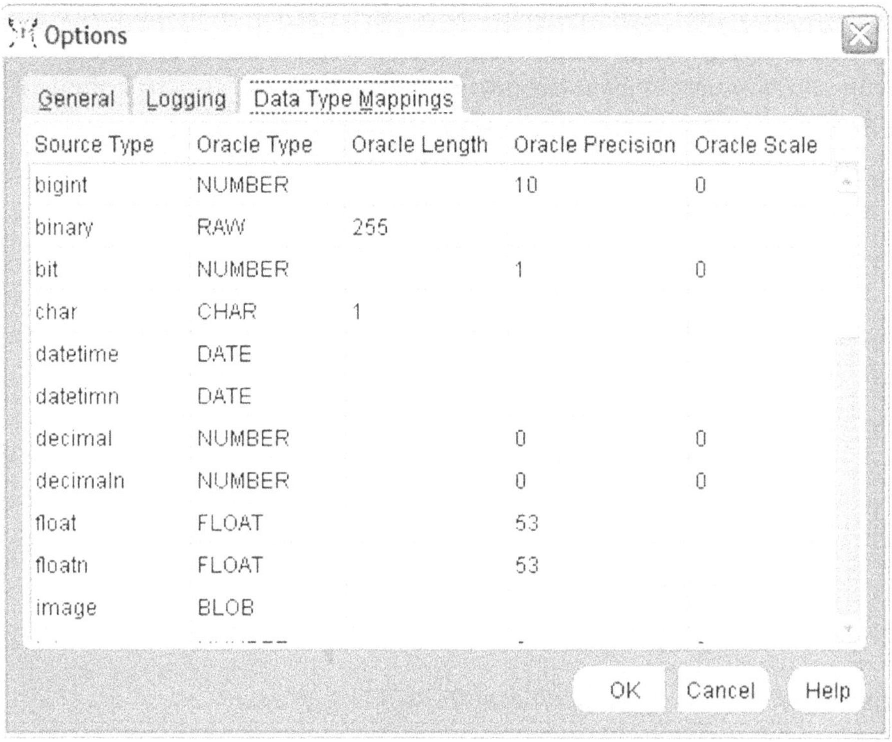

| Source Type | Oracle Type | Oracle Length | Oracle Precision | Oracle Scale |
|-------------|-------------|---------------|------------------|--------------|
| bigint | NUMBER | | 10 | 0 |
| binary | RAW | 255 | | |
| bit | NUMBER | | 1 | 0 |
| char | CHAR | 1 | | |
| datetime | DATE | | | |
| datetimn | DATE | | | |
| decimal | NUMBER | | 0 | 0 |
| decimaln | NUMBER | | 0 | 0 |
| float | FLOAT | | 53 | |
| floatn | FLOAT | | 53 | |
| image | BLOB | | | |

**Figure 7.55:** *Data Type Mappings in Options Menu for OMWB*

The Data Type Mappings window displays the current data type conversion settings from the source database to Oracle. The OMWB provides options to change the data type conversions to Oracle to resolve any type mismatch errors, as will be seen later in the chapter. The next item to be covered is the Parser Editor tools in the OMWB.

## Code Parser Editor

The OMWB provides a feature-rich editor called the Code Parser Editor to modify the code between third party databases including MySQL and

Microsoft SQL Server 2000 to Oracle SQL and PL/SQL. To access the parser editor, select the source model for MySQL or MS SQL Server.

The first step in using this function is to make the changes to the schema object for the SQL Server 2000 source model. To complete the parser operation, select the object, whether it is view, trigger, or stored procedure, to parse and then either right click on the object or choose the Object-> Parse menu selection to complete the process. The parser icon is also a third option to parse the schema object.

**Figure 7.56:** *Parse Schema Objects from OMWB Object Menu*

Once the schema object has been parsed, the OMWB will display the status.

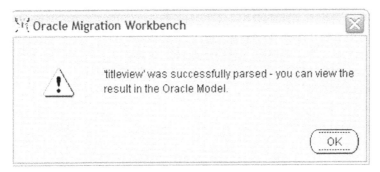

**Figure 7.57:** *Completed Parse Example*

To access the parser options window in the OMWB, select the left tab for the source model, which in this case would be the SQL Server 2000 source model.

The OMWB allows the user to parse triggers, views, and stored procedures to customize the migration process to Oracle.

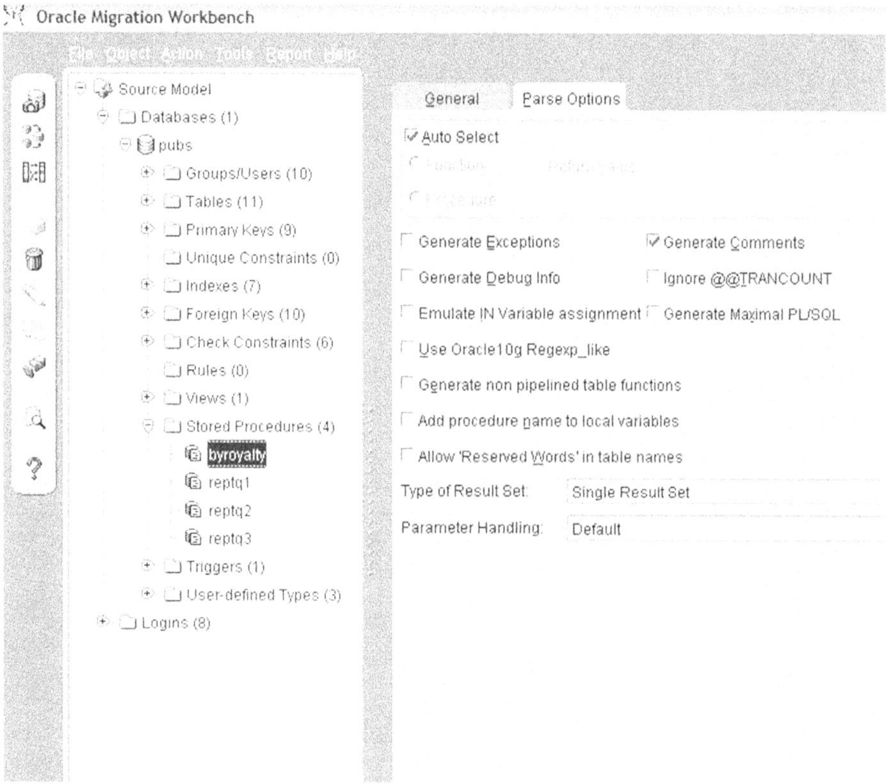

**Figure 7.58:** *Code Parser Editor Options*

The parser editor provides extensive options to change variable assignments and mappings for triggers, views, and stored procedures. Furthermore, it offers the ability to add comments and debugging information to the code as these objects are migrated from MySQL and SQL Server to Oracle.

Now that the subject of the various editors and tools has been introduced for the OMWB, next to be introduced are the editors and tools available with the migration workbench functions for SQL Developer and Oracle.

# SQL Developer Editors and Tools

From SQL Developer 1.5 and on, the latest versions of migration tools provide an integrated development environment (IDE) that offers single-console full functionality to migrate third party databases to Oracle 10g and 11g. The main menu for migration tools provides the following set of editors and tools to manage the procedures for migrating to Oracle as shown in the following figure.

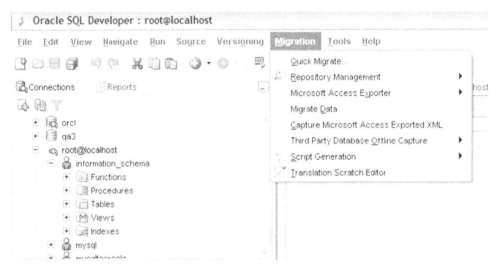

**Figure 7.59:** *Migration Tools and Editors Menu Screen for SQL Developer*

SQL Developer 1.5 and later releases provide editors and tools to perform quick migrations as well as options to manage the repository for migration related tasks. This is also in addition to script generation tools and offline capture utilities.

## Exporter for Migrating MS Access to Oracle

The Exporter provides the option to migrate databases from Microsoft Access to either or both SQL Developer and Oracle Application Express. A quick example of how to export MS Access to SQL Developer will be shown in the next figures.

Select the Microsoft Access Exporter tool from the Migration menu toolbar in SQL Developer.  The exporter splash screen will open and the Exporter Wizard will prompt selection choices.

**Figure 7.60:**  *MS Access Exporter for SQL Developer*

The tool provides the choice to migrate from MS Access databases to SQL Developer and/or APEX.

**Figure 7.61:**  *Exporter Options for SQL Developer 1.5*

Once the migration is complete, it will be available in SQL Developer. SQL Developer also provides the option to migrate XML databases in MS Access to Oracle as well.

## Translation Scratch Editor for SQL Developer

The Translation Scratch Editor is a fantastic tool in SQL Developer that provides conversion testing and assistance when migrating third party database SQL and stored procedures such as those from T-SQL on SQL Server to Oracle SQL and PL/SQL. The editor provides windows for both the third party database as well as the target Oracle environments.

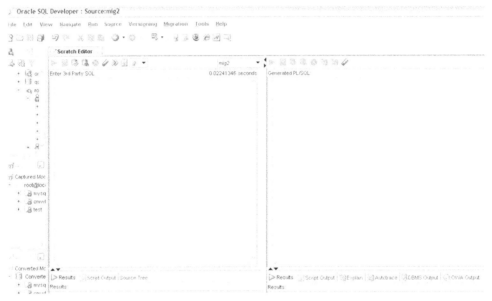

**Figure 7.62:** *Translation Scratch Editor in SQL Developer*

# Troubleshooting Migration Issues: Common Problems and Solutions

Now that the editors for migration tasks with SQL Developer for Oracle have been introduced, the most common issues and solutions to migration problems can be investigated. These often occur when migrating third party databases to Oracle while using the OMWB and the SQL Developer Migration products.

# Problems with Source and Target Model Mapping

Problems that occur with migrations to Oracle from MySQL and SQL Server databases involve a mix of code mapping errors, conflicts with names for roles, privileges and objects as well as architectural differences in schema objects that are migrated to Oracle.

## Schema Conflicts between Source and Target Models

One common error that occurs during migrations to Oracle from SQL Server and other third party databases is a result of existing database schema objects, security conflicts and other related matters. ORA-01921 is shown in the below error message.

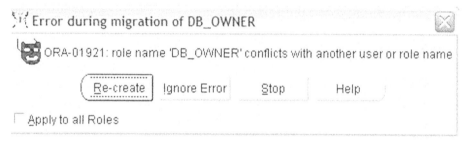

**Figure 7.63:** *Errors During Migration of Schema Objects to Oracle*

The error exemplified previously occurred in the test migration to Oracle from SQL Server 2000 because the user or role name, as referenced by the above ORA-01921 error message, already exists in the target database. In order to resolve the error message during the migration process, choose the re-create option in the error box.

The code parser editor is another valuable tool when conflicts occur with migrating schema objects such as triggers, views, and stored procedures to Oracle from MySQL and MS SQL Server 2000. This utility in OMWB provides the ability to edit and modify code to resolve data type and code mismatches.

## Incorrect Source to Target Database Connection Settings

The database connection for the source third party database is often incorrect, which generates connectivity errors between the client, network, JDBC or ODBC driver and target server. The same issue is true for the target Oracle 10g or 11g database. All of the username and password settings must be correct or the migration tasks will fail.

## Constraint Violation Errors During Migration

When the migration steps are performed from the source database model to the new target Oracle database, constraint violations and conflicts will cause failures in the migration of associated tables, indexes, triggers and other schema dependent objects. In order to resolve these constraint violations, the relationships need to be reviewed between the dependent objects. Furthermore, constraint violations must be resolved or migration will not be possible for these objects.

Now that the most common issues have been examined that may occur when performing migrations to Oracle by using the OMWB, it is time to address common problems that arise when using the newer migration suite of tools with SQL Developer.

# Issues with SQL Developer Migration Tools

Oracle has invested substantial efforts and costs into the next generation of development and migration tools with SQL Developer. Many of the past bugs that plagued users with the OMWB have been resolved with SQL Developer. However, as is the case with any newer software product and release, current issues do exist that may cause problems with migrating databases to Oracle with SQL Developer Migration Workbench.

In the following pages, the most frequent problems that result when migrating third party databases to Oracle with SQL Developer will be covered.

## Problems with Quick Migrate for SQL Developer 1.5

SQL Developer provides various methods to migrate from MySQL and MS SQL Server 2000/2005 to Oracle 10g/11g. The biggest issue that commonly occurs is with the Quick Migrate functionality with SQL Developer's latest releases. Although not officially sanctioned as a bug from Oracle, the Quick Migrate tool does have some limitations and problems with the migration of MySQL databases to Oracle. The most frequent types of errors generated by SQL Developer when performing migration related tasks are java error message exceptions due to various incident conditions.

EXAMPLE CASE: When performing an online capture using either Quick Migrate or standard capture, SQL Developer generates a series of Java error messages similar to the following:

```
java.sql.SQLException: Protocol violation
atoracle.jdbc.driver.DatabaseError.throwSqlException(DatabaseError.java:112)

at oracle.jdbc.driver.T4C7Ocommoncall.receive(T4C7Ocommoncall.java:150)
at oracle.jdbc.driver.T4CConnection.logoff(T4CConnection.java:464)

at oracle.jdbc.driver.PhysicalConnection.close(PhysicalConnection.java:1175)
```

- The Problem:

  - The capture process will either fail or hang for MySQL to Oracle

- Cause:

  - Unknown, Possible Bug in SQL Developer 1.5 release

In discussions on the OTN forums for Oracle migration tools and SQL Developer, the example case is a known issue and requires a manual workaround procedure to resolve when the migration from MySQL to Oracle is performed with Quick Migrate and other capture tools in SQL Developer. Here is a viable workaround solution:

Create a Windows *cmd* script, call it *sqldeveloper.cmd* and put the following entries in the script:

```
SET ORACLE_HOME=%CD%
```

Save the command windows script as *sqldeveloper.cmd*. Copy the script to the base installation directory for SQL Developer:

```
cd c:\SQLDeveloper1_5\sqldeveloper-5338\sqldeveloper
```

Start SQL Developer with the command script that was created earlier. Here is an example of the procedure. First, open a Windows shell prompt window and execute the following scripts:

```
prompt> sqldeveloper.cmd sqldeveloper.exe
prompt> sqldeveloper.exe
```

After the Windows script has been created and a new session for SQL Developer 1.5 has been started, the repository will need to be cleaned up to perform the migration correctly.

Here is the workaround for SQL Developer 1.5:

1. From the Migrate menu, delete the current repository and create a new schema in Oracle target database; call it mig2.

2. Create a new repository in SQL Developer 1.5.

3. Right mouse click on the MySQL 5.x database and choose Capture.

The capture should now be successful and resemble Figure 7.64:

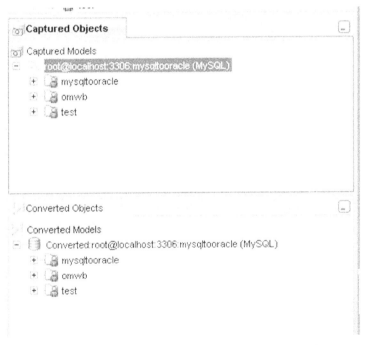

**Figure 7.64:** *Captured Model for MySQL in SQL Developer 1.5*

## Incorrect JDBC Driver Versions for SQL Developer

The third most common problem that occurs when using SQL Developer to perform migrations to Oracle exists in the driver layer for JDBC connections to third party databases. If the incorrect version is installed and/or not configured properly, migration will fail and SQL Developer will hang on java exception errors flooding the log window. The next chapter will review the correct versions and installation requirements for these drivers with SQL Developer.

Now that the most common problems that arise with migrations to Oracle with SQL Developer have been touched upon, complete the test case migrations from Microsoft SQL Server 2000 to Oracle 10g with the OMWB. SQL Developer can also be used to migrate from MySQL 5.x to Oracle in the next section.

# Completing the Initial Migration Using OMWB

Now that the various editors and utilities available for the OMWB and SQL Developer Migration tools have been reviewed, complete the migrations for Microsoft SQL Server 2000 to Oracle 10g and MySQL to Oracle 10g using these powerful migration tools. First, finish the migration from Microsoft SQL Server 2000 to Oracle 10g using the Migration Workbench in the following example.

Step 1: Start the OMWB

Open a new session for the OMWB and connect to either the default repository or the custom repository that was created earlier.

Step 2: Choose Migrate to Oracle in the OMWB

Choose the migration option to migrate the Oracle source model that was created earlier by either selecting the migration icon on the left pane or the Action-> Migrate to Oracle option:

**Figure 7.65:** *Migrate to Oracle Option with OMWB*

The following icons on the left panel in the OMWB warrant further explanation as they play an important role in the migration operations for the OMWB. See Figure 7.66:

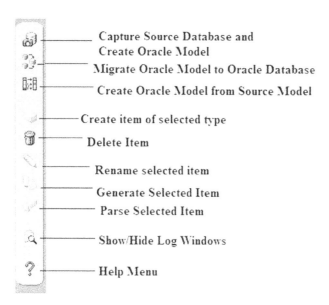

Capture Source Database and
Create Oracle Model

Migrate Oracle Model to Oracle Database

Create Oracle Model from Source Model

Create item of selected type

Delete Item

Rename selected item

Generate Selected Item

Parse Selected Item

Show/Hide Log Windows

Help Menu

**Figure 7.66:** *OMWB Tools*

Step 3: Migration Wizard, Initial Screen

Follow the default for the initial migration wizard screen in the OMWB and choose Next.

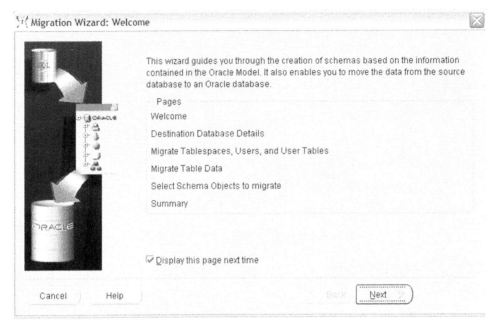

**Figure 7.67:** *Migration Wizard Initial Screen with OMWB*

Step 4: Enter Destination Information

Now enter the parameters for the target Oracle 10g database that will contain the newly migrated database, as shown in Figure 7.68, then click Next to continue.

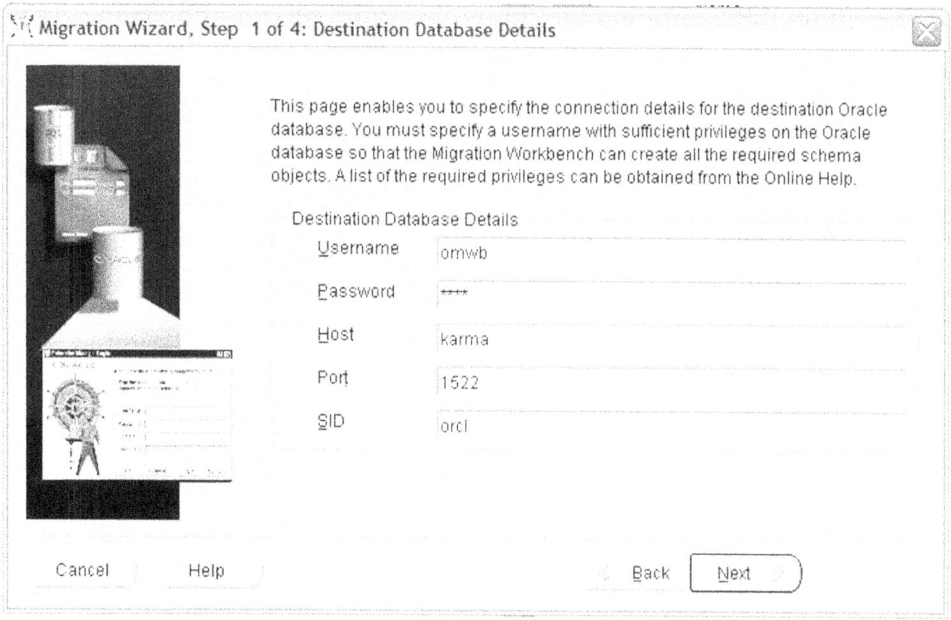

**Figure 7.68:** *Destination Database Information Migration Details*

Step 5:  Migration Wizard: Migrate Database Schema Objects

The next step of the migration will move all of the Microsoft SQL Server 2000 database and schema objects to Oracle. Since the tablespaces and associated schema objects were created earlier when the source models were built, choose to not re-create these objects as they already have been created. Then click Next to continue.

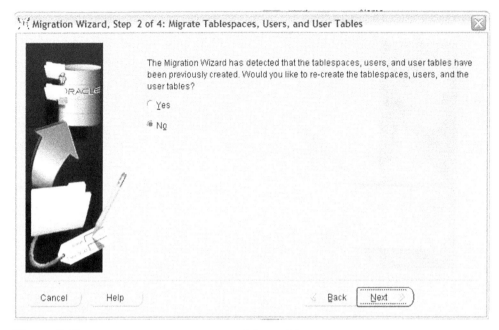

The Migration Wizard has detected that the tablespaces, users, and user tables have been previously created. Would you like to re-create the tablespaces, users, and the user tables?

      Yes

      No

Cancel      Help                                     Back      Next

**Figure 7.69:** *Migration Wizard, Migrate Schema Objects*

Step 6: Migrate Table Data from MS SQL Server 2000 to Oracle

The next step in the migration wizard presents the option to either migrate the table data from Microsoft SQL Server 2000 to Oracle or to defer the task. Since it has not been previously done, migrate the data from SQL Server 2000 over to Oracle. Choose the option to do so by selecting Yes, then Next.

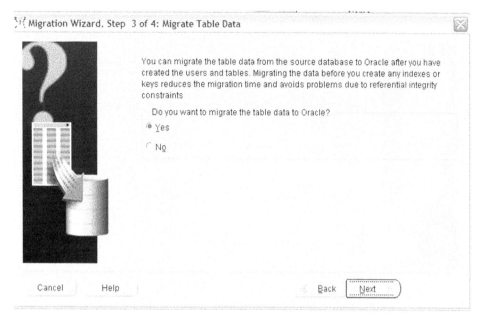

**Figure 7.70:** *Migrate Table Data from MS SQL Server 2000 to Oracle*

Step 7: Select Schema Objects to Migrate to Oracle

Since performing a complete database migration from Microsoft SQL Server 2000 to Oracle is desired, select all schema objects, as shown in the next example, with the Migration Wizard.

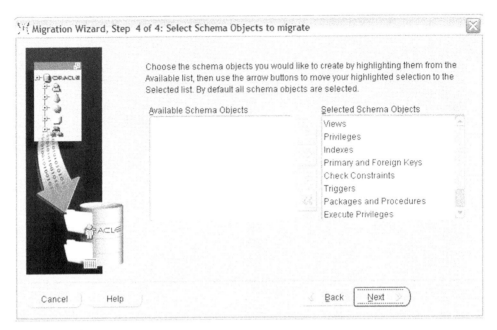

Choose the schema objects you would like to create by highlighting them from the Available list, then use the arrow buttons to move your highlighted selection to the Selected list. By default all schema objects are selected.

Available Schema Objects

Selected Schema Objects

Views
Privileges
Indexes
Primary and Foreign Keys
Check Constraints
Triggers
Packages and Procedures
Execute Privileges

Cancel     Help                    Back     Next

**Figure 7.71:** *Migrate Schema Objects*

Once the schema objects have been selected for migration, click Next.

Step 8: Migration Wizard Summary and Confirmation

The OMWB will display the summary window next and confirm the choices made before it performs the database migration.

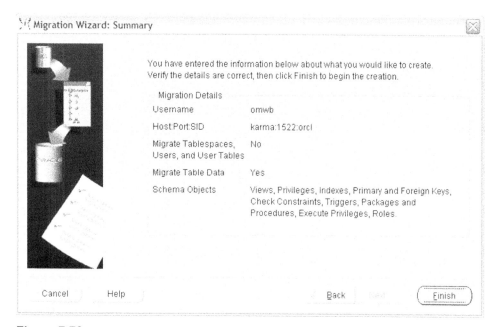

**Figure 7.72:** *Migration Wizard Summary and Confirmation Page*

Choose Finish to complete the migration. The log window will appear with a status window for the migration processing to Oracle.

Step 9: Migration Log Window

The Migration Workbench will provide the status of the migration procedures in the log window, which can be disabled if desired.

**Figure 7.73:** *Migration Status Screen*

It will then load the table data first from the SQL Server 2000 source model before migrating the data to Oracle.

Step 10: Complete Migration and Resolve Errors

At the next stage, the migration has completed but with errors that will need to be addressed and resolved.

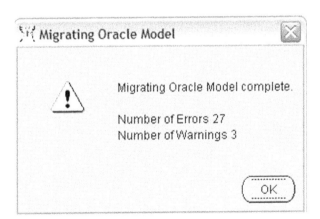

**Figure 7.74:** *Completion for Migration Process*

The next task is to generate the database migration report to resolve open issues and complete all migration tasks for Oracle.

By default, the OMWB will place the database migration reports under the *C:\omwb\log\Database* directory. These are opened using a web browser that has been certified as compatible with the OMWB such as MS Internet Explorer or Netscape. Particularly useful is the detailed report that contains all of the migration details from SQL Server to Oracle as seen in Figure 7.75.

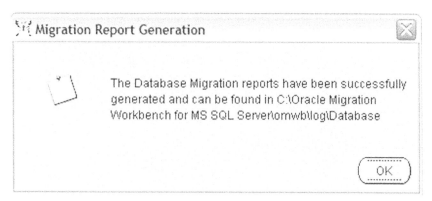

**Figure 7.75:** *Migration Report Generation*

The Database Detailed Report is the best starting point to examine all of the details for the completed migration. This is because from there, all of the items can be investigated further.

## Database Detailed Report

| | |
|---|---|
| **Capture Date:** | 18-05-2008 20:53:38 |
| **Migration Workbench Release:** | ( Build 20050629 ) Production |
| | MySQL 4.X Plugin, Production Release 10.1.0.4.0 Microsoft SQLServer 2000 Plugin, Production Release 10.1.0.4.0 |
| | Oracle JDBC driver Release 10.1.0.4.0 |
| | Connected to karma:1522:orcl as omwb |
| **Source Database(s):** | pubs |

**Figure 7.76:** *Database Detailed Report for Migration to Oracle*

The source database from MS SQL Server 2000 pubs has been migrated to Oracle 10g. Details on the release for the OMWB and associated plugins are covered in the report. Now the items are presented for the objects migrated to Oracle from SQL Server as shown in the next figure.

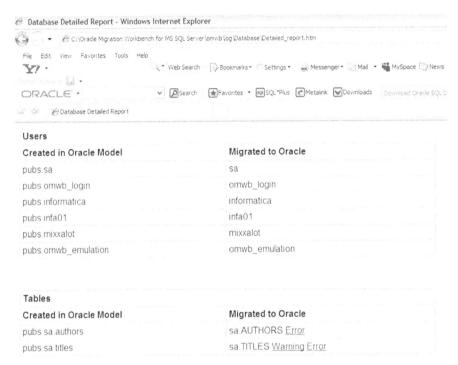

**Figure 7.77:** *Database Detailed Report for OMWB Migration*

It is important to examine and resolve the open errors and warnings as part of the migration process to clean up failed objects that were not migrated successfully to Oracle from MS SQL Server 2000. Now that the test pubs database has been migrated from MS SQL Server 2000 to Oracle 10g using the Migration Workbench, a test case will be presented using the latest migration tools from Oracle in SQL Developer to migrate from MySQL 5.x to Oracle 10g or 11g.

# Completing the Initial Migration Using SQL Developer

Oracle provides comprehensive steps for migrating third party databases to Oracle 10g and 11g in the SQL Developer User Guide for all releases of SQL Developer. Covered earlier were the preliminary steps for the migration from MySQL to Oracle in the online capture and source model build for the MySQL and Oracle target databases. Now that these models have been built, the final step is to migrate the actual data from MySQL to Oracle.

For the data migration process, SQL Developer provides options to generate online and offline data move scripts and DDL scripts to Oracle. In order to migrate the data from MySQL to Oracle, the Migration menu item needs to be selected in the toolbar for SQL Developer as shown in the next figure.

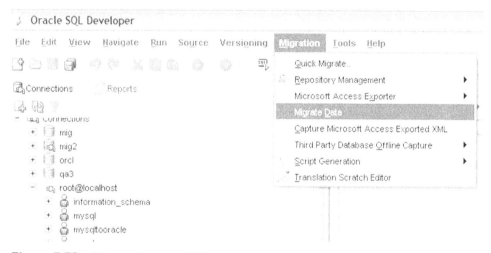

**Figure 7.78:** *Migrate Data in SQL Developer 1.5*

After the Migrate Data option is selected from the SQL Developer Migration menu, SQL Developer will prompt for the source and target connections.

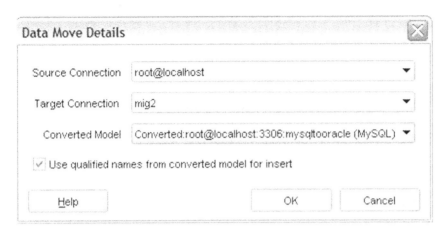

**Figure 7.79**: *Data Move Details for SQL Developer Migration with MySQL*

The Data Move Details window requires the user to input the source connection for MySQL, the Oracle target database connection, and the converted model that was created earlier for the migration to Oracle from MySQL. Once the entries are approved, click on the OK button to proceed with the data migration.

The actual data migration time will depend on the quantity and type of MySQL data to be moved to Oracle. If there is a substantial amount of data to migrate off of MySQL to Oracle, perhaps the use of offline data move scripts will be more useful to perform the data migration during a maintenance window period.

## Generate Data Move Scripts with SQL Developer

In addition to the automated procedures that were presented earlier in the chapter, SQL Developer also provides useful scripts to move data. The Data Move Scripts can be generated for later execution as part of a comprehensive migration project from MySQL to Oracle by using these scripts in SQL Developer.

To access the menu to create the data move scripts in SQL Developer, select the Migration submenu as shown in the following example.

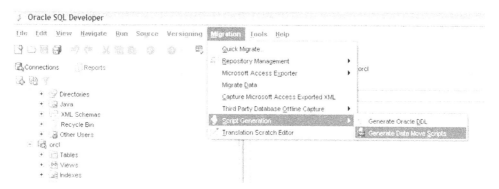

**Figure 7.80:** *Generate Data Move Scripts in SQL Developer 1.5*

The Generate Data Move Scripts will open a wizard to assist in creating the move scripts for data to Oracle from MySQL or the chosen third party database. It will ask for the directory to store the offline capture scripts as shown in the next figure.

**Figure 7.81:** *Generate Offline Data Move Scripts for MySQL with SQL Developer 1.5*

In addition to the method for data move scripts, as shown above, SQL Developer also provides custom offline capture scripts for MySQL. The process to implement and create these offline capture scripts will be explained in the following examples.

# Offline Capture Scripts for MySQL Using SQL Developer

SQL Developer provides the ability to create offline capture scripts for third party database environments in the Migration menu. The scripts will be created and saved to use later during the migration of MySQL and other databases to Oracle. The following example shows how to access the offline capture script feature.

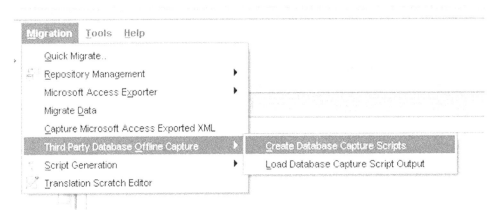

**Figure 7.82:** *Third Party Database Offline Capture Scripts in SQL Developer*

When the Create Database Capture Scripts selection is chosen, SQL Developer prompts to select the platform that will be used to create the new offline database capture scripts.

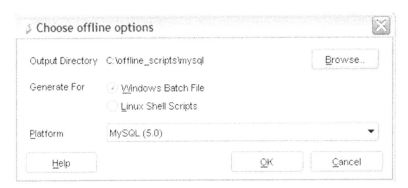

**Figure 7.83:** *Offline Capture Options for SQL Developer*

Here, the choices provided for offline capture scripts include the operating system platform (Windows or Linux) as well as database platforms like MySQL, Sybase or SQL Server, for instance. The next example will use Windows batch files for MySQL 5.x databases to generate the offline database capture scripts with SQL Developer. In the figure above, the offline scripts will be stored in the *c:\offline_scripts\mysql* directory. After the offline database capture scripts are generated, the location and file names are provided for the new offline capture scripts:

**Figure 7.84:** *Script Generation Complete for Offline MySQL Scripts*

Now take a look at what these offline database capture scripts look like so that how SQL Developer migration works under the covers can be better understood.

The main offline database capture script for MySQL is called *master_5.bat*. As can be observed from the code shown below, it uses the *mysqldump* utility to perform the offline database capture in addition to Windows batch shell commands.

🖫 **master_5.bat**

```
@ ECHO OFF
REM @(#)master_5.bat
REM
REM Copyright 2006 by Oracle Corporation,
```

```
REM 500 Oracle Parkway, Redwood Shores, California, 94065, U.S.A.
REM All rights reserved.
REM
REM This software is the confidential and proprietary information
REM of Oracle Corporation.


SET user=SET_USER_NAME
SET host=SET_THE_HOST
SET password=SET_THE_PASSWORD

IF %user%==SET_USER_NAME GOTO ERROR_CONDITION

IF %host%==SET_THE_HOST GOTO ERROR_CONDITION

IF %password%==SET_THE_PASSWORD GOTO ERROR_CONDITION

SET SEED=%RANDOM%

ECHO SEED=%SEED% >> mysql5.ocp

ECHO SELECT VERSION()> version%SEED%.sql

mysql -u%user% -p%password% -h%host% < version%SEED%.sql >version%SEED%.txt

mysqldump -u%user% -p%password% -h%host% --xml --no-data --all-databases >
alldbs%SEED%.xml

ECHO alldbsfile=alldbs%SEED%.xml >> mysql5.ocp

ECHO select SCHEMA_NAME from information_schema.schemata where (SCHEMA_NAME
NOT IN ('information_schema','mysql'));> showdatabases.sql

mysql -u%user% -p%password% -h%host% < showdatabases.sql
>temp_databases%SEED%.txt

FOR /F "tokens=*" %%A IN (temp_databases%SEED%.txt) DO IF NOT
%%A==SCHEMA_NAME call get_table_5.bat %%A

ECHO SELECT TABLE_SCHEMA, TABLE_NAME, VIEW_DEFINITION, DEFINER  FROM
INFORMATION_SCHEMA.VIEWS;> showviews%SEED%.sql

mysql -u%user% -p%password% -h%host% < showviews%SEED%.sql>views%SEED%.txt

ECHO  SELECT ROUTINE_SCHEMA,ROUTINE_NAME , ROUTINE_TYPE , DEFINER FROM
INFORMATION_SCHEMA.ROUTINES; > routines_name%SEED%.sql

mysql -u%user% -p%password% -h%host% <
routines_name%SEED%.sql>temp_routines%SEED%.txt

FOR /F "tokens=1,2,3,4" %%A in (temp_routines%SEED%.txt) DO IF NOT
%%A==ROUTINE_SCHEMA  CALL get_stored_proc_5.bat %%A %%B %%C %%D

ECHO table_info=all_tabs%SEED%.txt>> mysql5.ocp

ECHO column_table_info=all_col_data_tabs%SEED%.txt>> mysql5.ocp

ECHO constraint_table_info=all_constraints_tabs%SEED%.txt>> mysql5.ocp
```

```
ECHO max_column_info=all_cols_tabs%SEED%.txt>> mysql5.ocp

ECHO index_info=all_index_data_tabs%SEED%.txt>> mysql5.ocp

ECHO views_info=views%SEED%.txt>> mysql5.ocp

ECHO routines_info=routines%SEED%.txt>> mysql5.ocp

ECHO version_info=version%SEED%.txt>> mysql5.ocp

GOTO :CAPTURE_DONE

:ERROR_CONDITION
ECHO You need to enter either user or host or password at the beginning of
script.
GOTO DONE

:CAPTURE_DONE
ECHO Processing completed - files generated for MySQL Offline

:DONE
pause
```

To perform the offline capture, these MySQL scripts will need to be executed against the source MySQL database environment.

# Generating Schema and DDL Creation Scripts

Now that the offline database capture script utilities have been explained, it is time to review how to generate scripts for the MySQL to Oracle schema and DDL capture process within SQL Developer. As has been seen with the other migration tools, the capture scripts that generate the DDL and associated schemas are called from the migration submenu of the main SQL Developer toolbar. This is exemplified in Figure 7.85:

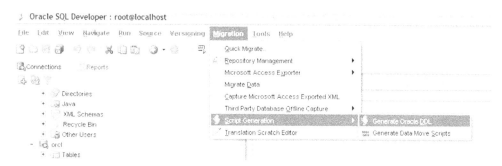

**Figure 7.85:** *Script Generation Options for Oracle DDL in SQL Developer*

Begin by exploring the generation of new Oracle DDL scripts. To create the new Oracle DDL, select Script Generation-> Generate Oracle DDL from the Migration menu in SQL Developer. The options for choosing the source model are presented in the figure below.

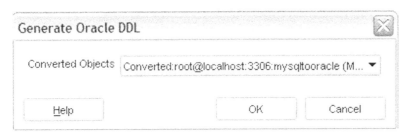

**Figure 7.86:** *Generate Oracle DDL from MySQL with SQL Developer 1.5*

One note of interest comes to mind - the source model for MySQL to Oracle must have been captured prior to generating new Oracle DDL using this utility. Since the prerequisites were completed earlier, choose the MySQL converted model database from the drop down menu box, as in Figure 7.87.

**Generating Oracle SQL**

| Object Type | No of Objects Generated |
|-------------|-------------------------|
| User | 3 |
| Schema | 3 |
| Package | 3 |
| Table | 8 |
| Sequence | 1 |
| Trigger | 1 |

Generation Done

☐ Automatically close the dialog

Close

**Figure 7.87:** *Generating Oracle SQL Progress in SQL Developer*

Once the generation process has completed, the new DDL scripts will be stored in the default directory for SQL Developer.

**Figure 7.88:** *Completion Window for DDL Generation in SQL Developer*

Now examine the new DDL scripts for Oracle to review the output configurations. The following code depot sample script portrays the required DDL to create the new users and schema objects for the migrated database.

### 🖫 OracleGeneratedDDL.sql (partial)

```
SET SCAN OFF;
CREATE USER mysqltooracle IDENTIFIED BY mysqltooracle DEFAULT TABLESPACE
USERS TEMPORARY TABLESPACE TEMP;
GRANT CREATE SESSION, RESOURCE, CREATE VIEW TO mysqltooracle;
CREATE USER omwb IDENTIFIED BY omwb DEFAULT TABLESPACE USERS TEMPORARY
TABLESPACE TEMP;
GRANT CREATE SESSION, RESOURCE, CREATE VIEW TO omwb;
CREATE USER test IDENTIFIED BY test DEFAULT TABLESPACE USERS TEMPORARY
TABLESPACE TEMP;
GRANT CREATE SESSION, RESOURCE, CREATE VIEW TO test;
connect mysqltooracle/mysqltooracle;

create or replace PACKAGE mysql_utilities AS
identity NUMBER(10);
END mysql_utilities;
/

/

CREATE TABLE bonus (
  ename VARCHAR2(10 CHAR),
  job VARCHAR2(9 CHAR),
  sal NUMBER(10,0),
  comm NUMBER(10,0)
);

GRANT SELECT, INSERT, DELETE, UPDATE, REFERENCES ON bonus TO omwb;
GRANT SELECT, INSERT, DELETE, UPDATE, REFERENCES ON bonus TO test;

CREATE TABLE dept (
```

```
  deptno FLOAT NOT NULL,
  dname VARCHAR2(14 CHAR),
  loc VARCHAR2(13 CHAR)
);

GRANT SELECT, INSERT, DELETE, UPDATE, REFERENCES ON dept TO omwb;
GRANT SELECT, INSERT, DELETE, UPDATE, REFERENCES ON dept TO test;

CREATE TABLE emp (
  empno NUMBER(10,0) DEFAULT '0' NOT NULL,
  ename VARCHAR2(60 CHAR),
  job VARCHAR2(50 CHAR),
  mgr NUMBER(10,0),
  hiredate DATE NOT NULL,
  sal FLOAT,
  comm FLOAT,
  deptno NUMBER(10,0) NOT NULL
);

GRANT SELECT, INSERT, DELETE, UPDATE, REFERENCES ON emp TO omwb;
GRANT SELECT, INSERT, DELETE, UPDATE, REFERENCES ON emp TO test;

CREATE TABLE salgrade (
  grade NUMBER(10,0),
  losal NUMBER(10,0),
  hisal NUMBER(10,0)
);

GRANT SELECT, INSERT, DELETE, UPDATE, REFERENCES ON salgrade TO omwb;
GRANT SELECT, INSERT, DELETE, UPDATE, REFERENCES ON salgrade TO test;

connect omwb/omwb;

create or replace PACKAGE mysql_utilities AS
identity NUMBER(10);
END mysql_utilities;
/

/

CREATE SEQUENCE  msemp_empno_SEQ
  MINVALUE 1 MAXVALUE 999999999999999999999999 INCREMENT BY 1  NOCYCLE ;

CREATE TABLE msbonus (
  ename VARCHAR2(10 CHAR),
  job VARCHAR2(9 CHAR),
  sal NUMBER(10,0),
  comm NUMBER(10,0)
);

GRANT SELECT, INSERT, DELETE, UPDATE, REFERENCES ON msbonus TO
mysqltooracle;
GRANT SELECT, INSERT, DELETE, UPDATE, REFERENCES ON msbonus TO test;

CREATE TABLE msdept (
  deptno FLOAT NOT NULL,
  dname VARCHAR2(14 CHAR),
  loc VARCHAR2(13 CHAR)
);
```

If the DDL generation scripts for Oracle were created by using the option within the left panel section for the Converted Model, than the script output will appear in the right pane. The next figure shows an illustration of this.

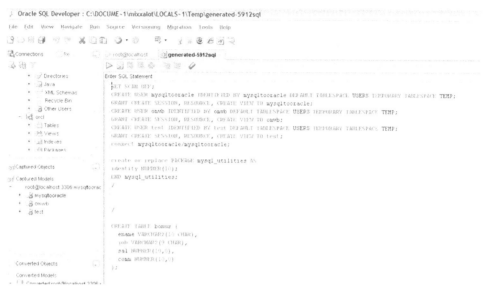

**Figure 7.89:** *DDL Generated Script Display for Oracle in SQL Developer*

On the other hand, if a different method is desired, open the SQL scripts using the user's favorite editor or within the SQL Developer environment.

Further instructions and information on deployment for Oracle DDL generated scripts are available in the Oracle SQL Developer documentation.

# Conclusion

In this chapter, various tools and editors available for performing complex migration tasks to Oracle with the OMWB and SQL Developer tools have been explained. Online and offline capture tasks have now been shown in more detail as well as common problems that may arise in the migration process to Oracle when deploying these tools. Solutions to these issues were also presented along with further illustrations on how to map the source database model to the target Oracle environments to complete the initial migration procedures.

The next chapter will provide a capstone to the migration tasks and procedures with a discussion of optional tools and editors to provide for verification and validation of the newly migrated Oracle environment by using the OMWB Verification Tool. Using Oracle Application Migration Workshop (APEX) with SQL Developer will also be explained.

# References

OMWB Reference Guide for MySQL 3.22, 3.23, 4.x
Migrations Release 10.1.0 for Microsoft Windows 98/2000/NT/XP
Part B13911-01, Oracle Corporation

OMWB Reference Guide for SQL Server and Sybase
Adaptive Server Migrations Release 9.2.0 for Microsoft Windows
98/2000/NT/XP, Part B10254-01

OMWB Frequently Asked Questions (FAQ) Release
9.2.0 for Microsoft Windows 98/2000/NT/XP, Part B10258-01

Oracle Database SQL Developer Installation Guide, Release 1.5, Part E12153-02
Oracle Database SQL Developer User's Guide, Release 1.5, Part E12152-03
Oracle Database SQL Developer Supplementary Information for MySQL Migrations, Release 1.5, Part E12155-01

Oracle Database SQL Developer Supplementary Information for Microsoft SQL Server and Sybase Adaptive Server Migrations, Release 1.5, Part E12156-01

Oracle OTN Forums for Migration Topics
http://forums.oracle.com

Oracle Metalink Support Failed to disable constraints: Data move; Note: 468452.1

# Understanding the Oracle Database Migration Utilities

*"Confusion is the first step in understanding the migration tools and utilities for Oracle SQL Developer and the OMWB"*

## Introduction

In the last few chapters, the Oracle migration process was described for online and offline captures with both SQL Developer and OMWB tools. Previous chapters have shown how these tools are essential for a smooth migration from MySQL and Microsoft SQL Server 2000 third party databases to Oracle 10g and 11g environments. This chapter will expand on database migrations to Oracle by focusing on the verification tools and editors that can be used to resolve tricky issues for code translation from MySQL and Microsoft SQL Server to Oracle.

# OMWB Verification Tool

The verification tool is available from Oracle on the following download: URL:http://www.oracle.com/technology/tech/migration/dmv/index.html Oracle provides a free tool, The Database Migration Verifier (DMV), available for Microsoft SQL Server and Sybase database environments to perform additional migration verification checks as part of a migration project toolkit. The verification tool is available from Oracle on the following download:

- http://www.oracle.com/technology/tech/migration/dmv/index.html

Unfortunately, the verification tool is not currently available for other third party database platforms. What is available is another tool called SwisSQL that provides similar functionality in terms of the verification and validation process for mapping third party database schemas to Oracle.

Provided by AdventNet Software, the SwisSQL products are compatible with

> 🔔 SwisSQL can be downloaded for free, along with more details from their website: http://www.swissql.com/oracle-migration.html

most third party databases and fill in the gaps that the migration tools do not provide from Oracle.

The DMV tool is free of charge and it offers many utilities to verify that tables and schemas have been migrated from SQL Server to Oracle correctly. The following section outlines the prominent features of the DMV tool.

## Features of the Oracle Database Migration Verifier Tool (DMV)

The DMV tool was introduced in Chapter 3. It is worth repeating what the Oracle DMV has in the way of features:

- Source-to-target database comparison for all tables, indexes, views, functions, stored procedures, and triggers

- Verification that objects exist in both the source database and target Oracle database

- Checking for table column order

- Checking for the existence of the table column with the ability to produce a NULL value

- Tests to verify that the stored procedures and functions exist in the newly migrated Oracle Database

- Checking the data type, scale, precision, length, and default for table columns, functions, and stored procedures between source and target

- Checking the argument order for stored procedures and functions

- Single row count checks for all user tables to verify the integrity of the migrated data

- Providing a DMV report that summarizes the results of all verification checks at schema and data level

- Allowing the use of Java Database Connectivity (JDBC) to simultaneously connect to the source database and Oracle Database

- Providing a Java command line interface enabling the integration of the tool into an existing test harness.

It is recommended that one uses the Oracle DMV tool for Sybase and SQL Server databases that are migrated to Oracle. If SQL Developer is being used to perform database migrations, there are built-in reports to provide database comparisons between the source third party database and the target Oracle database. These reports collect statistics on the migration objects. SwissSQL from AdventNet Software also provides excellent third party schema comparison tools as well as the tools from Quest Software and other third party database tools vendors.

# Installation Process for OMWB Verification Tool

The installation process for the DMV tool is a simple procedure of downloading and configuring the jar file. Note that an example of installation for Microsoft SQL Server 2000 was given in Chapter 3.

# Requirements for DMV Installation for Oracle

The primary component required to install the DMV tool is the correct version of the Java Development Kit (JDK) software. Listed below is the minimum software that must be installed based on the source database platform:

- JDK 1.3.x or later driver

- Microsoft SQL Server 2000 Driver for JDBC

- Sybase jConnect 4.5 for JDBC

- Oracle Database 10g JDBC Driver for Oracle 10g, and later database releases, for the target Oracle database

# Summary of Steps to Install and Configure DMV for Oracle

The following guide is a set of instructions to install and configure the DMV.

Step 1

Download and extract the *dmv.zip* file from Oracle technical site listed next:

- http://otn.oracle.com/tech/migration/dmv

Step 2

Edit the properties file for SQL Server called *dbinfoss2k.prop* located in the *dmv_install_dir\config* directory. The properties file will need to contain the correct source and target database connection settings for the following parameters:

- Class path for the JDBC driver

- Source database URL, user name, and password

- Oracle Database URL, user name, and password

Step 3

Save the properties file once all settings have been added.

An example property file for SQL Server 2000 is shown next with settings for the JDBC and source to target database configuration settings.

### 🖫 dbinfoss2k.prop Configuration File for Oracle DMV

```
# Oracle Database Migration Verifier Properties File for
# Microsoft SQL Server 2000
# Developers Release 1.0.0
#
# File Name: dbinfoss2k.prop
#
# Update this file to specify the JDBC driver connect URLs for
# your environment. This is used
# by the Oracle Database Migration Verifier (Database Migration #Verifier)
to connect to your
# Microsoft SQL Server 2000 database and verify against the
#Oracle Database.
#
#
# Edit the properties file for your environment. A sample
# Microsoft SQL Server 2000 properties file, dbinfoss2k.prop,
# is located at the following directory:
#
#    dmv_install_dir\config
#
#
#=====================================
#  GENERIC JDBC CLASSPATH SETTINGS
#=====================================
#
#

    ORACLE_HOME\jdbc\lib
#
# where ORACLE_HOME is the Oracle home directory specified by the
# %ORACLE_HOME% environment variable on Windows or the
# $ORACLE_HOME environment variable on UNIX.
#
# Microsoft SQL Server 2000 JDBC Drivers
#=========================================================
# For Microsoft SQL Server 2000 JDBC drivers, enter the location #
msbase.jar, msutil.jar, and mssqlserver.jar files.
# By default, these files are installed into the following
#
#    C:\Program Files\Microsoft SQL Server 2000 Driver for #JDBC\lib
#
# Example of JDBC Classpath
#==============================
# JDBC.ClassPath = d:\\oracle\\ora92\\jdbc\\lib\\classes12.jar;
# C:\\Program Files\\Microsoft SQL Server 2000 Driver for
#JDBC\\lib\\msbase.jar;
# C:\\Program Files\\Microsoft SQL Server 2000 Driver for
#JDBC\\lib\\msutil.jar;
# C:\\Program Files\\Microsoft SQL Server 2000 Driver for
#JDBC\\lib\\mssqlserver.jar
#

JDBC.ClassPath = C:\oracle\product\10.2.0\db_1\jdbc\lib;
```

```
C:\Program Files\Microsoft SQL Server 2000 Driver for JDBC\lib\msbase.jar;
C:\Program Files\Microsoft SQL Server 2000 Driver for JDBC\lib\msutil.jar;
C:\Program Files\Microsoft SQL Server 2000 Driver for
JDBC\lib\mssqlserver.jar;

#=======================================================
# Microsoft SQL Server 2000 JDBC CONNECTION SETTINGS
#=======================================================
# Enter the JDBC URL for the Microsoft SQL Server 2000 database.
# You can use a Microsoft SQL Server 2000 JDBC URL similar to the following
format:
#
# Example of the Microsoft SQL Server JDBC URL
#=======================================================

Source.url =
jdbc:microsoft:sqlserver://karma:1433;databaseName=pubs;selectMethod=cursor;


# Enter the Microsoft SQL Server database user name.  The default for
Microsoft SQL Server 2000 is sa.

Source.username = sa


# Enter the Microsoft SQL Server database password.  The default for
Microsoft SQL Server 2000 is sa.

Source.password = sa

#=======================================================
# ORACLE JDBC CONNECTION SETTINGS
#=======================================================
# Enter the URL for the Oracle9i Database or Oracle Database 10g.
# Oracle uses the JDBC thin driver that is 100% Java.
# You can use an Oracle Database URL similar to the following

Target.url = jdbc:oracle:thin:@karma:1522:ORCL


# Enter your Oracle Database user name:

Target.username = omwb


# Enter your Oracle Database password:

Target.password = omwb

# Plug-in Classes
#===================
DatatypeMap.ClassName = oracle.mtg.schemaverifier.map.SQLServerDatatypeMap
Source.queryClassName =
oracle.mtg.schemaverifier.query.SQLServer2KQueryComponent
Target.queryClassName =
oracle.mtg.schemaverifier.query.Oracle9iQueryComponent
```

# Using the Oracle Database Migration Verifier

The DMV obtains the source and target database configurations from the properties file. This establishes connections and performs the database comparisons. Then the DMV outputs the results to a text based report, which can be given a name or the default will be named as *DMVReport.txt* if only the directory is specified.

To use the DMV, the following steps will need to be performed.

1. Open a new windows command prompt.

2. Enter the following command to start the Oracle DMW:

```
java -jar dmv_install_dir\dmv.jar PropertiesFilePath ReportStorePath
```

The *dmv_install_dir* is the base directory where the DMV was installed.

The *PropertiesFilePath* is the directory and file name for where the properties file is stored for the DMV.

In the case of SQL Server 2000, the default sample properties file is called *dbinfoss2k.prop*.

The *ReportStorePath* references the directory and file name for the DMV report file generated by the utility after a comparison is performed.

Now that the use and function of the DMV tool has been explained, next to be covered are the various editors and tools for the OMWB and SQL Developer.

# Using OMWB Editors

In the last few chapters, the various tools and features on how to perform database migrations from MySQL and Microsoft SQL Server to Oracle using the OMWB and SQL Developer migration environments were covered. In this section, some of the other utilities that can aid the fine-tuning of the database migration tasks will be examined. Since most of these tools for OMWB have already been detailed, there will only be a review of the logging window and migration script generator tools.

## Log Window Tool in OMWB

In the OMWB environment, the most critical tool during a migration operation is the ability to monitor status for errors. This is also helpful if needing to pause or cancel a migration should an incident arise.

To access the log window in the OMWB, select the Tools-> Log Window menu item from the main Tools menu as shown in the following example.

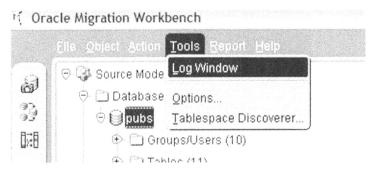

**Figure 8.1:** *Log Window from OMWB Tools Menu*

The log window will display what options are available to choose from for configuration with respect to status for a migration task performed by the OMWB. The logging tool is critical for monitoring activities from the source database to Oracle target environment during the migration process. In the following example, the default log window contents are displayed.

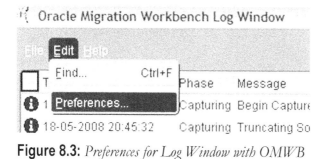

| Time | Phase | Message |
|---|---|---|
| 18-05-2008 20:45:32 | Capturing | Begin Capture of Source Model |
| 18-05-2008 20:45:32 | Capturing | Truncating Source Model |
| 18-05-2008 20:45:39 | Capturing | Source Model Truncated |
| 18-05-2008 20:45:39 | Capturing | Truncated tables from MASTER database |
| 18-05-2008 20:45:39 | Capturing | Source Model Truncated |
| 18-05-2008 20:45:39 | Capturing | Loading Source Model |
| 18-05-2008 20:45:39 | Capturing | Loading tables from MASTER database |
| 18-05-2008 20:45:39 | Capturing | Loading SS2K_SYSDATABASES |
| 18-05-2008 20:45:39 | Capturing | Loading SS2K_SYSLOGINS |
| 18-05-2008 20:45:39 | Capturing | 8 rows inserted into table SS2K_SYSDATABASES |
| 18-05-2008 20:45:39 | Capturing | 7 rows inserted into table SS2K_SYSLOGINS |
| 18-05-2008 20:45:39 | Capturing | Loaded tables from MASTER database |
| 18-05-2008 20:45:39 | Capturing | Loading Source Model For pubs |
| 18-05-2008 20:45:39 | Capturing | Loading SS2K_SYSPERMISSIONS |
| 18-05-2008 20:45:39 | Capturing | Loading SS2K_SYSUSERS |
| 18-05-2008 20:45:39 | Capturing | Loading SS2K_SYSPROTECTS |
| 18-05-2008 20:45:39 | Capturing | Loading SS2K_SYSCOLUMNS |
| 18-05-2008 20:45:39 | Capturing | 89 rows inserted into table SS2K_SYSPROTECTS |
| 18-05-2008 20:45:39 | Capturing | 37 rows inserted into table SS2K_SYSPERMISSIONS |
| 18-05-2008 20:45:39 | Capturing | 16 rows inserted into table SS2K_SYSUSERS |

**Figure 8.2:** *Log Window Display in OMWB*

The log window displays all activities for the capture process based on the configuration preferences that are set for monitoring tasks for migrations. In order to customize these monitoring tasks, tailor the messages that are displayed in the log window for the OMWB by editing the preferences as shown in Figure 8.3.

**Figure 8.3:** *Preferences for Log Window with OMWB*

Once the preferences are opened for log operations with the OMWB, a variety of options to configure the monitoring tasks are shown. For example, one may choose to only display errors that occur with the migration phase from SQL Server to Oracle, allowing the white noise that is not relevant for the monitoring tasks to be filtered. So uncheck the other boxes and filter as shown in the next figure.

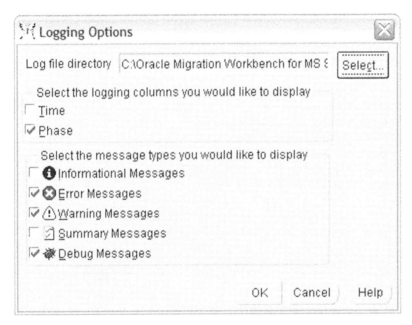

**Figure 8.4:** *Logging Options for OMWB Log Window*

After selecting the logging options and refreshing the log window, it only shows the failed operations and warning messages by phase of the operations performed by the OMWB. This is useful when diagnosing and troubleshooting to pinpoint the time and place of migration errors.

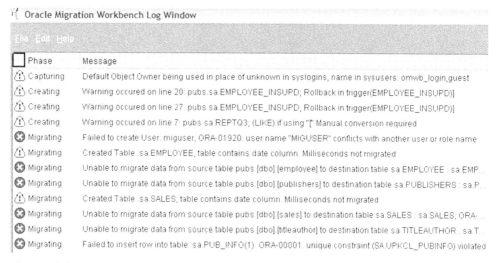

**Figure 8.5:** *Updated Log Window for Warnings and Errors with OMWB*

If a particular error message string needs to be found, use the Find option to locate that particular message as shown in Figure 8.6 below.

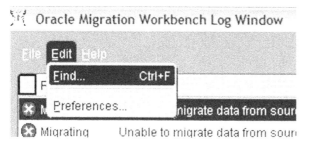

**Figure 8.6:** *Using the Find Function with Log Window for OMWB*

If all occurrences of the Oracle constraint errors that took place during the migration need to be seen, search for the ORA-00001 error message:

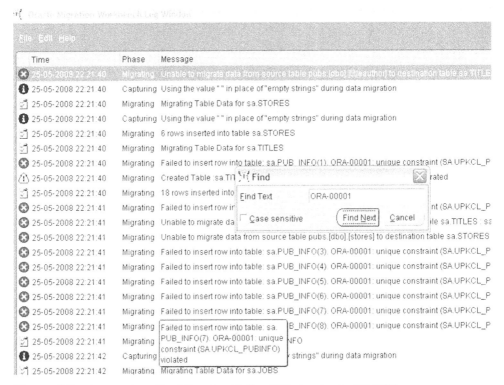

**Figure 8.7:** *Output from Find Search with Log Window in the OMWB*

The log window options provide a useful tool for monitoring the status of database migrations to Oracle with the OMWB. Now begin exploring the generation tools available in the OMWB.

## Migration Script Generation

The OMWB provides a nifty feature to generate migration schema creation scripts for the new database environments. To access the feature, which can be used for either the source third party database or target Oracle environments, go to that function within the Action menu as shown below.

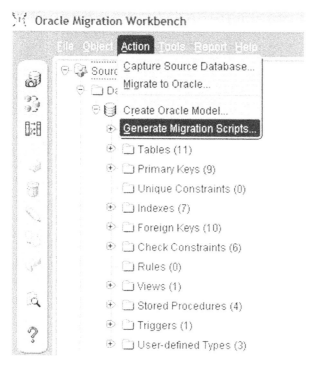

**Figure 8.8:** *Generate Migration Scripts in OMWB Action Menu*

The options have appeared for the schema object selection in the following example.

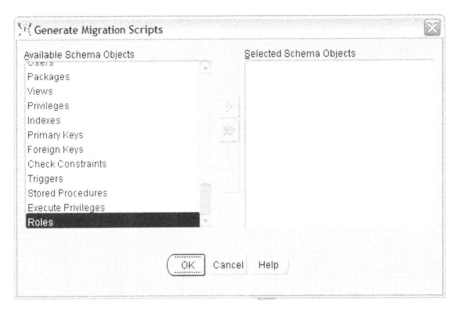

**Figure 8.9:** *Generate Migration Scripts Main Selection Window*

When the Generate Migration Scripts option is selected from the drop down Action menu within the OMWB, the choice is offered to create a script for all or some of the objects in the source database schema. For example, one can choose to create a new generated script for only schema user and table objects as shown in Figure 8.10.

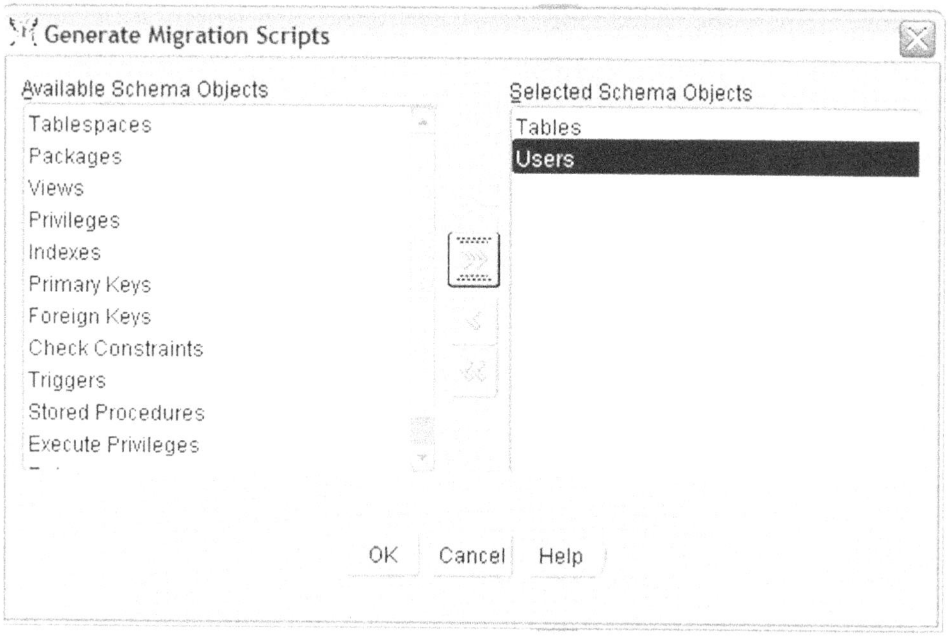

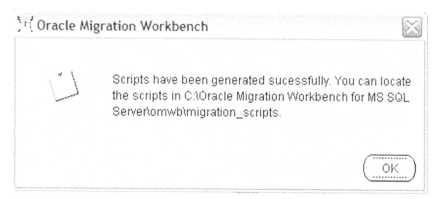

**Figure 8.10:** *Generate Migration Scripts for User and Tables with OMWB*

After the selection has been made to generate migration scripts for the user and table objects, the OMWB gives the location for the newly generated scripts.

**Figure 8.11:** *Completed Scripts for Tables and Users with OMWB*

Now examine the output for these newly generated scripts. By default, the OMWB will generate two scripts called *create.sql* and *drop.sql* in the default installation directory for the OMWB. Below is a listing for the *create.sql* script available in the code depot.

### 💾 create.sql

```
------------------------------------------------------------------
-- These are the SQL statements to create the objects from
-- the Oracle Model in an Oracle database.
------------------------------------------------------------------
REM
REM Start Tables
REM

REM
REM Message : Created Table :sa.AUTHORS
REM User : omwb
CREATE TABLE sa.AUTHORS(AU_ID VARCHAR2 (11) NOT NULL,AU_LNAME VARCHAR2
 (40) NOT NULL,AU_FNAME VARCHAR2 (20) NOT NULL,PHONE CHAR (12) NOT
NULL,ADDRESS
 VARCHAR2 (40)  ,CITY VARCHAR2 (20)  ,STATE CHAR (2)  ,ZIP CHAR (5)
,CONTRACT
 NUMBER (1,0) NOT NULL) TABLESPACE USERS;
REM
REM Message : Variable STARTVAL will store the value that we will use to set
the START WITH value for sequences
REM User : sa

VARIABLE startval NUMBER;

ALTER TABLE sa.AUTHORS  MODIFY (PHONE DEFAULT ('UNKNOWN'));
REM
REM Message : Processed defaults for table :sa.AUTHORS
REM User : omwb

REM
REM Message : Created Table :sa.TITLES
REM User : omwb

CREATE TABLE sa.TITLES(TITLE_ID VARCHAR2 (6) NOT NULL,TITLE VARCHAR2 (80)
 NOT NULL,TYPE_ CHAR (12) NOT NULL,PUB_ID CHAR (4)  ,PRICE NUMBER (19,4)
  ,ADVANCE NUMBER (19,4)  ,ROYALTY NUMBER (10,0)  ,YTD_SALES NUMBER (10,0)
  ,NOTES VARCHAR2 (200)  ,PUBDATE DATE NOT NULL) TABLESPACE USERS;


ALTER TABLE sa.TITLES  MODIFY (TYPE_ DEFAULT ('UNDECIDED'));
ALTER TABLE sa.TITLES  MODIFY (PUBDATE DEFAULT (SYSDATE));
REM
REM Message : Processed defaults for table :sa.TITLES
REM User : omwb

REM
REM Message : Created Table :sa.STORES
REM User : omwb
```

```
CREATE TABLE sa.STORES(STOR_ID CHAR (4) NOT NULL,STOR_NAME VARCHAR2 (40)
  ,STOR_ADDRESS VARCHAR2 (40)  ,CITY VARCHAR2 (20)  ,STATE CHAR (2)  ,ZIP
 CHAR (5)  ) TABLESPACE USERS;
REM
REM Message : Processed defaults for table :sa.STORES
REM User : omwb

REM
REM Message : Created Table :sa.EMPLOYEE
REM User : omwb

CREATE TABLE sa.EMPLOYEE(EMP_ID CHAR (9) NOT NULL,FNAME VARCHAR2 (20) NOT
 NULL,MINIT CHAR (1)  ,LNAME VARCHAR2 (30) NOT NULL,JOB_ID NUMBER (5,0)
 NOT NULL,JOB_LVL NUMBER (3,0)  ,PUB_ID CHAR (4) NOT NULL,HIRE_DATE DATE
 NOT NULL) TABLESPACE USERS;


ALTER TABLE sa.EMPLOYEE  MODIFY (JOB_ID DEFAULT (1));
ALTER TABLE sa.EMPLOYEE  MODIFY (JOB_LVL DEFAULT (10));
ALTER TABLE sa.EMPLOYEE  MODIFY (PUB_ID DEFAULT ('9952'));
ALTER TABLE sa.EMPLOYEE  MODIFY (HIRE_DATE DEFAULT (SYSDATE));
REM
REM Message : Processed defaults for table :sa.EMPLOYEE
REM User : omwb

REM
REM Message : Created Table :sa.PUBLISHERS
REM User : omwb
```

These DDL scripts can be executed against the target Oracle database to complete migration testing and other migration tasks as opposed to using the online capture and apply methods. The *drop.sql* script is generated and, as listed below in the code depot, will remove these objects.

## 💾 Drop.sql

```
REM
REM Start Users
REM

REM
REM Created User :sa
REM User : omwb
DROP USER sa CASCADE;

REM
REM Created User :omwb_login
REM User : omwb
DROP USER omwb_login CASCADE;

REM
REM Created User :informatica
REM User : omwb
DROP USER informatica CASCADE;

REM
```

```
REM Created User :infa01
REM User : omwb
DROP USER infa01 CASCADE;

REM
REM Created User :mixxalot
REM User : omwb
DROP USER mixxalot CASCADE;

REM
REM Created User :omwb_emulation
REM User : omwb
DROP USER omwb_emulation CASCADE;

REM
REM End Users
REM

REM
REM Start Tables
REM

REM
REM Created Table :sa.AUTHORS
REM User : omwb
DROP TABLE sa.AUTHORS;

REM
REM Variable STARTVAL will store the value that we will use to set the START
WITH value for sequences
REM User : sa
;

REM
REM Processed defaults for table :sa.AUTHORS
REM User : omwb
;

REM
REM Created Table :sa.TITLES
REM User : omwb
DROP TABLE sa.TITLES;
```

As an extra function, the generation script tool is quite useful for dumping DDL statements for the database migration process.

# SQL Developer Migration Tools and Utilities

Most of the SQL Developer Migration tools and utilities were explained in previous chapters along with migration task examples about online and offline database capture for migrating databases to Oracle. In the following section, the translation scratch editor will be explained, which is one of the most useful migration tools in the latest version of SQL Developer.

# SQL Developer Translation Scratch Editor

One of the most challenging tasks involved with the migration of third party databases lies in the conversion of third party SQL and database stored procedures to Oracle SQL and Oracle PL/SQL code. This is because the majority of problems that occur when using the migration tools from Oracle involve code differences, between MySQL and Oracle, for example. To access the Translation Scratch Editor, which was introduced in Chapter 7, choose Migration-> Translation Scratch Editor from within SQL Developer tools menu by selecting the option shown in the figure listed here.

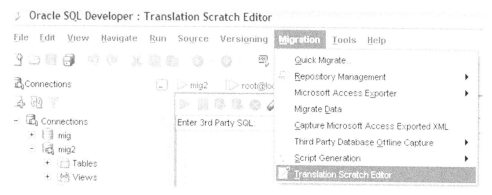

**Figure 8.12:** *SQL Developer Translation Scratch Editor*

Using the Translation Scratch Editor is a simple process. On the left corner, enter the source third party database SQL or stored procedure code. The right pane will show the newly translated Oracle SQL and PL/SQL code. Currently, the Translation Scratch Editor supports functionality for conversion mapping from Sybase SQL and T-SQL, MS SQL Server SQL and Microsoft SQL Server T-SQL stored procedures, and Access SQL to Oracle SQL and Oracle PL/SQL. The function toolbars and the various features that operate within the Translation Scratch Editor for SQL Developer will be explained next.

Within the SQL Developer Translation Scratch Editor, the following toolbar options exist, as shown in Figure 8.13. The translate functions are the most useful.

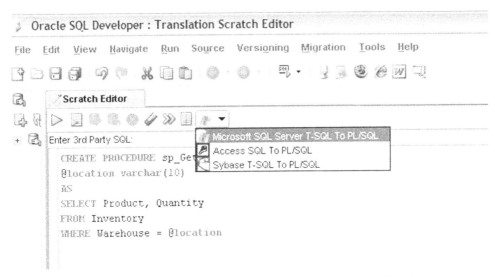

**Figure 8.13:** *SQL Developer Translation Scratch Editor Translator Function*

In this example, use the SQL Developer Translation Scratch Editor to convert a MS SQL Server 2000/2005 stored procedure to Oracle 10g/11g PL/SQL. Once the correct editor settings have been selected, choose the Translate button to convert the code from SQL Server T-SQL code to Oracle PL/SQL.

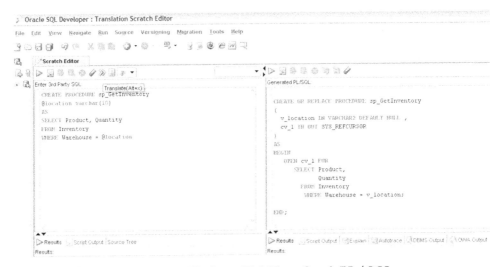

**Figure 8.14:** *Results for MS SQL Server T-SQL to Oracle PL/SQL*

Another helpful feature in the SQL Developer Translation Scratch Editor is the preview function called the Translation Diff Viewer. This is accessed from within the Translation Scratch Editor toolbar in SQL Developer. After the Translation Diff Viewer is called from the Translation Scratch Editor with SQL Developer, the code comparison is highlighted with differences and similarities shown in Figure 8.15.

**Figure 8.15:** *SQL Developer Translation Diff Viewer.*

Developers and DBA staff will find the code translation tools provided in the SQL Developer Translation Scratch Editor to be an invaluable tool in the arsenal for database migrations to Oracle.

## Installation for Database Plugins for SQL Developer

As was covered in previous chapters, the installation and configuration for the third party database plugin adapters for JDBC and ODBC connection is fairly simple and straightforward. Since new versions for SQL Developer connectors and plugins have arrived for the latest database releases of Oracle 10g and Oracle 11g for use with the migration workbench tools with SQL Developer 1.5 and future releases, it is worth mentioning the use of these plugins to avoid errors with the SQL Developer configuration for migrations to Oracle.

## Oracle APEX Migration Tools

The latest version of the Oracle Application Express (APEX) web development and migration tools provide editors with something that can be used when migrating MS Access databases to Oracle web enabled environments. Since the scope of using all of the many web development features for APEX is beyond the range of this text, only one of the migration tools available for APEX will be mentioned.

The migration of MS Access applications is performed via the APEX exporter tool as was discovered in Chapter 2. This feature can be called from either the SQL Developer Migration environment or from within the main Oracle Application Express menu. Using the menu driven graphical interface, MS Access databases can be quickly and easily migrated to Oracle using the exporter tool within the APEX environment.

# Conclusion

In this chapter, the Database Migration Verifier tool was introduced. It is used to check for post migration verification for newly migrated databases to Oracle. In addition, the various editors and utilities available for use in the pre- and post-migration tasks with SQL Developer Migration Workbench as well as for the OMWB and Oracle APEX environments were briefly explained. Lastly, the new installation requirements for using the new versions of the SQL Developer Migration Workbench tools for plug-in configuration of third party database drivers were reviewed. In the next chapter, methods for data verification procedures once the migration has been completed will be used to ensure that the migration has been accomplished in the best possible manner.

# References

Oracle Migration Verification Tool
http://www.oracle.com/technology/tech/migration/dmv/index.html

Oracle Migration Knowledge Base

---

http://www.oracle.com/technology/tech/migration/kb/index.html

SwisSQL Data Migration Tool
http://www.swissql.com/

Oracle Application Express (APEX) Main Site on Oracle Tech Net
http://www.oracle.com/technology/products/database/application_express/index.html

Oracle Application Express Migration Workshop
http://www.oracle.com/technology/products/database/application_express/migrations/mig_index.html

# Testing and Verification of Database Migration

*"Testing and Verification is an essential process to ensure that database migrations have been accurate and successful"*

## Introduction

The last several chapters have covered how to perform a database migration from MySQL and Microsoft SQL Server to Oracle using the currently available database migration tools from Oracle. One of the most important processes is about to begin.

Verification and testing is an essential part of the database migration project to Oracle to provide all of the stakeholders with the assurance and guarantee that data has been accurately migrated from MySQL and Microsoft SQL Server databases to Oracle. In this chapter, the focus will be on some best practices to validate and verify that the migration has been performed in an accurate manner. These steps will cover all of the required testing and verification phases as part of the critical verification and validation (V&V) process for database migrations to Oracle.

# Data Verification Testing

Data verification testing is the process of checking for data accuracy in terms of data quality. This process ensures that all aspects of the database information for schema objects, including tables, indexes, and stored procedure data, have been verified as intact and correct. For example, a good test to ensure that data verification is successful after a complex database migration would be to first execute row counts on the source database, such as MySQL or SQL Server. Then with the results, compare the row counts for all schema tables to the new target Oracle database to make sure that row counts match between the old source database system and the new target Oracle database environment.

Another aspect of data verification testing could also possibly include run times for batch jobs in the source to compare with that of the new target Oracle system. This ensures that execution plans are correct, and the optimizer is using up-to-date statistics.

# Performance Tuning

In line with the crucial step of data verification testing for completed migrations to Oracle is the phase for testing database and system performance for the newly migrated environment to Oracle.

Next will be a brief mention of some key points with Oracle database performance after migrations have been completed to ensure that performance is sufficient after the initial database migration. Complex assessments of all aspects of database performance is beyond the scope of this chapter and would require an entire text devoted to the subject matter, but beginning the examination will set the initial groundwork in motion.

Oracle provides excellent performance collection and monitoring tools with some Oracle 9i, 10g, and 11g releases. With Oracle 9i and earlier releases, Oracle provides Statspack to generate overall database performance reports and views such as *v$sql*, *v$sqlarea* and *v$sqltext* that can provide metrics on Oracle database performance.

For Oracle 10g, the new ADDM and AWR reporting and collection tools are available to capture performance tuning statistics and reporting analysis on database performance issues present in the new Oracle database environment. Oracle 11g provides the new SQL Performance Analyzer (SPA) for tuning newly migrated SQL statements that are top candidates for performance improvement. In addition to these tools for Oracle 10g and 11g, the new performance views for the new Active Session History (ASH) Wait Event such as *v$active_session_history* can be used to obtain statistics on performance.

Another key area of verifying database performance is to check that system and database statistics are up-to-date. If the database statistics for the newly migrated objects for Oracle are stale and not up-to-date, the optimizer in Oracle will not utilize the most efficient execution plan and suboptimal performance will result. The *dbms_stats* package in Oracle 10g and 11g allows the collection of up-to-date statistics for Oracle, as shown in the following example.

```
exec dbms_stats.gather_schema_stats( -
ownname          => 'MIGUSER', -
options          => 'GATHER AUTO', -
estimate_percent=> dbms_stats.auto_sample_size, -
method_opt       => 'for all columns size repeat', -
cascade          => true, -
degree           => 15 -
);
```

# User Acceptance Testing

Now that the data verification and performance review aspects of post-migration testing have been visited, the next phase to consider is the User Acceptance Testing, or UAT tasks. In a nutshell, UAT for the post-migration can be segregated into the following action items of deployment testing and functional testing activities for all involved stakeholders of the migration project.

# Deployment Testing

As part of the UAT process for post-migration deployment testing provides the assurance that no application or database issues exist in the newly migrated target Oracle database environment. Deployment testing requires validation that all of the major functionalities for the new database and application operate correctly without errors.

# Functional Testing

There are two cycles that compose the element of functional testing procedures for the UAT. The first phase of functional testing is to test all database and applications with the newly migrated data. This validates not the integrity but the functionality in using the newly migrated data.

The second phase of the functional testing for the UAT cycle is the sanity test process. This is a very brief run-through of the application's functionality for the newly migrated database in Oracle to assure that the system or methodology works as expected. In a sense, it is a focused but limited form of regression testing. The sanity tests measure that the migrated databases and applications have been accurately validated for usability.

# Quality Assurance (QA) Testing

After the UAT has been completed, the next phase in completing the verification and validation assurance process for the newly migrated databases to Oracle is the quality assurance or QA testing process.

Quality Assurance Testing is the complex process of working with end users, project staff coordinators, and developers to ensure that all of the code changes from development to test systems are accurate and ready for the migration to production environments. There are a few major paradigms in use for software development: Agile, Scrum, and Waterfall. These software development lifecycle methods influence the specific manner in which the applications and database testing procedures will be affected for the QA cycle. The Quality Assurance Institute provides the main body of standards for QA testing with software and applications. Next to be reviewed are the main areas of focus for QA testing for database migrations.

## Validation Testing

Validation testing provides checks for newly migrated data to Oracle when the user enters data into the database application the tester or end user knows is incorrect. For example, the tester would type in a character into a table entry that is expecting a numeric entry. The newly migrated Oracle database and application should thereby throw an error for the table entry.

## Data Compare Testing

The purpose of the data compare test phase for QA testing is to examine the output for database applications with specific parameters on the newly migrated target Oracle database. These parameters are compared to the source database's earlier sets of data with the same parameters that are known to be correct and accurate.

## Stress Testing

Stress testing is the process whereby the new Oracle database is used with a heavy load over a time period to measure performance and stability for demanding levels of load. For instance, one example of a useful stress test that could be performed for the newly migrated database to Oracle would be to run some large ETL or batch jobs by multiple users and measure the performance and availability over a window of several days.

## Usability Testing

The final phase usually associated with the QA test process after the database migration is usability testing. This involves the process of engaging new or unfamiliar users with the database application to try out the database applications. From this, they provide feedback to the development and QA team on what was experienced as difficult to accomplish so that the development and QA teams can improve the user interface and other features of the application.

# Conclusion

In this brief chapter, testing procedures were detailed that show the newly migrated database and application have been completed without errors in terms of data and user acceptance quality. Also explained were a few basic performance tuning tools and tips that may benefit technical teams in the analysis of database performance for the newly migrated environments to Oracle.

## References

Oracle Relational Migration Road Map
http://www.oracle.com/technology/tech/migration/maps/index.html

Oracle® Database Performance Tuning Guide 10g Release 2 (10.2), Part Number B14211-03

QA / Testing Technology Center
http://www.oracle.com/technology/tech/qa-testing/index.html

# Conclusion of Oracle Database Migration

*"And now our database migration to Oracle has been completed"*

## Book Conclusion

The long and challenging journey on best practices for migrating third party databases including MySQL and Microsoft SQL Server to Oracle using a variety of tools and methods has now been completed. It is important before, during and after completing a database migration to Oracle to remember that there is no such thing as a one–size-fits-all migration process. For some environments, the migration process may need to be automated using migration tools like OMWB and SQL Developer Migration Workbench to maintain online availability of production and other mission critical databases. For other migrations to Oracle, a more customized route may be necessary. As such, the tips and tricks provided in the methods for manual database migration to Oracle will be useful.

Since database migrations and related projects such as upgrades to Oracle involve potential risks and problems such as possible data loss and painful downtimes, this book was designed to point out a few available technologies that can help to mitigate risk with these database migrations to Oracle. One such technology is to implement a standby database server. Most third party database vendors offer this solution as part of their readily available technology stack of offerings.

For example, Microsoft SQL Server has Microsoft Cluster Server (MCS) which can be deployed when migrating from SQL Server to Oracle to avoid data loss risks as well as reducing expensive downtime during a migration project. MySQL has clustering technology as well but unfortunately, a detailed description is beyond the coverage possible in this book and would require another book in and of itself. IBM DB2 has a standby database option as well. Besides using a physical standby database and possible cluster solution, one can reduce costly downtimes by using replication technologies such as Quest Shareplex and Microsoft SQL Server replication if one wants to have a copy of the data available during the migration process.

# Lessons Learned From the Trenches

Here are some of my experiences at customer sites in the past for database migrations to Oracle from third party legacy platforms. One large-scale project involved migration of a 4TB Microsoft SQL Server 2000 data warehouse for imaging data to Oracle 10g (10.1) several years ago for a software company.

## Prepare, Prepare, Prepare!

In the above large scale migration project from Microsoft SQL Server 2000 to Oracle 10g, the project director initially scoped out the project for three months. However, after providing test plans and scripts, the estimate was pushed out to at least six months to perform the migration and testing to ensure all was successful.

## Call for Backup

One piece of advice that was recommended in the first chapter of the book was to make sure to take a cold or hot backup of the database before performing the migration. Also, test the backup. Just because a backup has been done is no guarantee that it is valid. I usually test my backups by doing a backup and clone to another server to make sure that my backup is valid and not garbage.

When the migration has been completed and all is working perfectly in Oracle, take a fresh backup again, this time in Oracle. Oracle 10g and 11g have this wonderful backup and recovery software tool called the Recovery Manager or RMAN that I tell all fellow DBAs and managers to use as it is rock solid and proven technology albeit having a cryptic syntax to the beginner. Downtime is bad news. However, data loss is unacceptable and grounds for termination at most companies. I once had a CIO ask me in the heat of a complex database recovery operation, "Ben, is the database going to come back up and when?" Fortunately, while it was New Year's Eve and I had been out with friends when I received the page and call, I had been the designated driver (not drinking anything but water!) and I was able to calmly answer with confidence after I completed the recovery operation for the large financial database.

## Standby to the Rescue

As busy DBAs, one often has to perform off-hours maintenance activities such as database migrations, upgrades and patching. Besides the dangers of losing data due to failed migrations without proper backups and other protective measures, downtime is costly and often impractical with today's 7x24x365 worldwide data centers and online global business operations.

Case in point: I performed some consulting work for clients in the past that had an Oracle RAC environment. One common misunderstanding about RAC is that many folks still believe that it is the panacea to data loss and downtime. It is not. While RAC is fantastic clustering technology that offers protection against a single node failure in a clustered environment, it does not protect against data loss from the RAC database because the way RAC works is that the cluster nodes all share the same database on shared storage. This means that RAC is still a single point of failure as far as data loss is concerned. It also means that downtimes must occur during upgrades, migrations and patching activities.

The solution to this problem is to implement what is called a standby database environment. Oracle offers this standby technology as part of Data Guard technology. By using a standby, a DBA can minimize downtime and prevent data loss while patching or performing database upgrades and migrations.

I hope that you as the reader have learned a lot of new tricks and tips to ensure a successful database migration to Oracle. Thank you for reading this book.

Ben Prusinski

# Appendix and Bibliography

OMWB User's Guide
Release 10.1.0.4 for Microsoft Windows 98/2000/NT/XP and Linux x86
Part No. B19134-01

Oracle Database SQL Developer's User's Guide
Release 1.1
B31695-01

# Index

# About the Author

## Ben Prusinski

Ben Prusinski is an Oracle Certified Professional with 10 years of full-time experience as a database administrator and has written numerous articles and white papers on database management. Ben is also an active member of the San Diego and Orange County Oracle and IBM DB2 User Group community, and he has published various articles for customers and user groups on data management.

Ben has been working with databases including Oracle, Microsoft SQL Server, IBM DB2 UDB, Informix, MySQL, and PostgreSQL since 1996 and has accumulated over a decade of practical knowledge and experience with complex database migrations and support on how to best achieve results with large database migrations to the Oracle platform.

Ben enjoys training in martial arts and tai chi as well as travel to exotic locations in his free time outside of working on Oracle databases. He has traveled to over 15 countries in Latin America and Asia and has a passion for learning new foreign languages as well as cultural traditions.

# About the Technical Editor

## Paulo Ferreira Portugal

Paulo Ferreira Portugal is a DBA with a decade of experience in IT and has worked as a DBA for 8 years. He is an Oracle Certified Professional (9i and 10g), IBM DB2 Certified (8 and 9 "Viper"), and an Oracle 11i Applications Database Administrator Certified Professional.

Currently, Paulo works as Senior Applications DBA for a company named F2C Consultoria in Rio de Janeiro/Brazil. F2C serves one of Oracle E-Business' largest clients in Brazil.

He has participated in the Oracle Beta Test 11i project using Data Guard, and is a specialist in High Availability tools like Oracle Data Guard, Oracle Streams and Oracle RAC. His clients in Brazil demand the most sophisticated services using tools like Oracle E-Business Suite 11i, Oracle OTM, Oracle Retail and Oracle BPEL with Oracle RAC 10g.

Paulo greatly enjoys what he does and is always improving his technical knowledge by attending events like Oracle Open World - San Francisco (2005 and 2006) and IBM Information on Demand – Los Angeles (2006).

## About Mike Reed

When he first started drawing, Mike Reed drew just to amuse himself. It was not long, though, before he knew he wanted to be an artist. Today he does illustrations for children's books, magazines, catalogs, and ads.

He also teaches illustration at the College of Visual Art in St. Paul, Minnesota. Mike Reed says, "Making pictures is like acting — you can paint yourself into the action." He often paints on the computer, but he also draws in pen and ink and paints in acrylics. He feels that learning to draw well is the key to being a successful artist.

Mike is regarded as one of the nation's premier illustrators and is the creator of the popular "Flame Warriors" illustrations at www.flamewarriors.com, a website devoted to Internet insults. "To enter his Flame Warriors site is sort of like entering a hellish Sesame Street populated by Oscar the Grouch and 83 of his relatives." – Los Angeles Times.
(http://redwing.hutman.net/%7Emreed/warriorshtm/lat.htm)

Mike Reed has always enjoyed reading. As a young child, he liked the Dr. Seuss books. Later, he started reading biographies and war stories. One reason why he feels lucky to be an illustrator is because he can listen to books on tape while he works. Mike is available to provide custom illustrations for all manner of publications at reasonable prices. Mike can be reached at www.mikereedillustration.com.